REFORM IN EUROPE

Reform in Europe
Breaking the Barriers in Government

Edited by

LIESBET HEYSE, SANDRA RESODIHARDJO,
TINEKE LANTINK and BERBER LETTINGA

Routledge
Taylor & Francis Group

LONDON AND NEW YORK

First published 2006 by Ashgate Publishing

Reissued 2018 by Routledge
2 Park Square, Milton Park, Abingdon, Oxon OX14 4RN
711 Third Avenue, New York, NY 10017, USA

Routledge is an imprint of the Taylor & Francis Group, an informa business

First issued in paperback 2018

A Library of Congress record exists under LC control number: 2006012537

Notice:
Product or corporate names may be trademarks or registered trademarks, and are used only for identification and explanation without intent to infringe.

Publisher's Note
The publisher has gone to great lengths to ensure the quality of this reprint but points out that some imperfections in the original copies may be apparent.

Disclaimer
The publisher has made every effort to trace copyright holders and welcomes correspondence from those they have been unable to contact.

ISBN 13: 978-0-815-39139-5 (hbk)
ISBN 13: 978-1-138-62032-2 (pbk)
ISBN 13: 978-1-351-15052-1 (ebk)

Contents

List of Figures

List of Tables

Notes on Contributors

Fleur Alink studied Political Science at the University of Amsterdam, the Netherlands. She worked as a Ph.D. fellow and teacher at the Department of Public Administration at Leiden University, the Netherlands (1999–2005). In her Ph.D. thesis (2006), she examines various institutional crises in the Dutch and German immigration sector to enhance our understanding of when and why some crises lead to reform, while others do not. She currently works at the Ministry of the Interior for the Expertise Centre for Risk- and Crisis Communication as a Research Officer.

Duco Bannink is a lecturer in Sociology at the University of Twente, the Netherlands. His Ph.D. thesis (2004) describes the reform of social security policies in the Netherlands. His research and teaching focus is on reforms in the welfare state, policy implementation, EU-governance, and social policies.

Frank Baumgartner is a Distinguished Professor of Political Science at Pennsylvania State University. His teaching and research interests include American national institutions, public policy processes, agenda-setting, interest groups, lobbying, legislative behavior, research design and measurement, and French politics. Together with other researchers, he heads the Policy Agendas Project and the Advocacy and Public Policymaking Project.

Bente Bjørnholt is a Ph.D. student at the Department of Economics, Politics, and Public Administration at the University of Aalborg, Denmark. Her research focuses on quality in public services, public accountability, management, and legitimacy.

Taco Brandsen is a lecturer at the Tilburg School of Politics and Public Administration, Tilburg University, the Netherlands. He studied English Language and Literature and Public Administration at Leiden University, and received his Ph.D. at Twente University. His fields of research include welfare state reform, the governance of public services, and non-profit management.

Gerard Breeman is a lecturer at the Department of Public Administration at Leiden University, the Netherlands. His Ph.D. thesis (2006) focuses on the role of trust in the Dutch agricultural sector. His interests include trust, policy-making, and collective action.

Francesca Gains is a lecturer at the University of Manchester. Her Ph.D. thesis (2000) addressed issues involved in the relationship between ministries and agencies. She is also the Research Coordinator for the Evaluating Local Governance (ELG) for the Office of the Deputy Prime Minister and Research Fellow of the Institute for

Political and Economic Governance (IPEG). Her research interests include NPM, political reform on local and central government levels, and New Labour politics.

Martijn Groenleer (M.A., Leiden University) is a Ph.D. student at the Department of Public Administration, Leiden University, the Netherlands. He conducts research on the creation and development of European Union agencies. He worked as a policy adviser with the Dutch Ministry of Foreign Affairs where he was a member of the task force coordinating the establishment of the International Criminal Court.

Michael Haus is a lecturer at the department of public administration/public policy and urban studies at the Institute for Political Science, Darmstadt University of Technology. He received his Ph.D. from Heidelberg University in 1999. His research interests are political theory, urban politics, and local government.

Jan-Kees Helderman is a lecturer in health policy and politics at the Institute of Health Policy and Management, Erasmus University Rotterdam in the Netherlands. After studying Urban Planning at the University of Nijmegen, he worked several years at the Department of Public Administration, Erasmus University Rotterdam. His research interests focus on comparative analysis of welfare state reform, particularly in housing and health care. He is Program Director of the Master Health Economics, Policy & Law at Erasmus MC.

Frank Hendriks is Professor in Public Administration at Tilburg University, the Netherlands. He was trained as a public administration and policy scientist at the joint Leiden University/Erasmus University program in Public Administration in the Netherlands and at Indiana University in the USA. In 1996, he obtained his Ph.D. from Leiden University. Frank Hendriks' fields of research include: urban planning and regional politics; comparative politics and policy making; political cultures and policy styles; institutional change and democratic renewal administrative systems, and state/society relations.

Liesbet Heyse studied Public Administration at Leiden University. In 1997, she completed a Masters in Political Science at Boston University, USA. In her Ph.D. research (2004), she analyses the decision-making processes in humanitarian aid NGOs. In addition, she was assistant editor of the Journal of Contingencies and Crisis Management (1999–2002). Since August 2002, she works as a lecturer at the Department of Sociology at the University of Twente. As of October 2004, she combines this position with a research position at the Department of Sociology/ICS at the University of Groningen. In addition, she is an associate member of the Leiden University Crisis Research Center.

Wendy van der Kraan is a Ph.D. student at the Institute of Management and Organization in the Health Care sector at the Erasmus University of Rotterdam, the

Netherlands. Her dissertation research focuses on demand driven care in the Dutch health care sector.

Sanneke Kuipers is a postdoc research fellow at Leiden University's Department of Public Administration in the project 'The Early Years of Public Institutions'. Her Ph.D. thesis (2004) at Leiden University compared social security reform in the Netherlands and Belgium. Her research focused on the occurrence of drastic policy change in social security policy in continental welfare states. Before, she worked in Stockholm at the Centre for Crisis Management Research and Training as a research assistant. Sanneke Kuipers runs the administrative center of a European crisis research network (ECMA). She recently worked as a visiting fellow at the Maxwell School of Citizenship and Public Affairs of Syracuse University in the USA.

Tineke Lantink studied Public Administration at Leiden University. In 2002 she completed her Master Thesis investigating the presence and extent of policy learning within the policy making process of Social Security Legislation (SUWI). After a two years traineeship at the Netwerkstad Twente, Tineke started her Ph.D. research at the Institute for Governance Studies (University of Twente) in September 2003. Her Ph.D. thesis focuses on contractual realities in quasi-markets and the role of principals in quasi-markets (e.g. the Dutch re-employment market).

Berber Lettinga is a Ph.D. student at the Institute for Governance Studies (University of Twente). In 2002, she graduated at the University of Twente in Public Administration (specialization: Organizational Management). Her master thesis investigated the impact of demand-led care on the relationship between family doctor and patient, based on sociological and economic institutional theories. Following her graduation, she joined the research team on governance and environmental issues at the CSTM/University of Twente. Since 2003, she has been working on her doctoral research which focuses on the relationship between governance and professionalism in health care. Berber Lettinga is involved in teaching organization sociology courses.

Julien van Ostaaijen is a researcher at the Tilburg School of Politics and Public Administration (University of Tilburg, the Netherlands). His research mainly focuses on local governance in Belgium and the Netherlands.

Mirjan Oude Vrielink-van Heffen works as a lecturer at the Department of Legal Studies at the University of Twente, the Netherlands. In 2001, she completed her Ph.D. dissertation on disputes between neighbours about noise. Her current research interests include public and private regulation of the public interest, quality care, and medical-technological innovations.

Melvyn Read works as a lecturer in Politics at the School of Politics & International Studies (Queen's University, Belfast, Ireland). He received his Ph.D. in Essex.

Teaching areas include British politics, MPs' voting behaviour in parliament, public policy, quantitative methods, and pressure groups. His primary interest is in the British political process, specifically in the role of Westminster.

Sandra Resodihardjo studied legal political science at Leiden University. Her M.A. thesis addressed the role of problem definitions in the fight between Greenpeace and Shell concerning the dumping of the Brent Spar. In her Ph.D. research (2006), she established which crisis-conditions led to reform in Dutch and British Prison Services. In the academic year 2003/2004, she worked as a teacher at the Department of Political Science at the University of Amsterdam. Since August 2004, she works as a lecturer at the Department of Public Administration, Leiden University, the Netherlands.

Acknowledgements

The idea for this book was initiated by Arjen Boin and Willem Trommel at a meeting of the Netherlands Institute of Government (NIG) Colloquium Institutional Rearrangement of the Public Domain. Members of the Colloquium swiftly jumped on the opportunity to combine international research to answer an age-old question: When does reform occur? Additional authors were asked to join, in order to create a comprehensive overview of different types of reforms in a number of West European countries.

During various meetings experts commented and discussed the chapters. We would like to thank the following people for their valuable feedback: Frank Baumgartner, Arjen Boin, Eefke Cornelissen, Marcel Hoogenboom, Oliver James, Martin Lodge, Martijn van der Meulen, Mick Moran, Maaike Moulijn, Marleen Romeijn, Sandra van Thiel, Leonique van Tol, Willem Trommel, Romke van der Veen, Michiel de Vries, and Kutsal Yesilkagit. Although these experts have contributed to this book by providing comments and suggestions, any errors remain ours and ours alone.

This book could not have been published without the help of various organizations. We would like to thank the Netherlands Institute of Government (NIG Colloquium grant), the NWO-British Council Partnership Programme (BW43–304), and the Netherlands Organization for Scientific Research (NWO ISW 460–05–001) for their financial support. Last, but certainly not least, we would like to thank Katleen Brummelhuis for efficiently handling the day-to-day operations of the international conference, and Maureen Donnelley and Ann Savoia for their editing skills.

Chapter 1

The Myths of Reform

Duco Bannink and Sandra Resodihardjo

The impossibility of reform

Reform is often presented in the literature as something that is nearly impossible to accomplish. Three myths support this pervading idea. The first myth states that the institutional structure of a policy sector will make reform impossible. Path dependency, lock-in effects, and paradigm block any chances for reform. The second myth holds that a strong disruption such as a crisis is required for institutional patterns to break. The third myth necessitates a strong leader who can stand up to the people blocking reform, create alliances, and use every resource available to push for reform. But even if a government routinely employs its resources to try to obtain reform, it remains difficult for actors involved – including strong leaders – to achieve reform (March & Olsen, 1995; Pollitt & Bouckaert, 2004). The focus on institutional stability and governments' inability to push for reform (Bovens & 't Hart, 1998) has created a pervading idea within social science that reform is rare and almost impossible to achieve.

Yet reform does occur. Departments in ministries become agencies (for instance, the Dutch Immigration Services or the Child Support Agency in England), new ministries are created (such as the Department of Homeland Security in the United States of America), and smoking in restaurants is banned.

In order to explain how reform can occur despite the tremendous barriers blocking reform, we will combine institutional and reform literature. Such a combination will help us to identify factors facilitating reform because institutional theories provide ideas to understand the inert and stable institutional environment we live in. We can, in a matter of speaking, turn around and look at these stability-inducing factors from another point of view: do these factors and variables that normally result in stability and inertia change during the reform process? If so, can we combine institutional and reform literature to generate a list of factors that facilitate reform?

Answering this question will result in achieving the aim of this study, which is to establish the factors that bring about reform in public policy sectors. This aim will be achieved by taking three steps. First, institutional perspectives and reform literature will be combined and discussed in this introductory chapter in order to generate a (theoretical) list of barriers blocking reform and factors enabling reform. The myths introduced at the beginning of this chapter will be explained in more detail when discussing these barriers and facilitators. Second, the case chapters will compare these barriers and facilitators of reform with the events that led to reforms in various policy sectors in different countries. Finally, the knowledge collected through these case studies will allow us to debunk the reform-myths and create a coherent overview of the factors that facilitate reform in the concluding chapter.

Our approach to reform complements studies such as Bovens, 't Hart, and Peters' *Success and Failure of Public Governance* (2001) which considered reform as a by-product of governments' efforts to manage challenges in the realm of governance while trying to explain reform on the level of national policy-making institutions. Our project deliberately focuses on reform – not on managing challenges to governance – while seeking explanations for these reforms at the policy sector level rather than the national level.

In order to be able to create a coherent overview of the policy sector reforms, the authors of the case chapters have structured their case descriptions in a unified manner, thereby focusing on the following questions. Which barriers prevented reform in the first place? Were these barriers present when reform was finally possible? If so, how were these barriers overcome? Moreover, did any of the factors described in the literature on reform occur in the policy sector and how did these factors affect reform barriers? Were other factors at work? Or, was a combination of factors needed for reform to occur?

Answering these questions requires that one understands what reform is about and which factors hamper and enable reform. These topics will be addressed in this chapter. Reform is defined in the next section, whereas section 3 presents an overview of the factors barring reform. Factors facilitating reform will be described in section 4. The last section addresses how the research was conducted and concludes with an overview of the various case chapters.

Conceptualizing reform

This study focuses on reform in policy sectors within the public domain of government. Government is 'conventionally organized around policy areas like economic policy or foreign policy' (Rayner et al., 2001: 319). Such a policy area is also known as a policy sector. In this study, reforms in various policy sectors are examined. Policy sectors in this study range from sectors dealing with soft policies, such as social welfare and health policy, to sectors covering hard policies such as immigration. Attention is paid to the reform of policy goals, instruments, and paradigms. Due attention is also directed at the reform of existing organizations within policy sectors, as well as changing established patterns between central government and executive agencies.

All cases share a commonality, in that the studied changes occurred in well-established institutional settings. An institutionalized policy sector displays two characteristics. First, a *policy paradigm* exists, i.e. there is an institutional identity. This identity consists of the values, norms, interests, opinions, ideas, goals, and means to achieve these goals (Brunsson & Olsen, 1997: 5). People working in a policy sector become accustomed to a certain way of doing things. They get used to the way we work around here. Goals have been set, and the ways to achieve these goals have been marked. Values and norms about which goals to achieve, and also how to respond to problems become incorporated into the sector as it becomes more and more institutionalized (Selznick, 1957). The second characteristic of an institutionalized policy sector is the existence of *organizational structures, decision-making procedures, and rules*. These elements can be formal as well as informal. Decision-making procedures, for instance, can be lined out in organizational manuals or laws. At the same time, an informal network on who should be consulted exists as well. Scott (1995) and Hall & Taylor (1996) show that existing strands of institutionalisms differ regarding the conceptualization of institutions. Selznick's (1957) infusion with value is relevant in a sociological approach to institutions. In this approach, belief and convictions structure action. According to the rational choice perspective, institutions are not so much organizations infused with value. Instead, institutions consist of rules and sanctions which structure action. In this study, both views are represented as we focus on the characteristic of policy paradigm (sociological approach) and organizational structures, decision-making procedures, and rules (rational choice approach).

In this study, we are not so much interested in incremental changes that eventually result in the unintended reform of a policy sector (Lindblom, 1959; Lindblom 1979; Rose & Davies, 1994: 37). Instead, our interest is in regard to how a reform package gets through the various policy-making stages. In this study we, therefore, focus on reform from the moment that it appears on the agenda to the moment the reform measure is enforced.

Reform can be defined in many ways, but in this study we are only interested in reform if it is characterized by the following three components: reform is *fundamental, intended, and enforced*. Fundamental reform implies a deviation from existing structures or paradigms (Dror, 1976: 127; Keeler, 1993: 434; Hall, 1993; Sabatier & Jenkins-Smith, 1993; Bonoli & Palier, 1998; Cortell & Peterson, 1999: 179, 182; Sabatier & Jenkins-Smith, 1999). This means that reform concerns the organizational structure of a policy sector, its paradigm, or both. A change in priorities would thus constitute fundamental reform, as would the introduction of new organizations within a policy sector. *Intended* implies that we are not interested in the unintended effects of years of incremental changes, but in the way some policy makers come to prefer, and are capable of, changing a policy's direction or the organizational structure of a policy sector.

Moreover, in this study, we are interested in *enforced* reform. Enforcement thus constitutes the third demarcating element of our study. We define reform as actually being put into force: the reform measure has survived all the policy-making stages and is now in place (i.e., the new policy is being executed). We do not define reform in terms of actual implementation or goal achievement for the very simple reason that it is very difficult to ascertain whether reform measures have been consummately implemented, or whether the implemented reforms have obtained the goals as intended by policy makers. Social science, political science, and public administration studies all show that the aims are either not obtained, or it is very difficult to measure whether the goals have been achieved (Hogwood & Gunn, 1993; Howlett & Ramesh, 1995; Fisher, 1995). For example, it is difficult to ascertain the reason why a certain reform was suggested and accepted in the first place. Moreover, changes in policy, organization, or paradigm produce negative side effects to a more or lesser extent (Sieber, 1981; Boudon, 1982; Beck, 1992; Engbersen & Van der Veen, 1992). We are not interested in a reform's success in terms of goal achievement, but we are interested in how reform measures survive all the policy-making stages. Hence, reform is defined in this study as the fundamental, intended, and enforced change of the policy paradigm and/or organizational structure of (an organization within) a policy sector.

> Reform is defined in this study as the fundamental, intended, and enforced change of the policy paradigm and/or organizational structure of (an organization within) a policy sector.

Our definition of reform includes various reform categories discerned by other authors. Categories of reform included in this definition are, for example, Pierson's (1994) systemic and programmatic types of reform, paradigmatic change (Hall, 1993; Sabatier & Jenkins-Smith, 1993), changes in the administrative organizations of a policy sector, and changes in policies administered. Furthermore, our definition of reform includes organizational reform as well as policy reform; two types of interrelated reforms, as one often affects the other. Consider, for instance, the introduction of New Public Management tools. Even though these instruments primarily revolve around organizational reform (e.g., introducing agencies or privatizing government organizations), they are accompanied by a change in paradigm (e.g., the state is no longer responsible for everything, instead the market should provide certain services). Conversely, policy reforms may only be achieved if they are accompanied by radical changes in the organizational structure of a policy sector. Although the interaction between organizational and policy reforms is not the central subject of our study, we acknowledge that such interaction may strongly affect the dynamics of reform processes.

Stability: Barriers to reform

There are many barriers to reform. In this section, we describe how the institutional context of a policy sector constrains reform. The purpose of this study is not to examine constraints, but instead to determine which factors contribute to reform. We will therefore only give a rough overview of the constraints that create the conditions under which reformers have to accomplish reform, what these constraints are about, how they operate, and what their effects can be.

In order to obtain a broad overview of these barriers, two approaches of the New Institutionalism will be used that represent two distinct theoretical positions. The calculus approach represents rational choice institutionalism, while the cultural approach reflects sociological institutionalism.[1] Both approaches suggest their own barriers to reform or at least their own way of looking at these barriers (Bannink, 2004). The calculus approach implies that actors act according to a logic of consequence; this approach directs attention to decision-making structures and procedures and the way institutions affect the *opportunities* available to political actors to influence policy-making. In this view, barriers to change exist where decision-making procedures provide limited leverage for actors preferring reform, i.e. where actors have limited opportunities to push for reform. The cultural approach, on the other hand, supposes that actors act according to a logic of appropriateness; this approach directs attention to the way institutions affect actors' normative and cognitive frameworks, their preferences, and their views of the world. In the cultural view, barriers to change exist because institutions produce *preferences* that resist reform (Hall & Taylor, 1996: 8).

Using these two views mandates that we take into account both characteristics of institutions when investigating existing reform literature to establish barriers to reform. The cultural approach directs our attention to the first characteristic (the paradigm) as infused values influence actors' preferences, whereas the calculus approach directs our attention to the second characteristic, as decision-making structure and procedures create and limit actors' opportunities to influence policy-making.

Examples of constraints are abundant in the literature on reform. From a calculus perspective, institutional constraints can be, for example, the decision-making rules within an organization or political system. Decision-making procedures affect the policy-making process. This is because a reform proposal has to go through a number of veto points (Immergut, 1992). The more veto points a proposal has to go through, the more difficult it is to get a proposal accepted. Each veto point presents an opportunity for another person to stop or change the proposal (Cortell & Peterson, 1999: 190). Steinmo and Watts (1995) and Skocpol (1996) argue that the fragmented structure of the American government, administration, and political system affects reformers' capacity to introduce new policies and administrative structures or reform existing ones. This is because – as in the argument on veto points – fragmented decision-making structures yield 'enormous power to intransigent interest groups' (Steinmo & Watts, 1995: 329). Moreover, Pollitt and Bouckaert (2004) argue that veto points are more abundant in a federal political system than in a system with a

---

1 Next to the sociological and rational choice institutionalism, a third variant of institutionalism that Hall and Taylor (1996) discern is historical institutionalism. This variant of institutionalism does not pursue a distinctive theoretical position, but offers an eclectic combination of both rational choice and sociological institutionalism, i.e. employing both a cultural and a calculus approach to action. Our own approach offers a comparable eclectic combination and can thus be considered to be historical institutionalism.

strong centralization of power. Consequently, it makes a difference in what type of political structure a reform proposal is made.

Furthermore, decisions from the past constrain reform capacities in the present. Past financial investments have resulted in sunk cost. Decisions to design the policy sector one way or another has resulted in investments in certain assets such as machines, software, and buildings. These are instances of *policy lock-in* (Pierson, 1998; 2000). Policy lock-in leads to *path dependence* – the idea that political choices made in the past circumscribe current political options. An oft-cited example of this effect is the fate of the QWERTY-keyboard; while originally designed to bring down typing speed (necessary since the early machines would falter at high speeds), it became the standard keyboard, because typists and others had invested effort to accommodate to the particular make-up (Wilsford, 1994).

Path dependency also occurs at the policy level itself, not just on the implementation level. Governments *inherit policy* from previous governments (Wilsford, 1994). Political leaders and organizational leaders are bound to uphold existing laws and policies. They do not have much leeway to add, amend, or end public policies (Rose & Davies, 1994: 1–4, 15–6). Bureaucratic leaders coming into office, for instance, will have to accept the budget allocated to their government agency, as well as how to allocate spending, because they also inherit obligations (Rose & Davies, 1994: 12).

In short, from a calculus perspective, institutional rules limit the capacities of actors who are willing to implement reform proposals at various levels. In contrast, the cultural approach to policy change and stability emphasizes how institutions produce preferences, norms, and values that tend to resist reform.

From a cultural perspective, the *policy paradigm* would be considered a barrier to reform. Such a paradigm is manifested in the routines and standard operating procedures in policy-making, and also in administration in a policy field. Furthermore, the paradigm is built around values that determine what is and is not acceptable in dealing with a problem or achieving a goal. As actors have been inculcated with the norms, values, and preferences presented in the paradigm, they are unlikely to support or suggest changes contrary to this paradigm. Instead, they are inclined to suggest changes that fit within the paradigm (Kaufman, 1995: 15–23; Boin & 't Hart, 2000: 13; 't Hart, 2000: 26–7). Hall (1993) argues that the more a reform proposal strays from an existing paradigm, the more this reform proposal will be resisted by policy makers and stakeholders alike. Policy makers tend to prefer to either adjust the settings of policy instruments (first order change) or to change the instruments (second order) before attempting to change the policy paradigm (third order change).

People working in institutionalized policy sectors are not only reluctant to accept reform because they have to face the policy they have inherited, but also because they may already *benefit* from the existing institutional structure. Hence, their preferences are structured by the institutional structure. Policy, for instance, creates benefits for people (including the institutions' clients), such as receiving subsidies or having the right to be consulted when new policy is made. People will be reluctant to give up these benefits (Korsten, 1993: 205; Pierson, 1994; Kaufman, 1995: 11–2). Another constraint is *vested interests*. People have invested their resources to obtain, for example, their current position or to create a new goal for their organization that has increased the esteem of their organization, as well as their own positions. If reform changes what they have obtained, their investment will be rendered almost useless (Leemans, 1976b: 88; Wilson, 1989: 131; Rose & Davies, 1994: 14; True, Jones & Baumgartner, 1999: 102; Shepsle, 2001: 324).

Moreover, reform is *upsetting and unsettling* for individuals (Leemans, 1976b: 88–9). The wish to maintain the status quo is particularly strong in the leaders of public organizations. These leaders feel obliged to protect their policy sector or organization in a way that is consistent with predominant values in the policy sector and government as a whole (Terry, 2003: 24). People unwilling to accept reform – for whatever reasons – can form an *anti-reform coalition*, for example, a strategic alliance aimed at blocking reform (Korsten, 1993: 205).

The institution's decision-making structure and procedures (resulting in calculus constraints) and paradigm (resulting in cultural constraints) do not operate independently from one another. Instead, the two characteristics (and their accompanying constraints) interact with, and may reinforce, one another. Furthermore, Pierson (1994) argues that the amount of interaction between these constraints and the strength of these constraints vary per policy sector. People who have privileged access to decision-making, for example, will have a strong incentive to defend their position. Steinmo and Watts (1995) discuss how such interaction of calculus and cultural types of constraints may unfold. They argue that the structure of decision-making systems in the United States affects the preferences policy makers pursue. The authors discuss President Clinton's plans for National Health Insurance. The implementation of this arrangement failed repeatedly because of the wide dispersion of veto points in the American polity. The continuous failure to implement such an arrangement, in turn, contributed to anti-government attitudes and a shift to a more voluntarist policy paradigm within the health insurance policy field. This shows that actors' preferences of what they want to achieve are not only structured by the institution's paradigm, but also by what is possible given the existing decision-making structures. As Steinmo and Watts (1995) explain, 'what we want is structured in some fundamental ways by what we can imagine achieving' (in the words of Hattam, 1993: 336).

In short, institutions produce a *double set* of stabilizing factors that create barriers to reform: institutions function against the emergence of preferences promoting reform while at the same time limiting actors' capacity and opportunity to push for reform (see column 1 of table 1.1 for an overview of these barriers). Considering these barriers, questions arise about how reformers come to desire such an achievement and how they are able to achieve it. People wishing to reform their policy sector face enormous obstacles. Even if they are capable of getting the proposal on the agenda without stumbling on constraints, reform proposals may still be obstructed in the decision-making stage (Bachrach & Baratz, 1970: 44; Caiden, 1991b; Cortell & Peterson, 2001; Patashnik, 2003). It is therefore an enormous feat if reformers, willing and able to overcome all the barriers to reform, get the reform proposal accepted and executed. This issue will be addressed in the next section.

> Considering the many barriers that hamper reform, it is a remarkable feat if a reform proposal survives all the policy-making stages and gets executed. The aim of this study is to establish how these barriers are overcome as well as determine the factors that facilitate such an outcome.

Change: Facilitators of reform

The calculus approach focuses on *opportunity structures* created by institutions, while the cultural approach concentrates on *preferences* instilled by institutions. The combination of the two shows that institutions consist of norms, rules, and routines that create stability in actors' preferences, and determine actors' interactions with one another. One knows what to expect from others, how to perceive and interpret others' actions, and one knows also how to act. Exactly because of this stabilizing influence, it is very difficult for reformers to reform institutions.

Following the view of the calculus approach, something has to happen to the decision-making procedures, and also the way such institutions affect the capacity of political actors to influence policy-making, if reform is to occur. Participants in a decision-making process could, for example, agree on new rules. Likewise, the cultural approach points towards changes in the paradigm if actors' preferences towards reform are to change. The question arises as to whether reform literature refers to these variables when describing the factors facilitating reform.

In the literature an often used explaining factor of reform is *the disrupted decision-making process* that is often preceded by a crisis, for example, a particular issue engulfed in flames of controversy (Brunsson & Olsen, 1997: 21). Baumgartner and Jones (1993), for instance, speak of the punctuated equilibrium model to explain reform (Krasner, 1988). In this model, long periods of stability and rest are characterized by incrementalism (Lindblom, 1959; Lindblom, 1979; Harrison, Hunter, & Pollitt, 1990: 9). These stretches of time are disrupted when an issue catches fire and draws the attention of media and stakeholders. Existing policies are then questioned and challenged. Policy makers are pressured to respond to and deal with the issue. Stakeholders demand new policy or changes in the existing policy. According to Baumgartner and Jones (1993: 10), the sudden appearance of a new issue disrupts the policy-making process (True, Jones & Baumgartner, 1999: 97). Once policy makers have dealt with the issue, stability will return.

Crises in policy sectors appear in many forms. To give an idea of the various ways in which a crisis can occur within a policy sector, three different types of crises will be briefly described. First, an incident such as the death of an asylum seeker or the escape from a high security prison can act as a focal point for media and Members of Parliament (MPs), who become aware that the policy sector is not functioning as it should. The negative attention of media and MPs, in which the functioning of the policy sector is severely criticized, results in a policy sector in crisis (Alink, Boin, and 't Hart, 2001). Second, negative media coverage – either preceded by a specific incident or not – can result in a negative image of the policy sector (McCombs, 1997; Terkildsen & Schnell, 1997). This, in turn, creates the need with the policy sector's policy makers to try to amend this negative image. Lastly, crises can be deliberately constructed by actors who want to reform a policy sector. These reformers can use crisis rhetoric to discredit the existing policy sector and to legitimize drastic change (Kuipers, 2006).

No matter how a crisis comes about, it could result in diminished support for policies and/or disruptions of the policy-making process. Consequently, reform-barriers will be diminished and it will be easier to introduce new policies and do away with old ones.

The diminishing of barriers, also known as a *window of opportunity* (Keeler, 1993: 437–442; Kingdon, 1995: 166; Cortell & Peterson, 1999: 185), does not necessarily result in actual policy reform. If no one acts upon the opportunity presented by the problems, reform will not follow. Agency is therefore required; actors (i.e. policy entrepreneurs) need to seize the moment presented by the diminished barriers and/or disrupted policy-making process to push for reform (Leemans, 1976a: 16–17, 33; Heffron, 1989: 156; Keeler, 1993; Hall, 1993; Rose & Davies, 1994: 105–6, 108–111, 178–9; Kingdon, 1995; Cortell & Peterson, 1999; Hay, 1999). Policy entrepreneurs include a range of people, from outside actors such as unions to inside actors such as civil servants, bureaucratic managers, and political masters (Keeler, 1993; Teske & Schneider, 1994; Kingdon, 1995: 122; Roberts & King, 1996; Richard & Smith, 1997; Cortell & Peterson, 1999: 183).

Another major factor cited in current reform literature to explain the occurrence of reform is *leadership*. Leadership is generally attributed to specific actors within policy sectors: those working within the executive branch of all levels of government (Terry, 2003: 4). Such actors are those at management level who are 'linked to innovative ideas and efforts to carry these ideas into effect, often attended by some risk to their organizations and to their own careers' (Doig & Hargrove, 1990: 7). The political persons in charge of a policy sector can be leaders as well ('t Hart, 2000). Leaders can either aim to conserve the status quo or reform it (Terry, 2003). Because of the aim of this book – establishing factors that facilitate reform – we are interested in the latter.

Reformist leaders can use the window of opportunity generated by a crisis. As such, they are part of the more encompassing concept of policy entrepreneur, which also includes other actors, from both inside and outside government, who can use the window of opportunity. However, whereas a policy entrepreneur is always dependent on the occurrence of a crisis to push for reform, reformist leaders can also push for reform without a crisis. Unfortunately, leadership literature is vague in its explanations of exactly how and when a leader can push for reform. The leadership literature states, in general terms, that reformist leaders have to take the right steps at the right moment if they want to achieve their goal. They have to be able to wheel and deal, form alliances, understand when the right time has come, and seize it (Doig & Hargrove, 1990; Olsen, 1991: 131; Brunsson & Olsen, 1997: 26; 't Hart, 2000). Leaders should be able to assess the situation and determine when it is appropriate to conserve the status quo, and when it is appropriate to opt for a reformist stance (Terry, 2003).

Other factors contributing to the execution of reform are factors that reformers – whether they are leaders or policy entrepreneurs – should take into account when trying to push their reform proposals through all the stages. Reformers need, for example, to try to go with the flow instead of swimming against the tide. In particular, their reform proposals should be compatible with current national and international trends, instead of being trendsetting (Olsen, 1991: 133; Caiden, 1991a: 133; Caiden, 1991b: 155; Brunsson & Olsen, 1997: 23). Reformers also have to seize the opportunity to push for reform when such an opportunity presents itself (Caiden, 1991a: 136). Moreover, reform plans have to be unambiguous, clearly defined, focused, and include good planning, instead of being broad and general (Dror, 1976: 129; Olsen, 1991: 134; Caiden, 1991a: 134; Caiden, 1991b: 159; Brunsson & Olsen, 1997: 24). Reformers should find backing for their proposals (Caiden, 1991a:135; Caiden, 1991b: 162). Once everyone within an organization is convinced of the need to implement this reform, it will be possible to overcome outsiders' resistance to this change (Olsen, 1991: 131; Brunsson & Olsen, 1997: 25). One way to procure this backing is to incorporate the wishes of the organization into the reform proposal (Olsen, 1991: 135), or to show that the proposal is feasible (Leemans, 1976b: 95). Another way to garner support for a reform proposal is through sheer force. In order to be able to do that, one must have power – to either coerce or sanction (Leemans, 1976b: 85). Reformers also need to have ample resources at their disposal. These resources not only consist of money, but also of time, qualified staff, and material (Leemans, 1976b: 90–93; Dror, 1976: 140).

According to reform literature, a majority of the barriers hampering reform can be tied to institutions. Actors are constrained by institutions in various ways, including the rules and decision-making procedures, the norms and values, previous policy-making, routinization, path dependency, lock-in effects, and vested interests. These barriers structure actors' options. *Structure* is 'the limit of action' (Smith, 1999: 30) and if barriers shift, structure changes. During disrupted policy-making processes (calculus approach), the decision-making rules (calculus approach), paradigms (cultural approach), and other constraints normally hampering reform may diminish. In other words, during disrupted policy-making processes, the institution's structuring capacities diminish.

For actors to indeed seize the moment, however, factors such as leadership, entrepreneurship (i.e. using the opportunity to push for reform), capabilities, and the ability to find backing for ideas – in other words *agency* – become important. Underlying these factors is the assumption that people's preferences will have to change in support of reform if they are to act at all. If policy-making actors were strongly attached to institutionalized policies, and the public were inclined to punish policy-makers for dismantling existing programs that provide public benefits (whether or not in a social policy sense of the word (Pierson, 1994)), then why and how would reformers' preferences change?

This question is all the more important because reform is associated with uncertainty. Actors cannot know in advance the extent to which they will be able to strive for their policy preferences in a reformed institutional set-up. Furthermore, reforming a policy sector may be costly in political terms. Governments may not want to implement reform measures in a politically visible manner because of the electoral hazards of imposing losses (Pierson, 1994: 17 ff.). Therefore, as Drazen and Easterly (2001: 134–5) argue, policy actors tend to 'out-wait' each other in a 'war of attrition'. Even in the face of considerable crisis, policy-makers may prefer not to implement reform measures themselves but await others to do so (Rodrik, 1996).

Consequently, it seems unlikely for actors to change their preferences, yet that is exactly the assumption underlying reform: actors have to act and use the lessening of institutional constraints to push for reform. This raises two questions. First, do preferences actually change? After all, research has shown that policy makers facing a crisis may actually be forced to pursue reform (Alink & Resodihardjo, 2002; Resodihardjo, 2004). Whether or not policy-making actors' real preferences have actually changed or these actors were merely forced to take specific actions, their actions indicate that they have changed, at least, the values attached to various factors in their environments.

Second, if preferences change, how and why do they change? Snyder and Mahoney argue that 'constitutive analysis' (1999: 112–3) might help explain what actors' preferences are, where these preferences come from, and how they have changed over time. Constitutive analysis aims at explaining both institutional stability and change by studying the institutional origins of the defenders and challengers of existing policy or administrative programs. An example may be found in Scharpf's (1987) game-theoretical interpretation of inflation and unemployment in Western Europe. Scharpf (1987) argues that – depending on the structure of decision-making institutions and on the strategies chosen by others – actors at times prove willing and able to adjust their preferences and strategies and become challengers of the existing institutional order.

In summary, reform literature states that reform may occur if someone is *willing* to use the situation to push for reform and if constraints have diminished. Together, the willingness to act (agency) and the ability to do so, as a result of diminished limits of action (structure), constitute facilitators of reform (see table 1.1 for an overview of barriers to and facilitators of reform). Barriers to reform exist where institutions determine both preferences and opportunities (see section 3). Reform is facilitated where actors are willing (agency) and able to withdraw from structural constraints and formulate alternative policies or policy paradigms, and where these actors are also able to be leaders or find adequate support to establish reform (see section 4).

At first glance, it seems as if the facilitators to reform are clear-cut. A closer look, however, reveals a pervading vagueness regarding two factors.

Table 1.1   Barriers and facilitators to reform

Barriers		Facilitators	
Opportunities	Preferences	Structure	Agency
Decision-making structures. Policy inheritance. Lock-in.	Paradigm, routinization, and internalised goals. Reform is disruptive.	Diminished barriers, such as a disruption in the policy-making process and the decline in support for the policy inheritance.	Change of preference. Leadership. Entrepreneurship. Go with the flow. Find support.

First, it is not always clear how to categorize specific barriers and facilitators. Imagine, for instance, a reform proposal in the health sector that is effectively resisted by the medical association. Both cultural and calculus-type barriers are prevalent: the medical association may not support reform because the current state of affairs strongly favours the position of doctors. At the same time, the medical association may be in a strong position to resist reform as a result of the association's place in the decision-making set up.

Second, current theory does offer numerous factors that could play a role in the reform process, but does not account for which factors are necessary and sufficient conditions for reform to occur. According to current literature on facilitators of reform, a variety of factors have to amalgamate if reform is to be effectively commenced and eventually executed. Both serendipity and omniscient leaders are vital if reform is to survive the agenda setting, decision-making, and execution stages.

During a crisis, for instance, the policy sector's functioning, policies, and paradigm are under attack. Exactly because they are under attack and support for these practices is low, it will be easier to change policies and paradigm. Barriers diminish, creating room to manoeuvre for policy entrepreneurs who wish to reform the policy sector. Yet, current literature does not tell us how and which barriers will diminish, how remaining barriers are overcome, and how reformers can use the window of opportunity. Moreover, the literature is equally unclear to what extent the facilitators listed should occur together if reform is to occur.

Current literature does not define the exact necessary and sufficient conditions for reform. It is unclear, for example, if: barriers need to diminish in order for reform to happen, which barriers will diminish under which circumstances, how remaining barriers are overcome, and how reformers can use the window of opportunity. Moreover, the literature is vague in addressing the extent to which the facilitators listed are to amalgamate if reform is to occur.

The question arises as to whether, and to what extent, these factors actually play a role in the reform process. Do other factors play a role? Or is a certain combination required? These questions bring us back to the aim of this study: establishing factors that facilitate reform. Case studies will help us to determine these factors. In the next section, an overview of the cases will be presented. The general outline of each case study will be addressed before briefly describing the content of each case chapter.

Myths and cases

A next logical step in the literature is a study that investigates which factors hamper and facilitate reform. The outcome of such a study will determine whether the reform myths introduced at the beginning of this chapter are fact or fiction. In order to be able to determine the factors hampering and facilitating reform, a qualitative case study is needed. Such an approach allows researchers not only to determine whether factors suggested in current literature actually come into play, but also to establish whether other factors may play a role – in contrast, researchers conducting a quantitative study are often limited to investigating a pre-determined set of variables. In other words, the qualitative case study approach allows researchers to remain open-minded and distil emerging themes from the data (Creswell, 2003: 18–9).

All selected cases have three features in common. First, all cases focus on reform as defined in this study, i.e. the reforms have survived the policy-making stages and have been executed. Second, every reform occurred in highly institutionalized policy sectors. Highly institutionalized policy sectors are characterized by strong barriers to change. Using a calculus and cultural approach to barriers, a list (table 1.1) was created that included barriers derived from the paradigm (infused values that determine whether actors actually want to change) and from the decision-making structures (creating and limiting actors' opportunities to influence policy-making) of the policy sectors. Taken together, the selected cases cover many of the barriers mentioned in this chapter. Third, the reforms occurred in West-European countries as a way to focus our research (table 1.2 presents an overview of the cases).

Although the cases share important characteristics, they also differ on various dimensions. This was intentionally designed as a way to ensure maximum variation sampling. This case selection method has the advantage of allowing researchers to 'describe the variation in the group and to understand variations in experiences while also investigating core elements and shared outcomes' (Patton, 1990: 172). Hence, it offers the opportunity to detect common patterns in a variety of settings and thus to identify the necessary and sufficient conditions of reform. Moreover, combining the similarities of the cases with variations between the cases allows for comparison and generalization to theory (Yin, 1993: 39).

The variation in the cases relates to differences in political systems, policy sectors and governmental levels of reform as well to the types of reform studied. The countries selected represent different political systems (e.g. federal versus centralized states). This benefits our analysis because cultural as well as political (i.e. state systems) dimensions can be considered when comparing the case findings (Pollitt & Bouckaert, 2004: 47). The selected cases vary regarding the government levels where reform occurred, i.e. European, national, and local level. The variation in government level involved improves our understanding of reform because we are able to include the influence of state level factors when determining factors impeding and facilitating reform. The cases also present a broad range of reforms. The cases include, for instance, NPM reform (home care), interactive/participative democracy reform (German building planning), organizational reform (Dutch social security), and European Union reform (introducing the super-levy). Finally, various policy sectors are included in this study. The case selection includes typical hard policy sectors (such as immigration), soft policy sectors (social welfare and home care) as well as mixed policy sectors (Rotterdam's encompassing safety policy includes issues such as police, dealing with drug addicted people, and street sanitation). All in all, the variation in the cases allows us to establish similarities as well as differences in reform patterns between the investigated cases.

Table 1.2   Overview of the cases in following chapters

Chapter	Case	Country	Level
2	Introducing super-levy in the EU	EU	Supranational
3	Housing reform	The Netherlands and the United Kingdom	National
4	Introducing quality standards in home care	Denmark and the Netherlands	Municipality and national
5	Constitutional change regarding the right to asylum	Germany	National
6	Introducing the ban on smoking	Ireland	National
7	Disability insurance reform	The Netherlands	National
8	Local authority reform	The United Kingdom	Municipality
9	Citizen participation in building planning	Germany	Municipality
10	Introducing an encompassing safety policy in Rotterdam	The Netherlands	Municipality

This study is limited to the extent that implementation is not considered. As has been explained in detail in section 2, implementation research requires different research methods and different data sets than the ones needed for this study (explaining the occurrence of fundamental, intended, and enforced change). Moreover, it is not easy to establish the level of implementation, i.e. have goals been achieved and, if so, to what extent? Consequently, implementation is not part of this study.

The study is also limited in terms of the potential for generalization by the nature of the case studies within. As with every study, not every case can be included. Consequently, there are the usual limits to generalization. However, we have tried to minimize these limitations by selecting cases as diligently as possible, thereby enhancing the generalization. As this study consists of a cross-section of cases in terms of state systems and state levels, reform types, policy sectors, and barriers blocking reform, we feel that if similar findings occur in various (and different) cases, we can generalize and debunk myths.

In order to analyze, compare, and generalize, we needed similar data from the cases. Hence, each case chapter has been constructed along strict lines. The first section of each case chapter is initiated with an introduction in which the reform is briefly described. In this section, the authors will also explain to the reader what renders the reform in question so remarkable. In the second section, authors describe why previous attempts, if any, failed. Based on the failed attempts, barriers to reform are established. If previous attempts were not present, possible barriers are listed based on logic and the characteristics of the policy sector. Third, attention is then turned to the reform, where the reform process is mapped out chronologically. Fourth, authors explain why reform could come about, paying special attention to facilitators to reform. In the fifth and final section of their respective case chapters, the authors link data found in their case with the theoretical notions described in this chapter. Do the factors in their case correspond with the existing literature or do we see new factors that interact with one another in complete new ways? The remainder of this chapter is a brief summary of the cases chapters.

Chapter 2 describes the introduction of a milk quota system in the European Community (1984) as a response to growing financial problems in the European Community (EC). A fundamental change swept through the European Community as the aims of agricultural policies changed from product-growth to growth-containment. The chapter describes how EC policy makers could take this radical decision.

Chapter 3 examines housing policy changes in the Netherlands. In 1989, the Dutch government announced reforms in housing policy. The authors explain how these reforms happened without any significant conflict between the actors involved. In order to better understand the Dutch experience, the Dutch housing reform process is compared to former British Prime Minister Margaret Thatcher's introduction of buying social houses.

Chapter 4 investigates the introduction of quality standards in long-term care in Denmark and the Netherlands – a measure introduced to assist governmental care providers working in a competitive market. In the Netherlands, this reform meant a break with traditional command-and-control regulation, while in Denmark the reform signified a break with Danish tradition of self-government. This chapter compares the two reforms.

Chapter 5 addresses Germany's constitutional change concerning the asylum procedure. For decades, Germany was known for its generous refuge law, which allowed numerous sanctuary seekers to enter and stay in the country. This chapter explores how and why German Parliament came to the decision to adopt one of the strictest asylum procedures in Europe in 1993 by reforming the German constitution.

Chapter 6 discusses bans on public smoking. On 29 March 2004, the smoke-free workplace regulations became law in Ireland. As a result, Ireland was the first country in the world to have a complete ban on smoking in the workplace – including pubs. The road to this accomplishment has not been an easy one, even though the idea for banning smoking from workplaces had been around for a long time. Considering the numerous people fighting the smoke ban in pubs, it is quite an achievement that the smoke-free regulation survived all the stages of policy-making, including the execution stage. This raises the question how we can explain this reform. The author of chapter 6 attempts to answer this question.

Chapter 7 studies the Dutch disability insurance policies and organizational structures which were reformed in the 1990s. It is argued that the reform of social security policies and organizational structures followed different paths as a result of differing preferences of the actors involved. The interrelation of policy and organizational reform, though, explains the dynamic of the process in this policy sector.

Chapter 8 addresses the introduction of a separation of powers in local government in the United Kingdom – a reform blocked in previous years by a combination of barriers at the national and local level. The New Labour government was able to make it happen through a combination of electoral mandate with strong support for the reform from the leadership and a reform proposal which gained the support of national as well as local actors. Local actors opposed to the unsettling reform chose the exit option leaving actors who were more willing to adopt the reform as they could see the benefits entailed into the new Act.

Chapter 9 describes the introduction of citizen participation in building planning in Heidelberg, Germany. Heidelberg was successful where other municipalities have failed: introducing a sustainable way to include citizens in the policy-making process. This chapter shows how the leadership of the newly elected mayor was vital to overcome the anti-reform coalition and any feelings of cynical disillusionment stemming from failed attempts to enhance citizen participation.

Chapter 10 discusses the fundamental changes in the safety policy in one of Holland's biggest cities: Rotterdam. This policy reform entailed a shift in focus within the municipality. This chapter explains how and why this reform was possible once a new right wing party – Leefbaar Rotterdam – was elected in the city council.

References

Alink, F., A. Boin, P. 't Hart (2001) 'Institutional Crises and Reforms in Policy Sectors: The Case of Asylum Policy in Europe' *Journal of European Public Policy* vol. 8 (2) pp. 286–306.

Alink, F., S.L. Resodihardjo (2002) *Conservative or Reformative – How trigger events turn around crisis managements approach during institutional crises*, Conference paper, *EGPA*, Potsdam (Germany).

Bachrach, P., M.S. Baratz (1970) 'Key Concepts: Decisions and Nondecisions' Bachrach, P., M.S. Baratz (eds) *Power and Poverty: Theory and Practice*, New York: Oxford University Press pp. 39–51.

Bannink, D. (2004) *The Reform of Dutch Disability Insurance: A Confrontation of a Policy Learning and a Policy Feedback Approach to Welfare State Change*, Dissertation: Enschede.

Baumgartner, F.R., B.D. Jones (1993) *Agendas and Instability in American Politics*, Chicago: University of Chicago Press.

Beck, U. (1992) *Risk Society: Towards a New Modernity*, London: Sage.

Boin, A., P. 't Hart (2000) 'Institutional Crises and Reforms in Policy Sectors' Wagenaar, H. (ed.) *Government Institutions: Effects, Changes and Normative Foundations*, Dordrecht: Kluwer pp. 9–31.

Bonoli, G., B. Palier (1998) 'Changing the Politics of Social Programmes. Innovative Change in British and French Welfare Reforms' *Journal of European Social Policy* vol. 8 (4) pp. 317–330.

Boudon, R. (1982) *The Unintended Consequences of Social Action*, London: Macmillan.

Bovens, M., P. 't Hart (1998) *Understanding Policy Fiascoes*, New Brunswick: Transaction Publishers.

Bovens, M., P. 't Hart, G.B. Peters (2001) *Success and Failure in Public Governance: A Comparative Analysis*, Cheltenham: Edward Elgar.

Brunsson, N., J.P. Olsen (1997) *The Reforming Organization*, Bergen-Sandviken: Fagbokforlaget Vigmostad and Bjorke AS.

Caiden, G.E. (1991a) 'Doing Something Different' Caiden, G.E. (ed.) *Administrative Reform Comes of Age*, Berlin: Walter de Gruyter pp. 131–149.

Caiden, G.E. (1991b) 'Guarding against Failure' Caiden, G.E. (ed.), *Administrative Reform Comes of Age*, Berlin: Walter de Gruyter pp. 151–169.

Cortell, A.P., S. Peterson (1999) 'Altered States: Explaining Domestic Institutional Change' *British Journal of Political Science* vol. 29 pp. 177–203.

Cortell, A.P., S. Peterson (2001) 'Limiting the Unintended Consequences of Institutional Change' *Comparative Political Studies* vol. 34 (7) pp. 768–799.

Creswell, J.W. (2003) *Research Design. Qualitative, Quantitative, and Mixed Methods Approaches*, Thousand Oaks: Sage Publications.

Doig, J.W., E.C. Hargrove (1990) 'Leadership and Political Analysis' Doig, J.W., E.C. Hargrove (eds) *Leadership and Innovation: Entrepreneurs in Government*, Baltimore: The John Hopkins University Press, abridged edition pp. 1–22.

Drazen, A., W. Easterly (2001) 'Do Crises Induce Reform? Simple Empirical Tests of Conventional Wisdom' *Economics and politics* vol. 13 (2) pp. 129–158.

Dror, Y. (1976) 'Strategies for Administrative Reform' Leemans, A.F. (ed.) *The Management of Change in Government*, The Hague: Martinus Nijhoff pp. 82–89.

Engbersen, G., R. van der Veen (1992) 'De onbedoelde effecten van sociaal beleid' *Beleid en Maatschappij* vol. 5 pp. 214–226.

Fisher, F. (1995) *Evaluating Public Policy*, Chicago: Nelson-Hall Publishers.

Hall, P.A. (1993) 'Policy Paradigms, Social Learning, and the State: The Case of Economic Policymaking in Britain' *Comparative Politics* vol. 25 (3) pp. 275–296.

Hall, P.A., R. Taylor (1996) 'Political Science and the Three New Institutionalisms' *MPIFG Discussion paper 96/6*.

Harrison, S., D.J. Hunter, C. Pollitt (1990) *The Dynamics of British Health Policy*, London: Unwin Hyman.

Hart, P. 't (2000) *Hervormend leiderschap: Over veranderingskunst in het openbaar bestuur*, Utrecht: Uitgeverij Lemma bv.

Hattam, V. (1993) *Labor Vision and State Power: The Origins of Business Unionism in the United States*, Princeton: Princeton University Press.

Hay, C. (1999) 'Crisis and the Structural Transformation of the State: Interrogating the Process of Change' *British Journal of Politics and International Relations* vol. 1 (3) pp. 317–344.

Heffron, F. (1989) *Organization Theory and Public Organizations: The Political Connection*, New Jersey: Prentice Hall.

Hogwood, B., L. Gunn (1993) 'Why 'Perfect Implementation' is Unattainable' Hill, M. (ed.) *The Policy Process: A Reader*, New York: Harvester Wheatsheaf pp. 238–247.

Howlett, M., M. Ramesh (1995) *Studying Public Policy: Policy Cycles and Policy Subsystems*, Ontario: Oxford University Press.

Immergut, E. (1992) 'The Rules of the Game: The Logic of Health Policy-Making in France, Switzerland, and Sweden' Steinmo, S., K. Thelen, F. Longstreth (eds) *Structuring politics: Historical Institutionalism in Comparative Analysis*, Cambridge: Cambridge University Press pp. 57–89.

Kaufman, H. (1995) *The Limits of Organizational Change*, New Brunswick: Transaction Publishers.

Keeler, J.T.S. (1993) 'Opening the Window for Reform: Mandates, Crises and Extraordinary Policy-Making' *Comparative Political Studies* vol. 25 (1) pp. 433–486.

Kingdon, J.W. (1995) *Agendas, Alternatives, and Public Policies*, New York: Longman 2nd edition.

Korsten, A.F.A. (1993) 'Beëindiging van beleid' Hoogerwerf, A., (ed.) *Overheidsbeleid. Een inleiding in de beleidswetenschap*, Alphen aan den Rijn: Samsom pp. 198–214.

Krasner, S. D. (1988) 'Sovereignty. An Institutional Perspective' *Comparative Political Studies* vol. 21 (1) pp. 66–94.

Kuipers, S. L. (2006) *The Crisis Imperative: Crisis Rhetoric and Welfare State Reform in Belgium and the Netherlands in the Early 1990s*, Amsterdam: Amsterdam University Press.

Leemans, A.F. (1976a) 'Overview' Leemans, A.F. (ed.) *The Management of Change in Government*, The Hague: Martinus Nijhoff pp. 1–62.

Leemans, A.F. (1976b) 'A Conceptual Framework for the Study of Reform of Central Government' Leemans, A.F. (ed.) *The Management of Change in Government*, The Hague: Martinus Nijhoff pp. 65–98.

Lindblom, C.E. (1959) 'The Science of 'Muddling Through'' *Public Administration Review* vol. 19 pp. 79–88.

Lindblom, C.E. (1979) 'Still Muddling, Not Yet Through' *Public Administration Review* vol. 39 pp. 517–526.

McCombs. M. (1997) 'Building Consensus: The News Media's Agenda-Setting Roles' *Political Communication* vol. 14 pp. 433–443.

March, J., J. Olsen (1995) *Democratic Governance*, New York: Free Press.

Olsen, J.P. (1991) 'Modernization Programs in Perspective: Institutional Analysis of Organizational Change' *Governance: An International Journal of Policy and Administration* vol. 2 (2) pp. 125–149.

Patashnik, E. (2003) 'After the Public Interest Prevails: The Political Sustainability of Policy Reform' *Governance: An International Journal of Policy, Administration, and Institutions* vol. 16 (2) pp. 203–234.

Patton, M.Q. (1990) *Qualitative Evaluation and Research Methods*, Newbury Park: Sage Publications.

Pierson, P. (1994) *Dismantling the Welfare State? Reagan, Thatcher, and the Politics of Retrenchment*, Cambridge: Cambridge University Press.

Pierson, P. (1998) 'Irresistible Forces, Immovable Objects: Post-industrial Welfare States Confront Permanent Austerity' *Journal of European Public Policy* vol. 5 (4) pp. 539–560.

Pollitt, C., G. Bouckaert (2004) *Public Management Reform. A Comparative Analysis*, Oxford: Oxford University Press.

Rayner, J., M. Howlett, J. Wilson, B. Cashore, G. Hoberg (2001) 'Privileging the Sub-sector: Critical Sub-sectors and Sectoral Relationships in Forest Policy-making' *Forest Policy and Economics* vol. 2 pp. 319–332.

Resodihardjo, S.L. (2004) 'Discourse and Funnelling: How Discourse Affected Howard's Leeway During the 1994–5 Crisis' *Journal for Crime, Conflict and the Media* vol. 1 (3) pp. 15–27.

Richards, D., M.J. Smith (1997) 'How Departments Change: Windows of Opportunity and Critical Junctures in Three Departments' *Public Policy and Administration* Vol. 12 (2) pp. 62–79.

Roberts, N.C., P.J. King (1996) *Transforming Public Policy. Dynamics of Policy Entrepreneurship and Innovation*, San Francisco: Jossey-Bass Publishers.

Rodrik, D. (1996) 'Understanding Economic Policy Reform' *Journal of Economic Literature* vol. 34 (1) pp. 9–41.

Rose, R., P.L. Davies (1994) *Inheritance in Public Policy: Change without Choice in Britain*, New Haven: Yale University Press.

Sabatier, P., H. Jenkins-Smith (eds) (1993) *Policy Change and Learning: An Advocacy Coalition Approach*, Boulder: Westview Press.

Sabatier, P., H. Jenkins-Smith (1999) 'The Advocacy Coalition Framework: An Assessment' Sabatier, P.A. (ed.) *Theories of the Policy Process*, Boulder: Westview Press pp. 117–166.

Scharpf, F. (1987) 'A Game-Theoretical Interpretation of Inflation and Unemployment in Western Europe' *Journal of Public Policy* vol. 7 (3) pp. 227–257.

Scott, W.R. (1995) *Institutions and Organizations*, Thousand Oaks: Sage.

Selznick, P. (1957) *Leadership in Administration: A Sociological Interpretation*, Berkeley: University of California.

Shepsle, K.A. (2001) 'A Comment on Institutional Change' *Journal of Theoretical Politics* vol. 13 (3) pp. 321–325.

Sieber, S. (1981) *Fatal Remedies: The Ironies of Social Intervention*, New York: Plenum Press.

Skocpol, T. (1996) *Boomerang: Clinton's Health Security Effort and the Turn Against Government in U.S. Politics*, New York: Norton.

Smith, M. J. (1999) *The Core Executive in Britain*, Houndmills: Macmillan Press Ltd.

Snyder, R., J. Mahoney (1999) 'The Missing Variable: Institutions and the Study of Regime Change' *Comparative Politics* vol. 32 (1) pp. 103–122.

Steinmo, S., J. Watts (1995) 'It's the Institutions, Stupid! Why Comprehensive National Health Insurance Fails in America' *Journal of Health Politics, Policy and Law* vol. 20 (2) pp. 329–372.

Terkildsen, T., F. Schnell (1997) 'How Media Frames Move Public Opinion: An Analysis of the Women's Movement' *Political Research Quarterly* vol. 50 (4) pp. 879–900.

Terry, L.D. (2003) *Leadership of Public Bureaucracies: The Administrator as Conservator*, New York: M.E. Sharpe 2nd edition.

Teske, P., M. Schneider (1994) 'The Bureaucratic Entrepreneur: The Case of City Managers' *Public Administration Review* vol. 54 (4) pp. 331–340.

True, J.L., D.B. Jones, F.R. Baumgartner (1999) 'Punctuated-Equilibrium Theory: Explaining Stability and Change in American Policymaking' Sabatier, P.A. (ed.) *Theories of the Policy Process*, Boulder: Westview Press pp. 97–115.

Wilsford, D. (1994) 'Path Dependency, or Why History Makes It Difficult but Not Impossible to Reform Health Care Systems in a Big Way' *Journal of Public Policy* vol. 14 pp. 251–284.

Wilson, J.Q. (1989) *Bureaucracy: What Government Agencies Do and Why They Do It*, New York: BasicBooks.

Yin, R.K. (1993) *Applications of Case Study Research*, Thousand Oaks: Sage Publications Inc.

Chapter 2

The 1984 Reform of the European Dairy Policy: Financial Crisis, French Leadership, and the Reappraisal of the EC's Core Values

Gerard Breeman[1]

Introduction

Forty years of European dairy policy

During its 40 years history, the European dairy policy changed from encouraging farmers to expand milk production, to severly restricting milk production. At its conception in 1964, all parties involved (i.e. farmers, member governments of the European Community (EC), the EC committee, and the representatives of the farmer unions) were convinced that agricultural production had to be supported in order to preserve the European food supply. The EC therefore encouraged farmers to increase their production and hence garantueed minimum prices.

In 1984, however, a policy reform took place that severely constrained the dairy production. At this time, Ministers of Agriculture agreed to impose a milk quota system to control the continuously rising milk production. Until then, the EC dairy policy had been so successful that it had caused large milk surpluses and major budgetary problems for the EC. After a few failed attempts to reduce milk production, the Ministers of Agriculture saw no other option but to impose a quota system. Based on their production level in 1983, all farmers received a fixed production quota. If they produced more milk than their quota allowed, they had to pay a levy, the so-called *superlevy*.

Over the years, the quota entitlements were reduced by 16% and the milk surpluses and budgetary deficits disappeared. Many observers of the EC dairy policy call the policy reform of 1984 a major success (Ettema, Nooij, Van Dijk & Van der Ploeg, 1995: 32). The quota system was intended to last for five years, but it has been in place for more than twenty years, and will be maintained until at least 2008.

---

1 The author would like to thank Leonique van Tol for her valuable help in gathering data for this chapter.

A paradigmatic change: From promoting to reducing milk production

The 1984 reform was the first time in modern agricultural history that state institutions limited food production. It was by all means a paradigmatic change of the Common Agricultural Policy (CAP), of which the dairy policy was a part (Bekke et al., 1994), because the quota system was considered a break with the 'traditional philosophy' of the CAP and with the 'founding-principles of the EC' (Haagsche Courant, 8 October 1983; FinancieeeleDagblad, 2 August 1983). If we define a policy paradigm as a common vision shared by members of a policy community, then in this case the pre-1984 vision was that agricultural production had to be promoted and the post-1984 vision was that it had to be restricted.

The road to this reform was difficult. The final policy proposal was preceeded by at least five attempts to reduce milk production, but these attempts were hampered by EC decision-making mechanisms, especially the rule of unanimity which gave all member states an equal opportunity to vote against policies that were harmful to their national interests. Member states only refrained from vetoing such policies if they were compensated on other issues. Consequently, many sweeping plans were vetoed, ended in weak proposals, or resulted in complicated package deals (Scharpf, 1988).

Given this condition, one may wonder why this 1984 reform was even formulated, let alone enforced. In this chapter we will try to answer this question and formulate some general propositions concerning policy reforms. We first discuss previous attempts to reform the dairy policy and the barriers that hindered these attempts. Then, we give a chronological account of European decision-making on the quota system. This description is followed by an explanation of how and why barriers were broken down. The last section provides some thoughts on policy reforms in general.

Previously failed attempts to reform the EC dairy system

From 1964 onwards, the European community supported milk production with great enthusiasm. These dairy policies, however, resulted in large production surpluses and the community sought a solution. Five attempts were made before the members accepted the superlevy.

Rising production surpluses

After the Second World War many European governments were preoccupied with recovering their nation's food supply. They devised plans that aimed 'to expand agricultural production by all possible means' (Tracy, 1989: 219). The generally held view was that agriculture warranted special attention. The foundation of the CAP is by and large considered the ultimate institutional consequence of this agricultural focus (Hendriks, 1995: 59). Although many European nations achieved self-sufficiency within twenty years after the war, agriculture continued to be a special policy domain. The protection of agricultural production had to be maintained.

The goals of the CAP were 'to (1) increase agricultural productivity by promoting technical progress and by ensuring the rational development of agricultural production and to (2) ensure a fair standard of living for the agricultural community, in particular by increasing the individual earnings of persons engaged in agriculture' (European Community 2002, article 33-EC: 48). To accomplish these goals, the Commission constructed a price and income system that guaranteed farmers a minimum price. The EC bought products against this so-called intervention price if the market price was lower than the minimum price. The dairy regime, one of the CAP-policies, was successful in meeting these objectives. The production increased continuously and farmers earned a fair income. However, within ten years after the establishment of the dairy regime, the consumption and export of milk fell severely behind production, which caused large production surpluses and serious financial burdens for the EC (see figure 2.1).

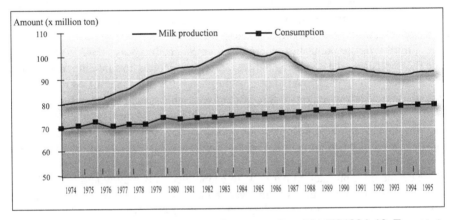

Figure 2.1   EEC milk production and consumption (NAJK 1984, 12; Eurostat; estimated consumption in period 1981–1995)

As a result of this guaranteed price system, the costs of the CAP rose rapidly. The overall Community budget doubled from ECU 18,400 million in 1980 to ECU 36,200 million in 1987 (ENA, 2005). The community's revenues, however, remained largely the same. The Commission therefore issued a strong argument that either the contribution of all member states had to be increased or the costs of the dairy sector had to be controlled.[2] Since the first option stranded on heavy protests from the poorest members, the Commission initially worked on the second option.

---

2   The contribution was 1% of the Value Added Tax (VAT) and the EC suggested to raise this up to 1.4%.

Finding solutions

In order to solve the overproduction of milk, the EC proposed and experimented with various policy proposals before the 1984 milk quota system was installed. Most of these plans, however, had no or a limited effect, or were simply not enforced at all.

The first attempt to control production was stipulated in a proposal from the then EC Commissioner for agriculture, Mansholt, in 1968. He believed that European farmers had to improve their efficiency by enlarging their businesses so that they would be able to compete on the world market. His solution was to promote structural policies that forced small farmers into an ultimatum: to either enlarge or, eventually, terminate their business. However, 'the plan proved too radical to be politically acceptable (…). It was seen as destructive for too many small family farms' (European Commission, 1994: 13). Many European member states vetoed it.

A second strategy to control production was to freeze the minimum guaranteed milk price for a period of time. Basically, this happened from 1968 to 1971, when the EC leveled the minimum price and increased it only slightly from 1971 onwards. Nonetheless, milk production continued to increase.

A third effort to control production was introduced in May, 1977. At this time, the EC implemented a bonus regulation for farmers in order to stimulate them to halt milk production, or even to quit farming altogether (the so-called SLOM regulation). It had some effects in regions where farmers were able – technically and structurally – to shift to other products and hence were interested in this bonus regulation. In most regions, however, the bonus regulation was unattractive. Pastures are, for example, not suitable to grow grain or crops on, and diary machinery is completely useless on an arable farm. The regulation was only attractive for farmers unable or unwilling to increase the milk production per cow. In economic terms they would be called the laggards. Consequently, the most innovative farmers and productive cows remained and milk production continued to increase (NAJK, 1984: 8).

The fourth attempt to control milk production came in September 1977, when the EC introduced the co-responsibility levy. Dairy farmers were forced to pay a certain amount of money per 100 kilos of milk.[3] The EC thought this would make the farmers co-responsible for overproduction. But to farmers, this levy was only considered as an extra tax, which had to be compensated with extra milk production (NAJK, 1984: 10–1).

The fifth attempt, from 1980 through 1981, was based on a proposal by the Commission to impose a superlevy on milk produced in excess of 99% of the amount delivered to the dairy factories in 1979. This meant that farmers had to pay a levy if they produced more milk in 1981 than they did in 1979 (minus 1%). However, the main EU decision-making institution concerning agricultural matters, the European agricultural Council, which consists of all European Ministers of Agriculture, rejected

---

3   Milk is expressed in kilos and not in litres because the amount of fat may vary.

this proposal because export possibilities had slightly improved in 1980, allowing EC surpluses to be sold against higher prices which would actually improve the EC's financial position.[4] Unfortunately, this export improvement did not last for long.

Barriers to reform the common European dairy system

Two barriers obstructed an effective reform of the European dairy system. The first barrier was the EC policy-making mechanism that constrained effective *decision-making*. The second barrier was the immobility of agricultural production factors that constrained the effectuation of the policy.

The EU decision-making system

Scharpf (1988) has notably discussed the constraining effect of the EC decision-making mechanism, and has shown that its rule of unanimity made decision-making ineffective. Scharpf posited that once member states benefit from a decision (given the assumption of national self-interest) they will not easily agree on adjustments. Only when new proposals aimed at improving the nation's overall position are made will member states refrain from using their veto. Scharpf named this deadlock situation the 'joint decision trap' of the European Community (Scharpf, 1988: 241; 1997: 144; see also De Groot, 1997: 78–9, 105, 133). Scharpf concludes that, due to this decision system, the 'joint European programmes seem to increase expenditures beyond the level that would be politically acceptable within a unitary government' (Scharpf, 1988: 255).

At least the first attempt to control milk production (the 1968 Mansholt plan) – if not more attempts – was blocked by this bargaining system. Mansholt's plan was vetoed because it was too ambitious in terms of common 'problem solving' (Scharpf, 1988: 255). In a memorandum to the Council, Mansholt suggested that the CAP had to be extensively reformed (Grant, 1997: 70–1; Dinan, 1994: 338–9). He wanted to introduce programs that would enable small farmers to withdraw from agricultural production and provide more opportunities for larger farms to increase their scale. This, he believed, would make European agriculture more competitive on the world market. The general reaction to his plan was disbelief, especially on the part of the French, who were particularly keen on protecting and supporting small family-run farms. The existing price and income policies did just that and 'encouraged marginal farms to stay in business' (Grant, 1997: 71). Consequently, the French and other members did not benefit from changing the status quo. They vetoed the plan.

---

4 Although the European Commission has much executive power, the European Council is the highest decision-making organ in the EU. The Council is referred to as the European agricultural Council when the Ministers of Agriculture of all member states are deliberating; it is named the general European Council when the Ministers of foreign affairs are involved; or simply the European Council when all head of states are negotiating.

The immobility of production factors

The immobility of agricultural production factors blocked any effective dairy reform. As discussed above, the SLOM regulation failed because of the immobility of pastures and machinery. Various agricultural economists claim that this immobility caused the continuous high level of milk production (Burger, 1993: 116–7; De Hoogh, 1994: 1–12). These economists argue that in most economic sectors, production factors are transferred when profits start to decline, while in agriculture they are not. Agricultural production factors are hard to transfer to other sectors. Consider, for instance, expensive agricultural machinery or agricultural know-how. Even if profits decline, agriculture's production factors generally do not shift, i.e. production levels will not decline.

Three of the previous attempts to control milk production clearly illustrate how this immobility of production factors constrained an effective effectuation. The freezing of the minimum milk price (attempt two), the SLOM regulation (attempt three), and the co-responsibility levy (attempt four) did not lead to a declining milk production. It turned out to be difficult for farmers to switch to other economic behaviour. They simply could not take part in the SLOM program, and they experienced the financial constraints of the freezing and the levy as extra declines in their incomes. Milk farmers saw no other option but to compensate their declining income with additional production. Consequently, the milk production increased.

Solving the problem: The introduction of the Superlevy

The EC fell into large financial problems because of its expensive agricultural policies. On three summits, Stuttgart (June 1983), Athens (December 1983), and Brussels (March 1984), the members of the Commission, as well as the European Minister of Finance and Foreign Affairs, pushed hard for agricultural reforms. The summits failed but, three days after the Brussels summit, the European Ministers of Agriculture under leadership of the French Minister of Agriculture, Rocard, reached an agreement on the dairy reform, which will be explained below.

Financial crisis

In 1982 the budgetary problems for the EC increased. Initially the prospects for dairy products were good: the world market prices were high. In April 1982, the Ministers of Agriculture of all member states (the Agrarian Council) therefore raised the guaranteed minimum price by more than 10% instead of the Commission's recommended moderate raise. In the second half of 1982, new financial burdens occurred. First, the British government claimed a refund for paying too much contribution. Its claim was accepted by other member states, but the states agreed neither on the amount of repayment nor how it was to be repaid. Second, the dairy sales stagnated resulting in packed warehouses and rising costs. Third, following good weather conditions, milk production had increased immensely. The EC therefore had to buy more surpluses, thereby oppressing its budget even further. In September 1982, the Commission announced it foresaw a severe financial crisis for 1983 (NRC, 8 September 1982).

Around this time, the Commission and the media presented the budgetary problems as a severe financial crisis. The Commission framed the weak budgetary position as a financial crisis, for the first time, in its 1982 annual report. The Commission specifically blamed the production surpluses of grain and milk for causing this crisis. The media covered the crisis with alarming headlines. Headlines read, for example, 'Completely Uncontrollable Milk Production' (Telegraaf, 19 February 1983) and 'The CAP Will Soon Become Unaffordable' (Volkskrant, 4 March 1983). This crisis rhetoric in the media continued throughout 1983, when more alarming numbers on the budgetary problems became public. In March 1983, the Commission claimed that the members had to increase their contribution in order to solve the financial problems. The Luxembourgian chairman of the Commission Thorn, stated that if the member states would not comply then this implied that the members were indeed 'rethinking the common agriculture policy and excluding Spain and Portugal from the EC would become necessary' (Volkskrant, 6 May 1983).

As a result, the European Ministers of Foreign Affairs and Finance met in May 1983 to discuss the budgetary problems and the Commission's request to increase the contribution – a request which they denied. Instead, they stated that the costs of the CAP and especially of the dairy policy had to be reduced first before they were willing to increase their contribution. The head of states affirmed this point of view on the Stuttgart summit in June 1983. However, they failed to formulate plans to reduce costs and the financial crisis continued on this last summit. The bottleneck was a disagreement on the raise of the contribution, the British rebate claim, and the CAP reform. British Foreign Minister Howe concluded that the EC had reached an 'extremely dangerous situation (…). Europe was about to go broke' (Reformatorisch Dagblad, 15 June 1983; see also Haagsche Courant 14 June 1983).

Reformation or devastation

Farmers and Ministers of Agriculture were not pleased with the Stuttgart summit's outcome. A farmer's magazine concluded that this was an apparent takeover of agriculture policy-making by the Minister of Finance and Foreign Affairs (Boerderij, 1 June 1983). The Ministers of Agriculture feared that the Commission or the Ministers of Finance would prepare far-reaching reform proposals that would be devastating for the CAP. To avoid such an outcome, the Ministers of Agriculture started devising less harmful reform proposals (Petit, 1987: 129–133).

When the Commission calculated that either the minimum guaranteed prices had to be lowered – with at least 10% or the co-responsibility levy raised with 12% to cover costs for 1984 – almost every Minister of Agriculture presented a reform plan. The proposal of the Dutch Minister of Agriculture Braks stands out because it was well-received by all others involved. Braks proposed to restrict the price and income system to such an extent that the costs of dairy policy would not exceed the EC revenues. If no restrictive measures were taken, Braks foresaw a re-nationalization of agricultural policies, i.e. the end of the common agricultural market, its compensating payments, and a reintroduction of levies on the internal European borders. Since Dutch farmers received the largest CAP-refunding, this would be 'disastrous for Dutch farmers' (Het Binnenhof, 25 July 1983). To avoid such catastrophic consequences, Braks emphasized the necessity of a quota system. Dutch farmer's magazines started supporting Braks' position by saying that 'painful choices are unavoidable' (Boerderij, 27 August 1983; 31 August 1983) and 'a re-nationalization is at stake' (Boer en Tuinder, 8 September 1983; 20 October 1983; Friesch Dagblad, 16 September 1983). Members of the European Parliament also feared a re-nationalization and agreed with Braks that reform was needed (Trouw, 11 October 1983).

While Ministers of Agriculture deliberated on the different reform proposals, the Commission retained the sense of crisis by threatening to discontinue its CAP payments if no additional money became available (Petit, 1987: 130). However, in September 1983, the European Parliament refused to meet the Commission's demands. The Parliament wanted cost reductions before additional money was allocated to the Commission because this allocation would only serve to strengthen the position of the Minister of Finance and Foreign Affairs. In response, and for the very first time in history, the Commission stopped CAP-payments on 10 October 1983, emphasizing that the EC suffered from a severe financial crisis. When a French representative accused the Commission of blackmail, the Danish Commissioner of agriculture Dalsager quickly responded that if no extra money was allocated, all EC payments would be discontinued, not only those of the CAP (Trouw, 13 October 1983).

The Commission's crisis rhetoric, its continuous demands for extra budgets, as well as the fear for re-nationalization of the agricultural policies, resulted in intensive pressure on all EC members to make haste with policy reforms. When, in November 1983, Commissioner Dalsager announced that milk production had again increased by 4%, farmer-representatives called for cooperation to restrain further production (Boerderij, 23 November 1983). France, the largest opponent to reform, immediately announced that severe action was needed. In reaction to the financial difficulties, France's Minister of Finance (Delors) surprised all EC members by consenting to a modest quota system. On the eve of the next summit of the heads of state in Athens, in December, 1983, the Dutch Minister of Agriculture stated that the willingness to reform the dairy policy was 'greater than ever' (NRC, 2 December 1983).

Deep core crisis

At the Athens summit, hopes were high that the financial crisis could be solved. A CAP policy reform was accepted, but negotiations failed dramatically. Although most representatives initially agreed on some kind of quota system, Ireland, and then Greece, wanted exemptions. When, in response to Irish and Grecian claims, Luxembourg and Italy put forth reservations as well, the annoyed French President Mitterrand called out that the French 'wanted to have an exceptional position too!' (Algemeen Dagblad, 7 December 1983). Quite obviously, the Dutch and Danish found this unacceptable and nothing came out of the meeting, 'not even a common statement' (Telegraaf, 7 December 1983).

The Athens summit had failed and most heads of state feared for the future of the EC. They posed the question as to whether European citizens could still have faith in Europe as a Community. Some argued that this crisis was not *just* another financial crisis or a agricultural policy crisis, but an institutional one, meaning that the legitimacy of the EU as an institution was at stake. Every aspect of the EC was open for discussion (Utrechts Nieuwsblad, 2 December 1983). Members of the European Parliament also feared for the EC's future. Some said that the failure of Athens illustrated how European leaders had lost their 'communitarian spirit' and were unable to represent general European interests (Petit, 1987: 34). Observers of the EC agreed with this position and concluded that 'the crisis had deepened and that the credibility of the EC was at stake' (FinancieeeleDagblad, 9 December 1983).

In response to this deep crisis, many called out for a reappraisal of the core values of the EC. The chairman of the European Parliament said, for example, that 'this failure should be a motive for a profound and common appraisal of the reasons of existence of the EC' (Algemeen Dagblad, 7 December 1983). Some recognized that the principal problem in Europe had been the members' continuous pursuits of national interests, and their lack of shared intentions. French president Mitterrand, who presided the EC in the first half year of 1984, stressed the importance of such shared values and intentions and pleaded for a 'return to the treaty of Rome – our Bible' (Algemeen Dagblad, 7 December 1983). With this reference to the establishing treaty of the community, he forcefully stressed that the very existence of the community was at stake. Petit (1987: 34) commented at the time, 'If the French Presidency too, does not manage to find answers to the vital problems of the continent, then the end of the Community would be in sight'.

French leadership

The media reported that the French were in a hurry: they planned new meetings in January and a new European summit in March. President Mitterand portrayed himself as a European leader, stating that 'France has a European calling and it is prepared to sacrifice itself' (Het FinancieeeleDagblad, 16 December 1983, 25 January 1984). The President told his cabinet that he would do everything in his power to find a way to deal with the financial problems (Het FinancieeeleDagblad,

9 December 1983). Supported by the President, the French Minister of Agriculture Rocard took the lead.

Rocard regarded the Return to the Treaty of Rome-statement not only an appeal to discuss the core values of the EC, but also motivation to change EC decision-making procedures. In Rocard's view, decisions in agricultural matters had to be taken by qualified majority voting, rather than by unanimity such as was written in Article 43 of the Treaty of Rome (European Community 2002; see also Het FinancieeeleDagblad, 9 December 1983). Rocard also stated that technical matters and broad political issues should not be mixed in package deals made at summits by the heads of states. Instead, technical matters had to be solved separately by expert ministers (Volkskrant, 14 December 1983).

Rocard allowed the Agricultural Council to vote by a qualified majority. He was entitled to do this because the voting procedures of CAP did not prescribe unanimity, although unanimous vote was the custom. As soon as Rocard noticed that no country represented communitarian interests, he even allowed the Council vote by simple majority (De Groot, 1997). Decision-making therefore proceeded much faster, and the Ministers of Agriculture felt that they had regained their policy domain back from the Minister of Finance and Foreign Affairs (Het Financieeeledagblad, 7 March 1984; 20 March 1984). Under Rocard's leadership, the Agricultural Council worked in a positive way to the new summit to be held on 19 and 20 March 1984 in Brussels. Rocard's ability to set the agenda and influence the decision-making process was strong. There was 'indeed a unanimity among those whom we interviewed that Mr. Rocard used these powers very effectively when he became President of the Agricultural Council' (Petit, 1987: 132–3).

Finally, a solution

During preparatory negotiations for the Brussels summit, the Ministers of Agriculture met from 12 until 14 March 1984. In the night of 13 and 14 March, they finally agreed to reform the dairy sector. Most importantly, they agreed that the total amount of milk production within the EC had to be reduced and that over-production would be subject to a punitive levy, i.e. the superlevy. The Ministers of Agriculture, however, did not agree on the exact amounts. Ireland, in particular, wanted a larger portion than the available quota. Nevertheless, with these agreements in mind most European leaders were no longer afraid of failure at the coming summit (Algemeen Dagblad, 15 March 1984).

Despite all efforts and hopes, the Brussels summit failed. British Prime Minister Thatcher refused to agree with anything, so long as she had not received a refund for paying too much to the contribution. Irish Premier Fitzgerald could not agree with any proposal by the French concerning the amount of milk quota; Fitzgerald left the meeting halfway through. The reactions to the summit's failure were bitter. Most heads of states insinuated that, in particular, Thatcher's resistance had caused the failure (Volkskrant, 22 March 1984) while Rocard and Mitterand were praised for their attempts. The French President stated bitterly, 'the ones who want to save the EC should do so in the coming weeks and I hope all ten nations want to save the EC' (Trouw, 22 March 1984).

Although the summit failed, the Ministers of Agriculture were very close to an agreement. They had continued their negotiations because every minister was willing, at least, to come to an agreement. Members of Parliament and the Commission urged the Agricultural Council to reach consensus on the interim agreements set up before the Brussels summit took place (Volkskrant, 23 March 1984). The only thorny issue they had to solve was Ireland's claim for a higher quotum.

On 29 March 1984, the Agricultural Council met. After two days of negotiations, all ministers but one were content about a package deal: the Dutch Minister of Agriculture Braks did not agree with an exemption for the Irish. Braks considered it unacceptable that all members had to cut their milk production, while the Irish were allowed to increase theirs. On the early morning of 31 March, Rocard forced a breakthrough by announcing that the Council would vote over the total package with a qualified majority. In the end, Braks voted in favour because he believed that the agreement contributed significantly to the solution of the deeper institutional crisis of the EC. As a result, the quota system was accepted unanimously. All ministers applauded for Rocard and praised him for his leadership. He responded by remarking that the general financial crisis was still not resolved, but that at least 'the Ministers of Agriculture had taken their responsibilities' (Volkskrant, 2 April 1984).

Thus, on 31 March 1984 the ministers finally agreed on a quota system based on an individually held quota of production of milk or a dairy product per year. If a farmer exceeded his amount, he would be subject to pay a punitive levy. Except for the Irish, the quotas were calculated on the total amount of milk-deliveries in 1981 plus 1%. This meant that all farmers were allowed to produce as much milk as they did in 1981 plus 1%. If they produced more, they had to pay a superlevy of 75% of the target price. The levy was raised step by step up to 115% in 2004, meaning that farmers had to pay more than they earned on all milk in excess of their quota (Council Regulations, 856/84; 857/84).

Facilitators and barrier breakers

Two events made the introduction of the milk quota policy possible: *crisis* and *leadership*. The financial crisis caused heated debate about the legitimacy of the dairy policy and about the core values of the EC. In turn, Rocard's leadership used these discussions to change the decision-making rules and push for the restrictive quota policy.

Crisis creation: Framing and maintaining

The Commission framed the budgetary position of the EC as a crisis in its annual report on 1982 and deliberately maintained a sense of crisis throughout the years of 1983 and 1984. It framed the crisis not only as a dairy problem, but as a general financial crisis, and soon the Minister of Finance and Foreign Affairs did the same.

The crisis increased to such an extent that in June 1983 agricultural matters were taken over by the Ministers of Finance. The Dutch Minister of Finance confirmed that they indeed had acquired control over the agricultural problems (Leeuwarder Courant, 28 July 1983, Haagsche Courant, 25 August 1983). The crisis of milk surpluses was thus redefined as a financial crisis and, later on, even as an institutional crisis whereby the whole institutional structure of the EC was threatened (Boin & 't Hart, 2000; Alink, Boin, & 't Hart, 2001). As one MP said it, 'all misery was coming together now' (Trouw, 11 October 1983).

Commissioners, Ministers of Finance, Foreign Affairs and some Ministers of Agriculture deliberately maintained the sense of crisis to maintain pressure for reform. The Dutch Minister of Agriculture Braks, Commissioner Dalsager, and the French Minister of Finance Delors, did so by persistently communicating their fear for a re-nationalization of agriculture. In their views, only one solution was possible: dairy policies had to be reformed to be in balance with existing budgets. British Foreign Minister Howe said that he deliberately blocked the raising of the agricultural budget 'in order to keep the pressure on cutting costs' (Het FinancieeeleDagblad, 21 July 1983). In September the Dutch foreign Minister Van den Broek confirmed that the denial for extra budget for agriculture was a 'means to keep the pressure on' (Het FinancieeeleDagblad, 22 September 1983). The deliberate attempts by the ministers and the Commission to remain pressure on the decision-making process by framing the situation as a crisis is previously described by Petit (1987). 'The cost of not taking a decision, which had caused the financial crisis, is considered as the engine of the bargaining process. Rocard *infused* his colleagues with a sense of urgency as well as a conscience that this was an opportunitie to seize' (Petit, 1987: 132–3).

The sense of crisis had two effects: it led to a shared goal, and it motivated the Ministers of Agriculture to create reform proposals. Many European Ministers and heads of states prioritized the financial problems of the EC over the agricultural policies. While frequently emphasizing the consequences of these problems, they increasingly started sharing intentions to take some serious action. Their shared goal was to come to a consensus to solve the budgetary problems. Consequently, the Ministers of Agriculture were pushed to formulate reform plans and they surprised each other with far-reaching proposals.

French leadership: Reappraising values and changing decision rules

The failure of the Athens summit in December 1983 resulted in serious debates about the core values of the EC and motivated the French to take a leading role in solving the crisis. The appeal to reappraise the core values of the EC generally reinstalled a kind of commonness among the representatives of the member states, and prepared them to make sacrifices. In their rhetoric, the French argued that they were willing to give up some of their national interests for the common good. The crisis thus resulted in a reappraisal of the core values which, in turn, solved the lack of shared intentions that had frustrated decision-making thus far.

The call to Return to the Treaty of Rome was interpreted by the French to include a re-evaluation of the decision-making rules. They became aware that the founding treaty of the EC mentioned the possibility of qualified voting in agricultural matters, but that unanimity had always been the unwritten standard decision-making procedure. The French Minister of Agriculture saw the crisis as an opportunity to break with this unwritten rule and introduce qualified voting. In short, the crisis situation was a window of opportunity for the French to change the decision-making mechanism, thereby avoiding the joint decision trap, and making the quota system possible.

In the end, the French were not only satisfied because they claimed to have secured the EU, but they were also happy that they were able to maintain the budgetary system with guaranteed prices for the dairy industry. Together with the Dutch and the Danish, they had benefited greatly from this system. They therefore had much reason to maintain the status quo. A reform without this redistributive financial system would have implied a serious financial problem for many small French farmers.

Two years later, the EU budget deficits were still not solved and, consequently, the contribution of all members had to be raised. The dairy sector, however, was off the hook. It had reformed itself, fixed the production, and was no longer seen as the problem. Still, the Frence, the Dutch, and the Danish benefited from the pricing sytem.

Explaining fundamental policy reform

This case illustrates that the institutional design of decision-making can be an immense barrier to policy reforms, as well as a facilitator for reform. The unwritten rule of unanimity in the EC decision mechanism had resulted in the continuous pursuit of national interests and the lack of commonness (Scharpf, 1988). For a long period of time, the rule of unanimity frustrated attempts at a solution for the milk surpluses. Only when a general financial crisis threatened decision-makers – and the Commission stopped the CAP payments – did shared intentions and a willingness to create sweeping policy reforms evolve. They only accepted far-reaching reform when decisive leaders had intentionally maintained crisis sentiments, changed the decision-making rules, stopped payments, and pulled the plans through (Dinan, 1994: 14).

At first glance, the case seems to indicate that policy reforms become acceptable only when an urgent crisis is upon decision-makers. This conclusion concurs with theories about crisis-induced reforms. These theories hold that sweeping policy reforms are mainly possible when crises create opportunities for policy entrepreneurs to promote reforms, and garner acceptance for them by all other decision-makers (Baumgartner & Jones, 1993; Kingdon, 1984). This case illustrates, however, that crisis-induced reforms are only possible after various non-radical attempts (i.e. attempts that do not overthrow the policy paradigm) have failed. Policy makers initially try to solve problems through simple adjustments to existent policy instruments (in this case, freezing the guaranteed prices and increasing the co-responsibility levy). When these attempts fail, policy makers may introduce new instruments (such as the SLOM regulation). If these measures turn out to be unsuccessful as well, policy makers can finally try to change the entire policy paradigm by using the crisis sentiments (Hall, 1993; Rose & Davies, 1994; Breeman et al., 2000).

In conclusion, crisis and leadership were factors facilitating paradigmatic policy reforms in this case (Petit 1987: 130–1). However, it seems that such reforms only occur once policy makers have attempted to solve problems in a way that is consistent with the existing policy paradigm. If these attempts fail, policy makers will be successful in framing the situation in terms of crisis because other actors will be more susceptible to crisis sentiments. By feeding and maintaining these crisis feelings, policy makers can act more decisively and push for reform. We therefore posit that previously failed attempts to reform a policy present two opportunities for those seeking to reform a policy: they allow crisis framing, and they facilitate more encompassing reforms later on (Hall, 1993).

References

Algemeen Dagblad (7 December 1983) *EG-top Athene: Geen enkel besluit.*

Algemeen Dagblad (15 March 1984) *Vol hoop over Eurotop.*

Alink, F, A. Boin, P. 't Hart (2001) 'Institutional Crises and Reforms in Policy Sectors: The Case of Asylum Policy in Europe' *Journal of European Public Policy*, vol. 8 (2) pp. 286–306.

Baumgartner, F.R., B.D. Jones (1993) *Agendas and Instability in American Politics*, Chicago: The University of Chicago Press.

Bekke, H., J. de Vries, G. Neelen (1994) *De salto mortale van het Ministerie van Landbouw, Natuurbeheer en Visserij: beleid, organisatie en management op een breukvlak*, Alphen aan den Rijn: Samsom H.D. Tjeenk Willink.

Boerderij (1 June 1983) *Kabinet vindt EG-uitgaven nu belangrijker dan boeren.*

Boerderij (27 August 1983) *Pijnlijke keuze in zuivelbeleid lijkt onvermijdelijk.*

Boerderij (31 August 1983) *De moeilijke keuze van het zuivelvraagstuk.*

Boerderij (23 November 1983) *Zuivelsector vergt nu overleg en samenwerking.*

Boer en Tuinder (8 September 1983) *Tijd van pappen en nathouden EG-landbouwpolitiek is voorbij.*

Boer en Tuinder (20 October 1983) *Europese gemeenschap moet snel maatregelen nemen.*

Boin, A., P. 't Hart (2000) 'Institutional Crises and Reforms in Policy Sectors' Wagenaar, H. (ed.) *Government Institutions: Effects, Changes and Normative Foundations*, Dordrecht: Kluwer, pp. 9–31.

Breeman, G., K. op den Kamp, M. Zannoni (2000) 'Mestproblemen en varkenspest: crisis en kansen in de landbouwsector' Boin, A., S. Kuipers, M. Otten (eds.) *Institutionele crises: breuklijnen in beleidssectoren*, Alphen aan den Rijn: Samsom pp. 114–143.

Burger, A. (1993) *Voor boerenvolk en vaderland: De vorming van het EEG-landbouwbeleid, 1959–1966.* Amsterdam: Het Spinhuis.

Council Regulation (EC) (1 April 1984) 'No 856/84 of 31 March 1984 Amending Regulation (EC) No 804/68 on the Common Organization of the Market in Milk and Milk Products' *Official Journal L 090*, pp. 10–12.

Council Regulation (EC) (1 April 1984) 'No 857/84 of 31 March 1984 Adopting General Rules for the Application of the Levy Referred to in Article 5c of Regulation (EC) No 804/68 in the Milk and Milk Products Sector' *Official Journal L 090*, pp. 13–16.

Dinan, D. (1994) *Ever Closer Union: An Introduction to European Integration,* Houndsmills, Basingstoke: Palgrave.

ENA (European Navigator) www.ena.lu, last accessed 19 December 2005.

Ettema, M., A. Nooij, G. van Dijk, J.D. van der Ploeg (1995) *De Toekomst: Een bespreking van de derde boerderij-enquete voor het nationaal landbouwdebat,* Doetinchem: Misset.

European Commission (1994) 'The Economics of the Common Agricultural Policy' *European Economy, Reports and Studies* (5), Luxembourg: Office for Official Publications of the European Communities.

European Community (24 December 2002) 'The Treaty Establishing the European Community' *Official Journal* C325/33, pp. 1–152.

Friesch Dagblad (16 September 1983) *Marktbeleid zuivel meest effectief met superheffing.*

Grant, W. (1997) *The Common Agricultural Policy,* Houndsmills: Macmillan Press.

Groot, T.C. de (1997) *Dertien is een boerendozijn: onderhandelingen in de raad van Ministers van landbouw over hervormingen van het Europese landbouwbeleid.* Delft: Eburon.

Haagsche Courant (14 June 1983) *EEG wil over hele lijn bezuinigen.*

Haagsche Courant (25 August 1983) *Europese landbouw aanvaardt rem op productie.*

Haagsche Courant (8 October 1983) *Kabinet wil rem op uitgaven EEG.*

Hall, P.A. (1993) 'Policy Paradigms, Social Learning, and the States: The Case of Economic Policymaking in Britain' *Comparative Politics* vol. 25 (3) pp. 275–296.

Hendriks, G. (1995) 'German Agricultural Policy Objectives' Wilkinson, A. (ed.) *Renationalisation of the Common Agricultural Policy?* Tonbridge: Combined Book Services.

Het Binnenhof (25 July 1983) *Boete voor boeren die te veel produceren.*

Het FinancieeeleDagblad (21 July 1983) *In vakantie doorwerken aan problemen EG financiering en landbouwbeleid.*

Het FinancieeeleDagblad (2 August 1983) *Koel onthaal voor EG-voorstel landbouwbeleid.*

Het FinancieeeleDagblad (22 September 1983) *Ministers wijken geen duimbreed van standpunten over EG-financiering.*

Het FinancieeeleDagblad (9 December 1983) *Haalt EG-landbouwbeleid eind 1984?*

Het FinancieeeleDagblad (16 December 1983) *Bevriezing EG-landbouwprijzen door financiele problemen onvermijdelijk.*

Het FinancieeeleDagblad (25 January 1984) *Frankrijk zet nu vaart achter oplossing problemen van EG.*

Het FinancieeeleDagblad (7 March 1984) *Fransen laten het in EG-raad steeds vaker op stemming aankomen.*

Het FinancieeeleDagblad (20 March 1984) *EG-top krijgt controversieel akkoord over landbouw op tafel.*

Hoogh, J. de (1994) 'Waarom eigenlijk landbouwpolitiek?' de Hoogh, J., H.J. Silvis (eds.) *EU-landbouwpolitiek van binnen en van buiten,*Wageningen: Wageningen Pres pp 1–13.

Kingdon, J.W. (1984) *Agendas, Alternatives and Public Policies*, Don Mills, ONT.: HarperCollins.

Leeuwarder Courant (28 July 1983) *Landbouwpolitiek in zwaar weer.*

NAJK (Nederlands Agrarisch Jongeren Kontakt), (1984) *Wie melkt er voort? De gevolgen van de superheffing voor inkomen, bedrijfsstruktuur en bedrijfsovername,* Utrecht: Imago-Landbouw.

NRC Handelsblad (8 September 1982) *EG-landbouwuitgaven dreigen dit jaar explosief te stijgen.*

NRC Handelsblad (2 December 1983) *Athene moet EG financieel gezond maken.*

Petit, M. (ed.) (1987) *Agricultural Policy Formation in the European Community: The Birth of Milk Quotas and CAP Reform*, Amsterdam: Elsevier.

Reformatorisch Dagblad (15 June 1983) *Europees landbouwbeleid kost teveel.*

Rose, R., R. Davies (1994) *Inheritance in Public Policy: Change without Choice in Britain*, New Haven: Yale University Press.

Scharpf, F.W. (1988) 'The Joint-Decision Trap: Lessons from German Federalism and European Integration' *Public Administration* vol. 66 (3) pp.239–278.

Scharpf, F.W. (1997) *Games Real Actors Play: Actor-Centered Institutionalism in Policy Research*, Boulder, CO: Westview Press.

Telegraaf (19 February 1983) *Zorg over enorme zuivelberg in EG.*

Telegraaf (7 December 1983) *Zelfs geen verklaring.*

Tracy, M. (1989) *Government and Agriculture in Western Europe 1880–1988*, New York: New York University Press.

Trouw (11 October 1983) *EG in bijna fatale crisis.*

Trouw (13 October 1983) *Opschorting in betaling van landbouwprodukten.*

Trouw (22 March 1984) *Onzekerheid troef na nieuwe Europese flop.*

Utrechts Nieuwsblad (2 December 1983) *Europese Gemeenschap: huis vol herrie dat niet mag instorten.*

Volkskrant (4 March 1983) *Landbouwbeleid is onbetaalbaar.*

Volkskrant (6 May 1983) *Europese Commissie vraagt lidstaten grotere bijdrage.*

Volkskrant (14 December 1983) *Nederland mede schuldig aan mislukken EG-top Athene.*

Volkskrant (22 March 1984) *Mitterand: Britten moeten nog wennen in EG.*

Volkskrant (23 March 1984) *Kabinet is sceptisch over stemmen bij meerderheid door EG-landen.*

Volkskrant (2 April 1984) *Europese Ministers sluiten moeizaam landbouwakkoord.*

Chapter 3

The Rewards of Policy Legacy:
Why Dutch Social Housing did not
Follow the British Path

Taco Brandsen and Jan-Kees Helderman[1]

Reform in Dutch housing

In 1989, during the third term of Prime Minister Lubbers, the Dutch government announced far-reaching reforms of the housing policy. Now, fifteen years later, it is clear that nearly all of the reforms that were proposed have indeed been adopted. The social housing reforms included budgetary cuts that gave way to a more fundamental reorganization of the relationships between the government and the housing associations. Two objectives lie at the heart of the reforms: the more efficient use of the capital that had accumulated over the years – which was stored in the social housing stock and the financial reserves of the housing associations – and the development of new governance relations between the state and the housing associations.

The climax of the reforms was the so-called Balancing and Grossing Operation (*bruteringsoperatie*), which took place in 1995 when, in a single stroke, the housing associations and the national authorities each wrote off the debts held by the other – over €16 billion in unpaid object subsidies against €17 billion in unredeemed government loans (NIROV, 1995). Many things are remarkable about the Dutch housing reform. From the Second World War until the late 1980s, Dutch housing policy was constrained and determined by external policy requirements and by the obligations entered into under earlier subsidy agreements (Van der Schaar, 1987; Helderman & Brandsen, 2004). Until the mid-1980s, Dutch housing policy seemed to be a classical example of the lock-in effects of previous policies. Yet in the 1990s, these lock-in effects apparently had lost their relevance in the sense that they no longer constrained reforms. Moreover, whereas the struggle against the housing-shortage used to be considered as one of the most politicized issues in the post-war Dutch welfare state, in the 1990s, reforms could be accomplished without

---

1   This chapter reflects ideas made in earlier studies by the authors, particularly Helderman & Brandsen, 2004; Brandsen, 2004; Brandsen & Helderman, 2004; Brandsen, Ribeiro & Farnell, 2006; Helderman, 2006.

any notable political and public attention. Dutch housing more or less underwent a silent revolution in which reforms could be accomplished without opposition from political parties (from the left) and interest groups (especially those of the housing associations) and without attention by the media and the wider public. But in international terms, too, the Dutch social housing reforms are considered to be remarkable: so far, for example, they have avoided the marginalization of the social housing stock that has taken place in Great Britain where the proportion of social housing in overall stock was severely reduced through sales and declining construction levels (Harloe, 1995).

This chapter examines how the reform in Dutch social housing was possible and why it did not result in a marginalized housing stock. In the UK, social housing production dropped off from the 1970s onwards, whereas Dutch construction levels during the 1980s remained close to those of the early 1970s (Harloe, 1995). In the early 1980s, moreover, the social housing stock in the UK was reduced by as much as a fifth (1.2 million homes) through the Right-to-Buy policy explained below, while in the same period the Dutch social housing stock continued to grow, its proportion in overall stock remaining fairly stable. Finally, contrary to what happened in the UK, Dutch tenants have not suddenly found themselves in a residual and marginal sector that caters only for the poor. Although this chapter focuses primarily on Dutch social housing, it will refer to the British situation as a contrast case. One must of course acknowledge the historically divergent course of Dutch and British housing policy, but many authors (as will be explained below) have regarded the British evolvement as typical and ultimately inevitable – an assumption that the Dutch recent history seems to question.

Social housing: A vulnerable policy sector?

Politics not only create policies, but policies also create politics. If there is one subset of policy areas from which this crucial lesson has been learned it certainly has been the welfare state. The development and expansion of social policy programmes in the welfare state, providing income maintenance, pensions, education, health care and housing, was part of a struggle over the role of the state vis-à-vis the market, but simultaneously it transformed the institutional context in which these political and social struggles took place (Esping-Andersen, 1996). Once enacted and implemented, social policy programmes themselves feed back into social politics and by doing so, transform the institutional constellation and political processes through which the welfare state develops over time (Skocpol & Amenta, 1986; Pierson, 1994). These insights have had important consequences for both causal analytic and historical interpretative studies of welfare state reforms. Instead of simply analyzing the impact of state-society relations and the socio-political power constellation on policy reform (politics creates policies), social policy reform should be analysed in a more fine-grained and dynamic way by tracing the political consequences of institutionalized policy programmes (policies create politics).

Arguably the most famous study on positive feedback and welfare state reform can be found in Paul Pierson's study *Dismantling the Welfare State* (1994), which addresses neo-conservative reforms undertaken in the 1980s by the Thatcher government in Great Britain and the Reagan administration in the United States – two critical cases in which reform of the welfare state focused primarily on dismantling the social services and reducing citizens' claims (retrenchment). Retrenchment is explicitly concerned with moving the welfare state toward a more *residual* role; either by cutting social expenditures; by restructuring social policy programmes (programmatic retrenchment); or by re-arranging the political environment (systemic retrenchment) in such a way that enhances the probability of such (residual) outcomes in the future (Pierson, 1994: 17).

Pierson's most important conclusion was that even for Thatcher and Reagan the welfare state turned out to be nearly impregnable. However, Pierson added a subtle qualification to his general resilience thesis: the extent to which the British and American welfare states had been resilient to neo-liberal reforms differed from one policy domain to another. What is particularly interesting for the present chapter is that in Pierson's study, social rented housing stood out as the case of what he called a vulnerable welfare programme. Contrary to what occurred in adjacent policy areas, positive feedback in housing did not lead to reform inertia, but instead created the conditions for a dramatic turnaround in British housing policy. In his own words:

> In housing, retrenchment advocates succeeded in establishing a self-reinforcing dynamic in which cutbacks led to weaker opposition, allowing further cutbacks. Had the government been able to apply these strategies effectively in other domains, the repercussions for the welfare state would have been serious; but housing was the exception rather than the rule (Pierson, 1994: 159).

For example, one of the most radical aspects of privatization to be successfully introduced under Thatcher was the so-called Right-to-Buy programme. Thatcher was able to offer a large number of tenants a home of their own – and thereby transform the political risks of retrenchment into political gain – simply by obliging the Labour-dominated council housing services to sell council houses to their sitting tenants for between 30% and 50% of their market price. At first glance, this is surprising because social housing could be expected to be a prime example of a sector in which policy feedback plays an important role. After all, the long life-cycle, high initial price and sheer immovability of housing all mean that houses built in the past have a considerable influence on supply and prices in the current housing market (Floor, 1971). In other words, policy feedback is physically located in the housing stock. Also, housing costs account for an important part of disposable income and house building represents an important investment market. Social housing policy is therefore often closely interwoven with socio-economic policy. One would rather expect a high degree of positive feedback in social housing and hence a firm obstacle to reform (Pierson, 1993).

Yet Pierson concludes the opposite and notes a striking openness of the housing field to reforms, which he ascribes primarily to the capital-good nature of the housing market, and to the fact that housing is characterized by one-off investments whose effects are spread over a long period of time. This made it easy for the Thatcher government simply to shift the cost of its policy (e.g. more limited availability of social rented housing) to the future, all while ensuring that the government would benefit from the revenues from the sale of council houses, both financially and politically (happy new home owners often voted for the Tory Party). Housing thus provided scope for neo-conservative reform that was not available in other policy areas of the welfare state. However, the consequences of the Right-to-Buy programme were dramatic: because only the worst rented accommodation remained, the public rental sector was marginalized.

It should be noted at this point that Pierson is not alone in his conclusion that housing is an extremely vulnerable policy area for welfare state retrenchment. Various international studies comparing social housing in the welfare state show that housing has developed into the wobbly pillar of the welfare state (Lundqvist, 1992; Harloe, 1995; Kleinman, 1996). Their claim seems to be confirmed by European housing trends; in nearly all European countries, the share of social housing stock has decreased, often in significant numbers, and has been increasingly reserved for the poorest sections of society.

Dutch social housing reforms seem to defy Pierson's conclusion in two ways. To begin with, reforms took place only after forty years of steady growth and numerous failed attempts to liberalize the housing market, as we will describe below. Furthermore, when the reforms finally did occur, they did not result in marginalization: in relative terms, the Netherlands still has Europe's largest and most varied public housing stock. The private non-profit housing associations own over two million homes, more than a third of all Dutch housing (see table 3.2). On the basis of their current market value, these homes give the associations estimated assets of €29 billion, which they are obliged under law to use for the benefit of housing needs (Ministry of Housing, 2004). In fact, the Netherlands seem to have gone further than any other country by stating that social rented housing can be self-supporting, in the sense that the mature social housing stock could function as a revolving fund. In other words, we are faced with a double question. If housing is as easy to reform as Pierson and others suggest, why did reforms in the Dutch system not occur earlier? And when reforms did happen, why did they not result in a marginalization of the social housing stock.

Historical barriers to reform: Private ownership and socio-economic policy

In spite of the supposed vulnerability of social housing to reform, no substantial policy reforms aimed at liberalising the housing market occurred until the early

1980s. Instead, Dutch post-war housing policy became locked-in by external socio-economic policy requirements and by obligations from long-term subsidy agreements. There were two main factors that created this lock-in situation during the 1960s and 1970s: (1) the stock was controlled by private non-profit housing associations rather than public organizations, and (2) social housing had become closely entangled with other policy areas. Both factors created not only a large social rented housing stock, but they also generated positive feedback in Dutch housing.[2]

Institutional contingencies: Private rather than public control

Because the Netherlands is a case par excellence of a corporatist (confessional) welfare regime (Esping-Andersen, 1990; Van Kersbergen, 1995), Dutch social housing policy has puzzled international researchers for a long time (e.g. Lundqvist, 1992; Barlow & Duncan, 1994). In the post-war era, the Netherlands have been able to build up one of the largest and most diversified social rented stocks in the world that caters not only for the lower incomes, but for the middle incomes as well. Hence, in their comparison of European housing systems Barlow and Duncan (1994: 31) concluded that Dutch housing seems to fit more closely into the social democratic regime type. Kemeny came to a similar conclusion. What is striking about the Dutch approach according to Kemeny (1995: 119), is the great preponderance of non-profit rented housing over profit rented housing (1995: 119). How and why did the Dutch achieve this social rented stock? Was it because of a political preference for a large and comprehensive social rented housing system, or are there other factors that can explain this particular outcome?

One important institutional aspect of Dutch social rented housing definitely fits into the corporatist regime type. Christian democracy in the conservative corporatist welfare regime developed its own political place between the free market and state-oriented socialism, which distinguishes it from social democratic welfare regimes and liberal welfare regimes. Based on the Catholic principle of subsidiarity and the Protestant principle of sovereignty, the state should not perform any functions that lower-level entities can perform (Van Kersbergen, 1995: 148). For housing, this meant that already in 1901, with the enactment of the Dutch Housing Act, it was decided that social rented housing should be devolved to private non-profit housing associations. Municipalities were only allowed to start their own housing companies when private initiatives failed. At the local level, each of the ideological (religious) pillars that constituted Dutch society was allowed to start their own housing associations. Financial contributions of the state to social housing were restricted to local and private housing associations, operating under a public regulatory regime. The only restriction was that the housing associations should exclusively serve the general interest in housing instead of the interests of their members.

---

2   The historical description of Dutch housing policy in this chapter owes a great deal to a small number of studies that have appeared over the last few decades, in particular Van der Schaar, 1987; Harloe, 1995; Kemeny, 1995; Faber, 1996; Brakkee, 1997; Faber, 1997.

Reform in Europe

The current model of Dutch social rented housing had its formative moment in the first years of the 20th century, but it took until the 1960s before the housing associations could really build up a stake in the Dutch housing market (see table 3.1). Although they were able to expand for a small period of time during the First World War, as soon as private housing investment had been recovered, their role was diminished again. In 1934, the Dutch government even decided that, from then on, housing associations were obliged to refund all the subsidies they had received, so that it was impossible for them build up any financial reserves. It was not before this policy was abolished in 1965 that they could really develop into modern housing companies. Also, in 1968, after a long period of deliberations and negotiations, the housing associations were finally given formal primacy over municipal housing companies (Faber, 1997). They were even allowed to invest in the middle segment of the housing market, under the crucial condition that for-profit landlords were allowed to build up a share in the social rented sector (which, in practice, the latter never took an interest in).

Table 3.1   Social housing stock by type of provider and in relation to the overall housing stock (CBS, 1989; Ministry of Housing, 2004)

Year	Private non-profit share of total stock	Local authority share of total stock	Overall social housing share of stock
1947	9%	3%	13%
1956	12%	11%	24%
1967	22%	13%	35%
1975	29%	12%	41%
1982	27%	7%	34%
1989	32%	6%	37%
1994	35%	2%	37%
1997	37%	0%	37%
1999	36%	0%	36%
2001	36%	0%	36%
2002	35%	0%	35%

The institutional contingencies of the Dutch social rented stock are important for three reasons. Firstly, housing associations represented a sort of compromise between the major political factions. As expressions of private initiative, they were the favourite housing provider of the Christian parties. This was not unimportant, since from 1954 to 1974, the Ministry of Housing was controlled by ministers from the religious parties. But the private nature of housing associations to some extent also accommodated liberal preferences, while their non-profit orientation appealed to the Social Democrats, even if the latter preferred the local authority provision.[3] Secondly, although the Dutch housing associations came under heavy state influence as time progressed, having little say over their own construction programmes and rent levels, the fact that they were privately owned made it extremely difficult from a legal standpoint to implement a radical and irreversible intervention in their assets. Finally, they maintained a strong lobby with the government. Having grown as extensions of a pillarized society, the housing associations were generally affiliated to one of the major ideological pillars (Catholic, Protestant, and Socialist) and maintained close links with political parties, both through their branch associations and informal social networks (Lijphart, 1968).

Social housing as an emergency exit

Equally important for the development of the social rented system, however, was the change in housing policy goals after the Second World War. At the end of the Second World War, the Netherlands found itself faced with immense housing shortages, higher than those of most European countries. During the war, construction had ground to a halt and many dwellings had been demolished or destroyed. The housing market was (still) wholly incapable of meeting such shortages. Not only were building materials and capital scarce, but private builders also delayed their investments in the hope that the economic conditions might soon improve. It was at this point that the state stepped in and started to plan and finance construction on a large scale. Housing policy became one of the most important instruments of socio-economic policy making in the Netherlands, a relationship that was to bring considerable benefits to the housing associations. With their size, the state-driven construction programmes in housing not only served the interests of those in need for housing, but they were of a major economic interest in terms of employment and investment. Furthermore, the level of rents paid by tenants were of great significance to government's wage and price policy, which was tied to the costs of living (of which rents make up a large share). Through construction subsidies invested in housing units (object subsidies), rents were generally brought to a level below cost. At a time when the government's main preference was for the economy to recover, it was important to keep wages low. Under pressure from the unions and the electorate, this was only possible given commitment to keep the costs of living low. As a consequence, any sharp rent rise was likely to cause controversy. Housing served as an emergency exit for socio-economic policy, with which it had become inextricably bound up and which created a lock-in situation that proved difficult to overturn in the years to come (Helderman & Brandsen, 2004).

---

3 By contrast, from the early twentieth century onward social housing in the UK came under the control of the local authorities, a choice that was more clear-cut from the start than it was in most countries (Harloe, 1995). Private non-profits were historically of relatively minor significance, though they have recently been on the rise (Kendall & Knapp, 1996; Mullins, 2000).

Reform in Europe

Previously failed reform attempts

The wish to build housing in large quantities and keep it cheap effectively thwarted any attempt to reduce state-driven construction, since private builders generally operated in the more expensive and more profitable segments. The protestant minister Van Aartsen (1959–63) tried to enact a programme of liberalization, arguing that local authorities and non-profits should only build housing for the poor sections of society. He lowered construction subsidies and targets for social housing, while raising those for the private sector. Simultaneously, he attempted to liberalize rents, which inevitably involved rises. Although initially successful, in the end, he was forced to retrace his steps as the social housing construction dipped while private construction did not pick up sufficiently. Overall construction rates were set to drop, which went against the political preferences of that time. Yet only local authorities and non-profits could meet the targets with any degree of certainty. There were also grave concerns that the rise in private construction would threaten the growth of cheap market segments, where shortages were still higher than in the housing market generally. The minister was forced to raise the construction targets for social housing closer to their former level. The liberalization was over before it had truly started (Van der Schaar, 1987).

Table 3.2   **Housing construction in absolute numbers (x 1,000) as spread over local authorities, private non-profit housing providers and for-profit builders.[4] (CBS, 1989; Ministry of Housing, 2004)**

	Total	Local authority share	Non-profits	For-profits
1946	1.6	0.4	0.2	1
1949	42.8	18.3	14.1	10.4
1959	83.6	24.7	22.9	36
1969	123.1	23.4	39.1	60.7
1979	87.5	2.6	23.8	61.1
1989	111	3.8	32.3	74.9
1994	87.4	1.1	23.6	62.7
1997	92.3	0.5	24.6	67.2
1998	78.6	0.4	17.3	61.0
2001	70.7	-	14.6	56.1

Van Aartsen's successors of the 1960s, the Catholic Bogaers (1963–67) and the Protestant Schut (1967–71), realized that the liberalization of housing policy would be impossible until the housing shortages had been effectively alleviated. Accordingly,

---

4   From 2000 onwards, local authority and private non-profit construction have no longer been measured separately, because the former is now negligible.

they quickly expanded the construction programme to record heights (see table 3.2). Between 1962 and 1967, social housing construction rose from 35% to 55% of total housing construction (Adriaansens & Priemus, 1986). As a consequence, total expenditures on housing subsidies as part of the of the Gross Domestic Product rose from 0.8% in 1950 to almost 4% at the end of the 1960s (Faber et al., 1996).

At the end of the 1960s, the government started to develop new instruments to control public expenditures. One of these was the introduction of the individual, income-related rent subsidy, an instrument that concentrated financial support on the neediest. The idea was that this type of subject subsidy might help bring down the less discriminate object subsidies. But on the whole, these attempts at reform were met with strong resistance within Parliament and from the housing associations (Van der Schaar, 1987). Minister Schut introduced a system of small yearly rather than large irregular rent rises, in the hope that these annual rent rises would face less opposition. It proved to be a gross miscalculation: the intense discussion over rent rises now returned on a yearly basis in the Dutch Parliament.

In the early 1970s, the Protestant Minister Udink (1971–1973) tried a head-on approach, setting ambitious targets for the harmonization of the rents in the housing stock and the abolition of object subsidies. Udink proposed two successive yearly rent rises of 10% in order to harmonize the rents of the stock with the new cost prices. Although these rent rises were at an unprecedented high level, it was argued that high inflation would largely mitigate their income effects. It was a window of opportunity to get rid of the object subsidy for once and for all. But in 1973, the government of Christian Democrat Prime Minister Biesheuvel fell, and the political tide turned with the centre-left government of the Social Democrat Den Uyl. In their programme there was no scope for 20% rent increases; instead, an increase of 6% was chosen (while inflation at the time was about 8%). Den Uyl and his cabinet saw housing explicitly as a merit-good that could be fostered only by means of continued state involvement (Ministry of Housing, 1974). All in all, there was no political support for radical reforms aimed at liberalization in housing policy. Housing policy was too strongly embraced by other policy areas, and vested interests were too strong.

The global recession that came at the end of the 1970s resulted in the collapse of private construction and the owner-occupied market, resulting in one of the most severe crises in the post-war housing market. The centre-right cabinet of Prime Minister Van Agt (1977–1981) was forced to return to anti-cyclical investments in social housing. Construction was encouraged by expanding subsidies, at a time when significant rent rises were politically unacceptable. Housing expenditure reached record highs. The Ministry of Housing partially succeeded in suggesting budget cuts by inventive bookkeeping, particularly by transferring the state loans to housing associations away from the regular budget. But housing expenditure was spinning out of control. Overall, total expenditure on social housing would eventually rise from approximately €0.9 billion in 1970 to €6.3 billion in 1988. In 1988, 60% of commitments on the budget of the Ministry of Housing consisted of subordinated payments as a result of the various subsidy schemes. In forty years' time, the effort to reduce public expenditures on housing and to liberalize the housing market (advocates of liberalization would say: to return to normal market conditions) had proved unsuccessful (Ministry of Housing, 1989).

Social rented housing at the crossroads: The process of reform

Between 1945 and 1982, Dutch housing policy had become completely locked-in by external socio-economic policy requirements and by obligations from long-term subsidy agreements. After 1982, however, the political climate in the Netherlands changed significantly. The political agenda became dominated by the need to reduce the government's budget deficit. Reforms started in areas that were considered to be the most vital or crucial part of the Dutch economy, given its high dependency on the world economy.

One way to achieve this was wage moderation. Yielding to pressure by the employers and the threat of government's imposed wage control, the trade unions abandoned their long-lasting claim to the automatic indexation of wages to prices. This resulted in the so-called Accord of Wassenaar that was reached under strong pressure from the then reigning centre-right government in 1982 after a long period of cumbersome negotiations between the representatives of employers and employees. This accord helped to lower the real exchange rate and thereby to restore the competitiveness of Dutch firms and products. The Accord of Wassenaar is generally considered to be the start of the miraculous recovery of the Dutch economy in the 1980s and 1990s (Visser & Hemerijck, 1997). After the Accord of Wassenaar in 1982, however, welfare state reform still had to begin in the Netherlands. Whereas wage moderation was aimed at improving the competitiveness of the Dutch economy, reforms in social security benefits, health care, education and social housing were generally aimed at restricting social entitlements to social provisions.

The start of the social housing reforms are usually thought to be tied to the publication date of the then new, integrated policy document in 1989, *Volkshuisvesting in de jaren negentig (Housing in the 1990s)*, under the responsibility of the Christian Democrat Heerma, junior minister of Housing in the centre-left government of Prime Minister Lubbers (Ministry of Housing, 1989). However, already in the early 1980s, changes were made that more or less paved the way for the 1989 policy paper. First of all, the Accord of Wassenaar meant that the direct link between rent policy and income policy was formally abandoned so that rent increases were no longer tested against their effect on incomes. From then on, rent policies could finally catch up. From 1982 until 1997, rents actually rose faster than building costs and inflation (Ministry of Housing, 1989). Secondly, in the mid-1980s, the legitimacy of previous housing policies became the subject of an intense political and public debate. Thirdly, by means of incremental adjustments and strategies of institutional layering and conversion[5], the risks and costs of housing investments and maintenance were gradually privatized to housing associations and individual consumers.

---

5   Institutional layering refers to the transformation of policy by means of adding new institutions to the established institutionalized system. Institutional conversion refers to the

A crisis of legitimacy: Opening the window

The first centre-right government of Prime Minister Lubbers imposed strict budgetary discipline upon the various ministries. Not surprisingly, housing became subject to these budgetary policies as well. While it had previously been fairly easy for the Ministry of Housing to pass on budget cuts by declaring expenditures on state loans for social housing simply as not being relevant for the Ministry's budget, in 1982 this game of *budget-obfuscation* was over when new budgetary rules were introduced by the Ministry of Finance (Faber et al., 1996). In 1985, the Social-Economic Council (SER), a policy advisory body in which both employers and employees are represented, openly wondered whether the object subsidy should not simply be abolished, if necessary even at the risk of a fall in building activity. In doing so, the SER referred to a soon-to-be published review of rent and subsidy policy, conducted by the Ministry of Housing under the supervision of the Ministry of Finance. The publication was to lead to the formulation of six possible cutback strategies in housing in the subsequent year (Ministry of Finance, 1985). The Council for Public Housing (RAVO), in which all the major interest groups in housing were represented, responded with shock and indignation over the policy review and the SER advice. Given the crisis on the housing market and the low levels in housing investments, government's involvement should be increased instead, it was claimed. Yet, the RAVO was fighting a rear-guard battle.

In 1986, a public Parliamentary Enquiry examined the rents and subsidy policies that had led to the expansion of housing expenditures as well as the functioning of the Ministry of Housing and its predecessor over the previous twenty years (Parlementaire Enquête Bouwsubsidies, 1988). The Parliamentary Enquiry was initiated at the request of the parliament after the publication of an article in one of the leading national newspapers. The article referred to fraud concerning housing subsidies by one of the leading institutional investors and the lack of control on these subsidies by the Ministry of Housing (De Volkskrant, 19 August 1986). While real fraud was never definitively proven by the Enquiry or an investigation of the judicature, the Enquiry had a dramatic impact on the legitimacy of past housing policies. All of the ninety public hearings undertaken by the Parliamentary Enquiry Commission were broadcasted live on national television and extensively reviewed and discussed by the press. Housing was pictured as a budget-maximising sector with a voracious appetite for subsidies. To limit the risk of any further political damage, the then responsible junior minister for Housing, Brokx, was forced to resign by his own Christian Democratic party even before the Enquiry was properly underway. Heerma, who was junior minister of Economic Affairs and member of the same party, succeeded him and came to office in 1987.

---

process of adapting existing institutions to new circumstances. In both instances, reforms are accomplished without the elimination of established institutions (Streeck & Thelen, 2005).

Privatising risks and containing costs[6]

One of Heerma's first political acts was to prepare a new, comprehensive policy document called *Housing in the 1990s*. The main purpose of the policy paper was to formulate a new vision of the role of the state in housing provisions. Abandoning the concept of merit-good that had been used to legitimize state intervention in the housing market, the paper defined housing explicitly as being an individual consumer good. Also, it was believed that the large-scale post-war housing shortages had finally been resolved. Therefore the responsibility of securing adequate housing could finally be given back to the market and to individual providers and consumers. In principle, direct government assistance was to be limited to households with below-average incomes through a limited programme of subsidized social rented housing and means-tested rent allowances. The rest of the population had to rely on the owner-occupied housing market or the liberalized rent market (Ministry of Housing, 1989).

Yet formulating a coherent and comprehensive vision on housing is one thing, formulating and implementing a workable policy programme is quite another. Although the policy paper can be conceived of as the seminal document of the housing reforms, it was preceded and succeeded by more incremental reforms in order to gradually adjust the housing system. The reforms that preceded and succeeded Heerma's policy paper drew on the fact that the housing market is characterized by supply in the form of stock, but this stock was now deployed for the purpose of funding cutbacks and institutional reforms in social housing. The common element in these reforms was that the financial costs and risks of housing investments and consumption were privatized to the housing associations, and also partly to the tenants.

The first step involved the reallocation of the risks associated with housing investments. Because state loans and government guarantees on capital loans were part of the Ministry's budget, these needed to be abolished. In order to do so, the Ministry more or less imposed upon the housing associations the establishment of the Social Housing Guarantee Fund (*Waarborgfonds Sociale Woningbouw, WSW*). The WSW is a private collective fund, established in 1984, to pool the risks of maintenance and housing improvement for participating housing associations. Although housing associations and municipalities had great difficulties with the replacement of government guarantees by a private Guarantee Fund, they realized that this was the only way to maintain a system of object subsidies in the long run. The WSW was financed by the contributions of participating housing associations. While it was originally intended for guaranteeing investments in housing maintenance and improvement only, in the 1990s, its scope gradually extended. Today, it guarantees

---

6   Several measures were taken in order to reform the rent, which are technically and economically too complex to do them full justice in this short overview. For more detailed analyses and explanations of these reforms, see Van der Schaar, 2003; Helderman & Brandsen, 2004; Brandsen & Helderman, 2004.

the capital loans for all the investments of almost 90% of the housing associations. The WSW arrangement gives housing associations an excellent reputation on the capital market and offers them a substantial reduction on the interest rates that they have to pay for their mortgages (Kempen, 1996).

Another fund, the publicly legislated Central Fund for Social Housing (*Centraal Fonds voor de Huisvesting*) had been added to the sector as a solidarity fund in 1988, anticipating the government paper, *Housing in the 1990s*. It was initially founded for the purpose of reorganising the finances of the housing associations, by whose contributions it was funded. But again, as with the WSW, its purpose and tasks gradually extended in the 1990s. In 1998, it was also given a role in the financial supervision and monitoring of the housing associations. Together, these two funds enhanced the stability of the social housing sector, making it virtually impossible for housing associations to go bankrupt. They are illustrative of the public/private constellation of the Dutch social rented system. By means of pooling the assets of participating housing associations (WSW) and by compulsory contributions (CFV) they established a firm basis for organized solidarity between the housing associations, and eventually paved the way for the abolition of the object subsidies in social housing as well as the establishment of a revolving fund in social housing in the 1990s.

Because rents had been rising faster than building costs since 1982, the gap between costs and revenues (rents) had grown smaller. But there were still many open-ended subsidy schemes that needed to be brought to an end. From 1988, various subsidy schemes were standardized, and devolved to the municipalities in order to put an end to the open subsidy schemes. Helped by low interest rates and the abolition of government loans, the government was eventually able to rid itself of the burden of ever-rising subsidies. Although this brought government expenditure under control, subsidies agreed to at an earlier date continued to weigh on the Ministry of Housing. In the 1991 mid-term review, an additional €0.6 billion was levied on social housing (Faber et al., 1996). To phase out the object subsidy as quickly as possible, after cumbersome negotiations, the treasury finally allowed the Ministry of Housing to make a large part of the necessary saving by raising the trend-related rent increase from 3% to 5.5% (Ibid.). The rise in expenditure anticipated for the individual rent subsidies as a consequence of the annual rent increase of 5.5% had to be absorbed completely by the social housing budget. From then on the annual rent increases were referred to as the *subsidieafbraakpercentage* – literally, the subsidy-destruction rate. In the 1992 Trend Report, the first reference was made to the abolition of the object subsidy (Heerma, 1992). The housing associations realized that the system of object subsidies had come to an end. Higher rents together with lower interest rates had helped to lower the amount of object subsidies that housing associations were entitled to.

A win-win situation

It was at this point that both the housing associations and the Ministry of Housing realized that they were facing a unique trade-off and a win-win situation. The provisional climax of the reform came with the Balancing and Grossing Operation (*bruteringsakkoord*), which was agreed upon in 1993 and implemented in 1995. After protracted negotiations in which future costs and risks of housing investments (with many uncertain parameters) had to be carefully calculated and fairly allocated, the representatives of the housing associations, the ministry, and the Association of Netherlands Municipalities agreed that all of the remaining object subsidy and then current government loans would be written off against each other. For housing associations and government alike, this represented a win-win situation. In a single stroke, the budget of the housing ministry would be relieved of one of its highest sources of expenditure, while the housing associations were assured of the remaining object subsidies. Ultimately, over 90% of the housing associations agreed to the operation, a near-unanimity that was sufficient for the government to approve.

With this, the financial independence of the housing associations had been achieved. Partly as a consequence of the Balancing and Grossing Operation, the share of social housing as a percentage of overall government expenditure fell from 8.7% in 1985 to 2.7% in 1998. At the same time, there were radical shifts between subsidy types. In 1990, 60% of subsidies consisted of object subsidies (Ministry of Housing, 1999). Since then, however, income-related subject subsidies have became the most common type. Nowadays, the housing associations (which have mostly converted themselves to foundations) receive only incidental subsidies from the state, which constitute only a very minor part of their revenues. Though still governed by specific regulation circumscribing the range of their activities, this is relatively light compared to the regime that existed before the reforms. The knot of rules and subsidies has been effectively cut through.

Explaining the reform: Crisis, leadership, and policy inheritance

A combination of three factors made the reform possible. First, the social housing sector was publicly disgraced, creating a crisis of legitimacy and opening a window of opportunity. Secondly, the policy makers handled the opportunity well. Finally, and perhaps most important, the inheritance of a past policy allowed a type of reform that would previously have been impossible.

Changing policy objectives and a crisis of legitimacy

One significant factor in enabling reforms was that the public image of housing was shattered. This was certainly related to a general shift in policy objectives. In the 1960s and 1970s, housing policy had become an important instrument for Keynesian anti-cyclical investment strategies. As such, it served many socio-economic policy goals. In the 1980s, when Keynesian economic ideas were abandoned, the ever-rising expenditure on social housing was increasingly problematic and its subsidy system was critically questioned. Throughout the 1980s and 1990s, the government's political agenda was dominated by socio-economic objectives such as curbing inflation and reducing the budget deficit. This meant that the link between policy on rents and policy on wages and inflation was formally severed, and that rent increases were no longer tested against their effect on personal income. Housing policy therefore became less tightly connected with socio-economic policy, and rents could finally catch up (Van der Schaar, 1987). The greatest shock, though, was caused by the Parliamentary Enquiry in 1986, which examined policy on rents and subsidies as well as the functioning of the Ministry of Housing over the previous twenty years. With the advantage of hindsight, the parliamentary enquiry opened a window of opportunity for more radical reforms.

Leadership: A gradual and depoliticizing approach

In explaining the reform, one must also recognize the cunning of the policy makers, particularly Heerma, in seizing the opportunity that opened up before them. Heerma came in after his predecessor succumbed to the massive financial scandal, and social housing was subject to intense scrutiny. He did not play the game of power, but of de-politicization. Rather than announcing a massive reform, as many of his predecessors since the 1960s had done, he had a trial-and-error way of working. New proposals were tested, evaluated, and, in many cases, silently formalized as new policy by the Committee for Experiments in Social Housing (*Stuurgroep Experimenten Volkshuisvesting* ((SEV)), an independent non-profit foundation created by the Ministry of Housing in 1982, exactly for this purpose. Its experiments included the decentralization of budgets, new methods for housing allocation, new methods of calculating the gross-rent incomes of housing associations and innovative forms of service provisions. The prevailing policy paradigm was not confronted in major debates, but slowly undermined by adjustment of existing instruments, by veiling measures in administrative terms, and by adopting a gradual approach that never hinted at a grand design – although, looking back, the reforms clearly amount to one.

Heerma was successful because he did not dismiss other political options, but kept reforms out of the public eye and, as much as possible, out of the formal political decision-making process. By excluding economically charged measures such as the sale of social housing (which would have led to serious opposition from his own party, the Social Democrats as well as the housing associations), it proved possible to undertake sweeping reforms (such as the devolution of financial risks to housing providers) under the guise of technicalities. It is telling that the Balancing and Grossing Operation, one of the greatest financial operations in the history of the policy field, was only announced midway through the reform process, and sold to a potentially hostile opposition of providers (who still had powerful political connections) as a clever accounting measure and potential win-win situation rather than as a fundamental change in state-provider relations. Not only did this work method facilitate the particular reforms Heerma undertook, it also kept other more radical and controversial options off the agenda. Incremental adaptations of the existing institutional frameworks meant that social housing was privatized and reformed step-by-step, not dismantled wholesale as it had been in Great Britain.

Positive feedback and the legacy of past policy

But why was this reform at all possible? It is the legacy of past policy that makes the Dutch experience decidedly different from the British one. Whatever one can say of Thatcher, it is not that she lacked leadership. As in the Netherlands, the British system of social housing had come under increasing criticism. But despite these apparently similar conditions, reforms in the two countries went in an entirely different direction. While some success factors for reform were achieved in the UK, the end result was a decline of social housing, whereas in the Netherlands the reforms led to a new, possibly more vigorous form of the social housing provision. The difference is that in the Netherlands, policy feedback eventually opened up policy options other than sell-out and marginalization. This challenges a widespread view in housing research that the British development towards a residual system is typical of an innate logic in housing policy, which cuts across national differences. It also challenges the view that the institutional structure of housing does not make any difference in explaining current developments in social housing across European housing systems (cf. Harloe, 1995).

The private character of social rented housing in the Netherlands explains why a Right-to-Buy scheme along Thatcher-esque lines was never really an option. A crucial difference between the British and Dutch social housing stocks was that the former was largely controlled by municipalities, whereas the latter was in the hands of private non-profit housing associations. With such legal, political and societal support, a reform of the Thatcher-type was simply impossible. The relatively independent position of the housing associations not only prevented the short-term capitalization of the stock, but also aided the development of an alternative reform strategy. The huge size increase, the fifty year time span and favourable regulation (e.g. permission to retain surpluses) had allowed the associations to gradually develop into modern housing companies, with large operational reserves and a well-maintained property. The consequences of the reform were also different from other countries: the housing stock, having grown over such an extended period, represented a diversity of architectural styles and locations. It also housed both lower and middle-income segments of the population. In short, the housing associations had matured to the point where they no longer needed the state. Their exposure to stronger market forces had become financially, commercially, and organizationally viable (Brandsen, 2004). It is perhaps ironic that the Dutch social housing reforms became possible precisely because previous attempts at liberalization had failed. It reminds us, however, of the crucial importance of timing and sequencing in policy reforms (Pierson, 2004).

Timing and sequencing, or ... could things had gone differently?

This immediately raises the question whether things could have gone differently if, at any moment in time, other choices had been made in Dutch housing, including opting for the status quo? What consequences could these alternative courses of action have had for the policy reforms under examination? The answers to these questions are not decisive or self-evident, since we simply cannot know what would have happened if things had gone differently or had not occurred at all. But it is clear, for example, that the Grossing and Balancing Operation in Dutch housing could only have happened at the particular point in time when the outstanding government loans and the future subsidy obligations were more or less at the same level. In the mid-1980s, this one-off-exchange would probably not have been possible and acceptable for both the housing associations and the state, nor would it have been such a positive-sum outcome in 2000, assuming that cutbacks in object subsidies would have continued at the same rate as before. In other words, by analyzing the causal sequence of reforms over time and in retrospect, we need to analyse the opportunities that actors (could) have had at particular points in time to reaching favourable outcomes, and then examine if and how they have taken these opportunities, or alternatively, why they simply missed the point. To paraphrase March and Olsen (1989) in their argument about the inefficiency of history, analyzing long term policy developments and policy reforms requires a clarification on why some histories (notably the Dutch) are nevertheless less inefficient than others (the British). It may very well be that taking a shortcut in welfare state reform is not always the most efficient path in the long run.

Conclusion: The benefits of policy feedback

Our case of the Dutch housing reforms reveals that policy feedback does not necessarily lead to reform inertia, but that it may generate the conditions for a radical policy shift as well. But the manner in which this took place was highly contingent on the timing and sequencing of policy reforms, as well as on institutional contingencies of the Dutch social rented sector.

Our analysis shows that Pierson's (2004) conclusion on policy feedback may be too limited, in the sense that it ignores the potential incremental effects of such feedback, in this case in the very tangible form of housing stock. The ability of positive feedback to act as a productive constraint remains unrecognized (Streeck, 1992). According to Streeck (1992), to support a socially benevolent development of policy, institutions must simultaneously impose constraints on, and provide opportunities for, individual actors. Constraints are necessary to prevent actors from seeking short-term solutions that may, in the end, lead to a tragedy of the commons, such as in the British housing system. Opportunities, in turn, have to be offered to adjust a policy system to new demands and challenges. The difficulty is that institutions must be designed in such a way that they can function as constraints and opportunities simultaneously; if they do just one and not the other, their capacity to facilitate and guide social policy reforms is likely to be low. The institutional structure of the Dutch social housing system in this respect functioned as a productive constraint. Although over time the government's attitude and goals concerning housing clearly changed, the will to reform had been present for decades. What ultimately changed was that it proved possible to realize those preferences by different means, not by scaling back the housing system in the form of retrenchment, but through a new decision-making option that had not existed previously. Though there were external factors facilitating the reform, it was essentially opened up from within the institutional legacy itself. Incrementalism and critical junctures found themselves working together.

If policies create politics, than the crucial question with respect to the relation between positive feedback and policy reform brings us back to Laswell's lesson that, in the end, politics is about *who* gets *what, when,* and *how?* That is, who is entitled to decide, and profit from, the inheritance of past policies (Helderman, 2006). In our analysis of the timing and sequences of Dutch social housing reforms, we have shown that the institutional structure of Dutch social rented housing turned out to be a productive constraint that, together with the positive feedback created by earlier housing investments, created the conditions within which more sustainable reforms could be made possible when Dutch housing arrived at a crossroad in its development. An interesting question is whether this is a peculiarity of housing (and of goods with similar characteristics), or whether it points to a driver of reform that has been overlooked within the conceptual framework of previous reform literature.

References

Adriaansens, C.A., H. Priemus (1986) *Marges van volkshuisvestingsbeleid,* WRR Voorstudies en achtergronden V50, Den Haag: Staatsuitgeverij.
Barlow, J., S. Duncan (1994) *Success and Failure in Housing Provision. European Systems Compared,* Oxford: Pergamon.
Brakkee, G. (1997) *Kroniek der gemeentelijke woningbedrijven,* Almere: Platform voor de Volkshuisvesting.
Brandsen, T., C.T. Ribeiro, R. Farnell (2006) *Housing Association Diversification in Europe,* Coventry: The Rex Group.
Brandsen, T., J.K. Helderman (2004) 'Volkshuisvesting' Dijstelbloem, H., P.L. Meurs, E.K. Schrijvers (eds), *Maatschappelijke dienstverlening: Een onderzoek naar vijf sectoren,* Wetenschappelijke Raad voor het Regeringsbeleid, Exploratory Study nr. 6, Amsterdam: Amsterdam University Press pp. 65–131.
Brandsen, T. (2004) *Quasi-Market Governance: An Anatomy of Innovation,* Utrecht: Lemma.
CBS (Central Bureau for Statistics) (1989) *Historical Series of the Netherlands 1899–1989,* The Hague: Sdu.
Esping-Andersen, G. (1990) *The Three Worlds of Welfare Capitalism,* Cambridge: Polity Press.
Esping-Andersen, G. (1996) *Welfare States in Transition: National Adaptions in Global Economies,* London: Sage.

Faber, A.W., J. van der Schaar, J.J. Koffijberg, H. Priemus (1996) *Volkshuisvesting in goud; verandering en continuïteit in beleid en organisatie van het Directoraat-Generaal van de Volkshuisvesting*, Den Haag: DGVH.

Faber, A.W. (1997) *In naam van de roos: verzelfstandiging van woningcorporaties*, Delft: Delft University Press.

Floor, J.W.G. (1971) *Beschouwingen over de bevordering van de volkshuisvesting*, Leiden: Stenfert Kroese.

Harloe, M. (1995) *The people's Home? Social rented Housing in Europe & America*, Oxford: Blackwell.

Helderman, J.K., T. Brandsen (2004) 'De erfenis van beleid: beleidsfeedback en hervorming in de Nederlandse volkshuisvesting' *Beleid & Maatschappij* vol. 31 pp. 74–85.

Helderman, J.K. (2006) *Bringing the Market Back in? The Politics and Policies of Market-oriented Reforms in Dutch Housing and Health Care*, Dissertation: Erasmus University Rotterdam.

Kemeny, J. (1995) *From Public Housing to the Social Market: Rental Policy Strategies in Comparative Perspective*, London: Routledge.

Kempen, B.G.A. (1996) *Niet uit liefde geboren: 12½ jaar WSW*, Huizen: WSW.

Kendall, J., M. Knapp (1996) *The Voluntary Sector in the UK*, Manchester: Manchester University Press.

Kersbergen, K. van (1995) *Social Capitalism: A Study of Christian Democracy and the Welfare State*, London: Routledge.

Kleinman, M. (1996) *Housing, Welfare and the State in Europe*, Cheltenham: Edward Elgar.

Lijphart, A. (1968) *The Politics of Accommodation. Pluralism and Democracy in the Netherlands*, Berkeley: University of California Press.

Lundqvist, L.J. (1992) *Dislodging the Welfare State*, Delft: Delft University Press.

March, J.G., J.P. Olsen (1989) *Rediscovering Institutions: The Organizational Basis of Politics*, New York: The Free Press.

Ministry of Housing (1974) *Nota huur- en subsidiebeleid*, Den Haag: Tweede Kamer.

Ministry of Housing (1989) *Volkshuisvesting in de jaren negentig: Van bouwen naar wonen*, Den Haag: Sdu.

Ministry of Housing (1999) *Evaluatie nota volkshuisvesting in de jaren negentig*, The Hague: Tweede kamer.

Ministry of Housing (2004) *Housing Statistics*, The Hague: Directorate-General for Housing.

Mullins, D. (2000) 'Social Origins and Transformations: The Changing Role of English Housing Associations' *Voluntas* vol. 11 pp. 255–75.

Nederlands Instituut voor Volkshuisvesting en Ruimtelijke Ordening (1995) *De politieke agenda van Tommel: Groenmarktberaad Volkshuisvesting*, 15 juni 1995, Den Haag: NIROV.

Parlementaire Enquête Bouwsubsidies (1988) *Eindrapport, Tweede Kamer, 1987–1988*, 19623, nrs. 30–36, Den Haag: Sdu.

Pierson, P. (1993) 'When Effect Becomes Cause, Policy Feedback and Political Change' *World Politics* vol. 45 pp. 595–628.

Pierson, P. (1994) *Dismantling the Welfare State?: Reagan, Thatcher and the Politics of Retrenchment*, Cambridge: Cambridge University Press.

Pierson, P. (2004) *Politics in Time: History, Institutions and Social Analysis*, Princeton: Princeton University Press.

Schaar, J. van der (1987) *Groei en bloei van het Nederlandse volkshuisvestingsbeleid*, Delft: Delftse Universitaire Pers.

Schaar, J. van der (2003) *Wonen en woonbeleid. Markten, instituties, instrumenten*, Amsterdam: Universiteit van Amsterdam.

Skocpol, T., E. Amenta (1986) 'States and Social Policies' *Annual Review of Sociology* vol. 12 pp. 131–57.

Streeck, W. (1992) *Social Institutions and Economics Performance*, London: Sage.

Streeck, W., K. Thelen (eds) (2005) *Beyond Continuity. Institutional Change in Advanced Political Economies*, Oxford: Oxford University Press.

Visser, J., A. Hemerijck (1997) *A Dutch Miracle: Job Growth, Welfare Reform and Corporatism in the Netherlands*, Amsterdam: Amsterdam University Press.

Chapter 4

The Introduction of
National Quality Policies:
A Comparison of Denmark
and the Netherlands

Mirjan Oude Vrielink-van Heffen, Wendy van der Kraan and
Bente Bjørnholt

Introduction

The health care sector is a complex public policy sector. The specific characteristics of
health care services, including information-asymmetry between patient and provider,
and professional and local autonomy, make it difficult to create a transparent system
in which all actions have accountability. Yet, politicians and the public demand
accountability systems for all policy sectors – even for such complex policy sectors
– with the intention of rendering visible what goes on in public organizations and
thereby ensuring that citizens receive the best service possible (Day & Klein, 1987;
Pollitt, 1993; Pollitt & Bouckaert, 1995; 2000).

One way of improving accountability is the introduction of quality standards.
In general, a national policy with quality standards enhances the transparency and
accountability of the health care sector, while simultaneously improving and ensuring
the provision of high quality, cost-effective care.

In the 1990s, quality standards were introduced in Denmark and the Netherlands.
This action represented a fundamental break from the past, as actors who were used
to determining how to account for the quality of their services were suddenly forced
to accept a nationwide policy requiring a more uniform quality management.

Considering the many vested interests at stake, it is surprising to see how the new
quality policy – a fundamental and intended change – was accepted and enforced so
smoothly in both countries. This chapter aims to explain this smooth transition.

For reasons of comparison, we focus on a particular type of care, i.e. long-term
care. Long-term care includes primarily care for the elderly, the handicapped, and
psychiatric patients, all of whom need lasting and frequent (daily) intensive attention.[1]

---

1 Long-term care defined on this website: http://www.minvws.nl/images/
2508976C%2Edoc_tcm11-54021.pdf.

In this chapter we focus on long-term care provided at people's homes. In Denmark this is referred to as eldercare, while in the Netherlands it is called home care.[2]

Following is a discussion of which barriers, presented in chapter 1, could have hampered the acceptance of the national quality policy and quality standards. Next, we present a historical overview of the introduction of quality standards in Danish eldercare and Dutch home care. An explanation of why potential barriers did not obstruct the reform, and which factors actually facilitated the adoption of quality standards, follows. The analysis is based on interim research results. Nevertheless, these and other research findings provide insight for a general understanding of conditions that facilitate reform.

Long term care in Denmark and the Netherlands

In order to demonstrate that the introduction of a nationwide quality policy was a fundamental break with the past, it is necessary to comprehend the political realms of Danish and Dutch home care, and specifically the relationship between public and private actors in the process of policy-making (Treib, Bärn & Falkner, 2005: 5). As figure 4.1 shows, the reform affected various actors at several levels of the Danish eldercare system and the Dutch home care system.

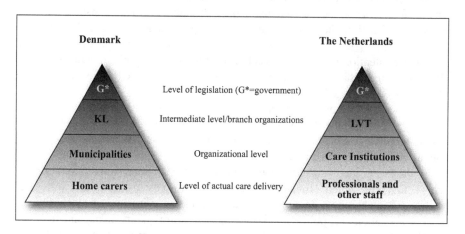

Figure 4.1   The institutional structure of the Danish eldercare system and Dutch home care

---

2   In the Netherlands care for the elderly includes home care, related social services and care provided by nursing homes and retirement homes (Okma, 2001:33). For reasons of comparison, we focus on the Dutch home care arrangements for it resembles the Danish eldercare in most respects.

The political dimension of governing long-term care plays out in a particular way. In both countries, the central government legally structures the provision of long-term care, while the main branch organizations in this sector (Kommunernes Landsforening (KL) in Denmark and the National Association for Community Nursing and Home Help (LVT) in the Netherlands) play an important role at the intermediate level.[3] The branch organizations, among other things, lobby on behalf of their members, organize benchmarks, and/or offer blueprint models that facilitate compliance with legal provisions. The national quality policies require Danish municipalities and Dutch care institutions to execute legal provisions regarding the quality of care.[4] In both countries, this mainly involves the setting up and monitoring of quality standards. Professional caretakers (called home carers in Denmark) are the ones who actually deliver long-term care at people's homes, and it is the responsibility of caretakers to comply with these quality standards. Although the behaviour of professionals and other staff at the shop floor determines whether the legislation has the intended effect, this book does not consider the (un)intended effects and effectiveness of reform (see chapter 1). Instead, we are interested in how reform – in this case the fundamental, intended, and enforced national policy on quality care – was achieved. This question is all the more interesting because of the many potential barriers that were present in both countries.

Expected barriers to reform

The introduction of a nationwide quality policy was accepted on the first suggestion. Consequently, there are no failed attempts from which to derive barriers that were successfully overcome. Nevertheless, it is possible to list potential barriers that could have blocked reform based on barriers presented in chapter 1.[5] Three barriers stand out. First, based on the existing paradigm regarding quality assurance processes (i.e. municipalities or medical professionals determine these standards for themselves), one would expect resistance to governmental interference in both countries. Second, the countries' decision-making processes could have restricted the opportunities for central government to enforce the new, national quality policy. Both central governments lack power to force the implementation of such a policy in a top-down manner and depend on local governments to enforce new policy; at the same time, local level actors have access to decision-making procedures (leading to a struggle

---

3   Since 1 July 2005 the National Association for Community Nursing and Home Help (LVT) changed its name in Z-org.

4   Sometimes Danish municipalities delegate the delivery of service to private suppliers, which municipalities increasingly do to comply with the 2002 requirement to offer citizens more than one supplier to choose from. However, for the purpose of clarity, we do not incorporate private suppliers in our figure as only few municipalities delegated the delivery of service to private suppliers in the period we have studied in this contribution.

5   In this chapter barriers are derived from a calculus approach (institutional rules) and a cultural approach (preferences) to institutions.

for power). Third, since the introduction of national quality standards would reduce the autonomy of Danish municipalities and Dutch care providers, it is logical to assume that they would have resisted such a reduction in order to protect their vested interests. In this section, these three potential barriers are discussed in detail.

Denmark

Introducing national quality standards conflicts with the policy paradigm in two ways. First, the Danish tradition of local self-government means that national interference in local policy is generally considered illegitimate since local governments are understood to protect local needs, which are distinguished from national needs. Second, eldercare is based on values of humanity that prompt the service to be tailored to citizens' individual needs. These values are difficult to combine with nationally standardized, and sometimes inflexible, quality measurements.

The paradigm is not the only barrier present in Denmark; there is also the decision-making barrier. Traditionally, local governments are responsible for Danish eldercare. Local governments have a high degree of autonomy in determining the service level, and they control the allocation of national grants and local taxes, as well as establish the content of eldercare. Additionally, local governments can influence policy processes at different levels and in different stages. In the decision-making stage, municipalities can exploit the corporative structure of the Danish system to influence the policy-making process. For example, they and other relevant interest groups are invited by the central government to participate in the decision-making process. Danish municipalities not only advocate their interest via the corporative structure, but also via the government's custom to circulate bills among influential actors for consideration before passing the bill. Furthermore, municipalities are major players when a decision has been reached; the municipalities have to implement policy and sanction non-compliance. Moreover, central government has little if any instruments to enforce policy.

Reform infringes upon the power and autonomy of local government, threatening their vested interests, while also being contradictory to existing norms and values (paradigm). Therefore, it would have been expected for municipalities to attempt re-establishing their power and authority in defining home care services by using the institutional structure to advocate their interests, vetoing any proposals that may harm such interests. In short, potential barriers that could have blocked the introduction of national quality standards stem from local governmental preferences (paradigm and vested interests), and opportunities to block and influence reform (decision-making procedures).

The Netherlands

Traditionally, quality control in the Dutch health care was considered the exclusive responsibility of the medical profession. Health care professionals primarily followed the professional standards from which norms concerning the quality of care were derived (Kasdorp, 2004). The new quality policy, however, implied governmental interference with the organizational aspects of the provision of care. This could have conflicted with the paradigm regarding quality assurance processes. In turn, professionals could have perceived this as an attempt to reduce their autonomy in determining if and how to account for their services.

The decision-making barrier that could have blocked reform is the result of public-private enmeshment. The Dutch central government is legally responsible to ensure equal access to high quality and affordable health care, but private institutions are responsible for the actual care provision. The private execution of public tasks defines the symbiotic relationship of private and public actors (Putters & Van der Grinten, 2001). The institutional arrangements resulting from this private-public enmeshment – which are typical for the Dutch health care sector including home care – present a barrier, as parties struggle for power. Though the government navigates policy by means of financial and legal instruments, its impact is limited. This is because care providers have the power to obstruct unwelcome plans that appear to disrupt their vested interests, or do not correspond with their professional norms and values.

Vested interests could have played a role in this case in two ways. First, the new national policy has severe financial consequences for care organizations; they are the ones who have to pay for the implementation costs of a quality management system. It seems likely that financial consequences would have resulted in resistance from organizations to accept the reform. One way to block the reform could have been, for instance, to argue that it would have been better to spend money on actual provision of care instead of measuring it. Second, the national quality policy affects vested interest at the shop floor of the organization. Traditionally, health care professionals are accustomed to assessment by peers on the basis of professional norms. However, the legal provisions regarding quality control hold managers responsible for the organizational aspects of care provision. From the managers' perspective, compliance with these rules requires at least some standardization of the professional activities by the organization, which could have lead to tension between managers and professionals. This tension could have, in turn, hampered reform when professionals refused to take part in activities related to the quality management system (which managers are legally required to set up and maintain, a concept that will be explained in the next section).

Course of events

Despite the expected barriers (paradigm, decision-making structures, and vested interests), reform measures were introduced. In this section, we describe the course of events in detail in order to identify what facilitated the reform. As will become clear, the introduction of national quality policies involved a process of self-regulation in which municipalities (Denmark) and branch organizations (the Netherlands) drew up quality standards.

Denmark

The introduction of quality standards in Danish eldercare was inspired by a Ministry of Finance rapport (Finansministeriet, 1995) which recommended that local decision-makers should actively participate in the formulation of quality goals, expected results, and the framework for local services. Even though the rapport is based on recommendations, it signals a first step in the direction of national interference with local autonomy. Eldercare was one of the first areas to adopt these recommendations, and in 1997 the Danish Parliament authorized the Minister of Social Affairs to define rules about the content, the level, and the delivery of local eldercare (Lovtidende, 1997).

Consequently, local autonomy in eldercare was challenged. Previously, the national focus on local services, and particularly long-term eldercare, had been mainly economic and it was considered the responsibility of local governments to determine the content and extent of services. During the 1980s, initiatives were introduced to increase decentralization, while at the same time national attention remained focussed on problems faced in the long-term care sector.

The 1997 law was one of the first attempts to gain more control over the quality of local services and it was meant to serve two goals. First, national government wanted to increase the quality of service because the media and the public perceived and portrayed long-term care as an underperforming sector in need of improvement. Second, the unclear terms in existing laws, regarding the allocation of local eldercare, violated the rights of the elderly because eldercare differed per municipality; some innovative municipalities had formulated quality standards while others had not. The new law was intended to improve the rights of the elderly by clearly stipulating what their rights were – including the quality of service they were entitled to receive (Socialministeriet, 1998a).

Despite national government taking control of the quality standards-issue in eldercare, distortion of the reform at the local level has been limited. Consider, for instance, the Kommunernes Landsforening (KL). This branch organization hardly opposed the national government's usurpation of control in the eldercare sector. On the contrary, the KL worked together with the Ministry of Social Affairs to develop procedures for formulating quality standards, and the KL also participated in investigations of quality standards' implementation. Moreover, the law has been implemented in over 90% of the municipalities, and local governments have shown their willingness to obey to the new law and adapt themselves to new conditions (Socialministeriet, 2000; 2002; 2003b). The municipalities did not resist the new law, despite the fact that they had good reasons and good means to do so. Instead, the majority of municipalities have complied with the national quality standards.

The Netherlands

In the 1970s, the Dutch government became interested in quality control. This interest came on the heels of growing political and societal criticism on the functioning of the medical profession, and the imbalanced relationship between professionals and patients. It took about two decades to draw up various quality bills. In line with the then common belief that society could be governed, the quality bills contained very detailed quality requirements. However, before these bills came into effect, a shift in policy paradigm occurred. The top-down view underlying the belief in the government's steering capacity was replaced by a less centralistic view focusing on market activity, deregulation, and self-regulation (Wagner et al., 1995: 5; Kasdorp en Van der Grinten, 1999: 38; Casparie et al., 2001: 21).[6] In line with this approach, the Dutch Minister of Health, Welfare, and Sport introduced a very ambitious grand design for a new health care system. The grand design represented a decentralized and market-based view on how health care should be structured. Initially, the plan to introduce a nationwide quality policy was part of this larger policy reform.

Between 1989 and 1992, several steps were taken to execute this grand design for the health care system, including the introduction of a nationwide quality policy. However, during the implementation of measures to arrive at deregulation and market activity in health care, political support became more and more hesitant and public support eroded even more so. Faced with mounting opposition, the Dutch parliament decided to shelve the debate and this led, ultimately, to the demise of the plan for a grand design (Okma, 2001: 37).

Surprisingly, this did not affect the decision-making process to create a national quality policy. However, instead of imposing very detailed quality provisions, the government turned to framework regulation which set the high quality care as objective, leaving care institutions room for manoeuvre in terms of specifying quality standards of their own.

The decision-making processes about the nationwide quality policy started in 1989 with a series of conferences – the so-called Leidschendam conferences (Casparie et al., 2001). Figure 4.2 presents a chronology of the various steps of these processes and the actors involved. At the first meeting, the parties involved (governmental agencies, branch organizations, patient/consumer organizations, professional organizations, and independent experts) signed a declaration of intent to design a nation-wide quality policy (Berkestijn & Colsen, 1989). In 1990, a follow-up conference was held to discuss the central elements of this quality policy (Kasdorp & Van der Grinten, 1999: 40). The following agreements were reached: care providers' branch organizations would initiate the creation of quality standards in close consultation with health insurers and patient and consumer organizations,

---

6 Previously, (home) care organizations had to meet very detailed governmental quality norms in order to be eligible for public funding.

Reform in Europe

quality management systems[7] would be used to ensure high quality care, and the central government would enact a law codifying the conference-agreements in order to ensure the cooperation of individual care providers.

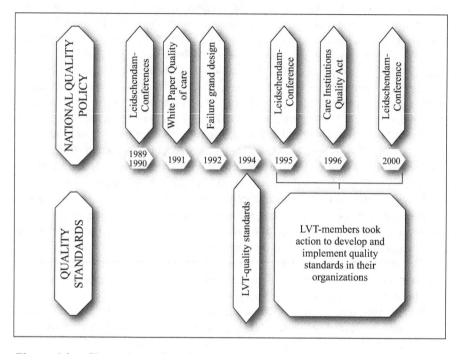

Figure 4.2   Chronology of the introduction of the nationwide quality policy

In 1991, the White Paper *Quality of Care* (Kwaliteit van Zorg; Ministry of Social Affairs, 1991) described the implementation process of the Quality bill. In 1996, the Dutch Parliament passed the Care Institutions Quality Act (Kwaliteitwet Zorginstellingen – KWZ). Primarily, the Quality Act codified the Leidschendam conference agreements following years of intensive consultations with interest groups and branch organizations. It allowed care institutions to pursue a quality care policy that suited their specific situation, while mandating that they systematically gather data on the quality of care provided, assess the delivery of care, and make necessary improvements.

In the home care sector, the National Association for Community Nursing and Home Help (LVT), a branch organization, had started to develop quality standards long before the Quality Act came into effect. In 1994, they set these standards as preconditions for membership. In preparation of the 2000 Leidschendam Conference,

---

7   Such systems exist of formalized procedures and actions for setting up and implementing quality policies, monitoring and auditing the results, and responding to shortcomings.

Sluijs & Wagner (2000) studied the progress in quality management activities during the period 1995–2000. Between 1995 and 2000, home care organizations made twice as much progress as other sectors (Sluijs & Wagner, 2000: 223).[8] In five years time, home care organizations introduced at least ten new quality activities. Another study revealed that the total number of quality activities in home care organizations doubled during this period (Klok & Van Heffen, 2004: 13). By 2000, practically all care institutions had implemented a quality management system that incorporated the LVT quality standards (IGZ, 2002: 9).[9]

This may seem slow, but the research findings show that other parts of the health care sector did not manage to make such progress. In the next section we will explain why the Dutch home care sector managed to set up and maintain quality management systems in such a relatively short period of time, whereas other health care sectors failed.

Unraveling the reform: Actual barriers and facilitators

Two factors explain how the adoptation of quality systems came about. The first factor includes the central government's awareness of existing decision-making structures and incorporation of relevant actors in the decision-making processes. Simultaneously, the central government provided a legally structured national quality policy that allows for bottom-up quality standards. By adhering to the decision-making structures, vested interests of municipalities and care institutions were taken into account, thereby avoiding potential barriers. A second explanation for the rather rapid reform pertains to a change in paradigm, regarding quality accountability towards external parties. Although the shifts in the paradigm in both countries are of a different nature, they have put the vested interests in a new perspective, causing a sense of urgency that, in turn, positively affected the willingness of executive actors to develop quality standards.

Prudent coping with the existing decision-making structures

Denmark From a vested interest perspective, maintaining local autonomy is essential for municipalities. We initially assumed that the reform would infringe upon

---

8   The progress was assessed on the basis of a written questionnaire sent to the directors of health care institutions in 1995 and 2000. The questionnaire measures the extent of the implementation of quality management activities.

9   All home care organizations implemented a quality management system, but their systems differ in the number of quality activities included (Sluijs &Wagner, 2003; Van Heffen & Klok , 2004). These differences at the organizational level may be due to cultural characteristics, such as innovative attitude of the employees, the hierarchical decision structure, and the degree to which organizations traditionally operate according to standardized methods. The home care sector does not differ in this respect from other subsections in the health care sector (Sluijs & Wagner, 2003: 225, 227).

this autonomy, thereby creating a barrier, as municipalities would want to disrupt the implementation process. As it turned out, however, the reform did not seriously threaten the power of municipalities and the structure of the Danish eldercare. Instead, the reform allowed local governments to specify the content of the quality standards, influence and control the criteria and the scope of the measurements, and sanction non-compliant organizations. At the same time, limited sanctioning power at the national level prevents national government from effectively sanctioning municipalities that do not formulate and adopt quality standards. In short, the structure of Danish eldercare leaves municipalities with a number of essential veto points and therefore municipalities' autonomy is not seriously threatened by the reform. Still, when the law was negotiated, no one could have foreseen this outcome. This raises a question as to why the KL and local governments did not strongly oppose the reform. Somewhat surprisingly, they actually pressured local governments to formulate and develop quality measurements. A change in paradigm explains this unexpected support for reform (see below).

The Netherlands   In the Netherlands, the central government initiated a debate among the main parties in health care. These parties installed a committee in charge of interviewing actors who were invited to a quality conference before the actual meetings in Leidschendam took place. Based on these interviews, this committee drew up a list of topics to be discussed at the conferences. The list offered a joint focus, thereby reducing the risk of clashing interests. Furthermore, the interviews revealed that all health care actors were concerned about the role of government. Their concerns reflected the frustration about the heavy-handed state regulation of the previous decades. The generally shared opinion was that government had to restrict its role in the health care sector by facilitating self-regulation instead of dictating regulations. This stimulated the actors to focus on mutual interests to make the self-regulation work.

Change of paradigm

Denmark   The vested interest perspective explains KL's and municipalities' stance towards the reform. Since their interests were not negatively affected by the reform, they had no need to fight the reform. However, the vested interest perspective does not explain how the idea of quality standards reached the public agenda in the first place. In order to answer that question, it is necessary to consider the environment in which the eldercare sector operates (March & Olsen, 1983: 283ff; Moe, 1989; Winther, 1994: 23; Wilson, 1989: 203; Van Dooren & Van de Walle, 2002). Prior to the introduction of quality standards, no attempts had been made by national government to interfere with the content of local long-term care, partly because such initiatives were generally considered inappropriate. It is, therefore, unlikely that national policy-entrepreneurs wished to promote illegitimate standards in an area so publicly visible.

But values traditionally linked to eldercare changed during the 1990s, and this change was preceded by a drastic alteration in the sector's political environment. A changing image and values and understanding of eldercare explains why long-term care was one of the first sectors to adapt quality systems.

In the 1990s, eldercare was associated with poor performance, inefficiency, and bad quality following intense media debate filled with stories and visual images of elderly people living in miserable conditions (Socialministeriet, 2003). At the same time, home carers were being accused of laziness during work hours, even drinking coffee instead of attending to their duties. In the beginning, the stories about a malfunctioning care sector were not spread by policy entrepreneurs but by the media. Another compounding factor was the possible threat to the local economy. Eldercare had always been the largest expense of local governments, and the aging population would only create an even heavier burden on the local government's budget (Finansministeriet, 2002).

Thus came the need to control eldercare, specifically by increasing the quality while controlling the costs. Decision-makers were forced to pose as managers interested in rational control and influencing lower level government. The sector's image changed from one defined by humanistic values to a sector that not only malfunctioned, but also violated the rights of the elderly. This changed image opened a window of opportunity for national government to interfere with local eldercare. Local government could not escape these reforms because they needed to restore their image. Hence, the focusing events changed the paradigm and made various national actors interested in interfering with and controlling local eldercare (Baumgartner & Jones, 2002).

Considering the circumstances, quality systems seemed an appropriate tool because they signalise rationality, accountability, and control. The change in paradigm progressed simultaneously with the introduction of a new trend in West European countries: the modernization of public administrations with an emphasis on quality systems, accountability, responsibility, and standardization (Pollitt, 2003; Pollitt & Bouckhaert, 2000). Through quality standards as the instruments of control, the possibility for national reformers to succeed increased, since these standards were compatible to international trends. At the same time, a small number of municipalities who had already introduced quality standards were increasingly portrayed as modern and innovative municipalities. Hence, an image in favour of quality systems emerged, making it easier to advocate for such systems.

At the same time, the changed paradigm made it difficult for local government to escape reforms. Municipalities needed an instrument with which they could rebuild their reputation as effective and accountable organizations serving the interests of local areas and their citizens. One public official, part of one of the most progressive municipalities in adopting quality standards, explains as follows: 'When [politicians] meet extensive criticism, [they] need something to lean against in order to demonstrate that things are going well' (Fokusgruppeinterview-Ældreservice, 2004). Politicians decided to lean against quality assessments because they symbolize a modern institution open to criticism and changes. Quality assessments seemed appropriate tools because they illustrate a drive towards modernity and efficiency, and seem to be obvious solutions for accountability and control problems. At that time, quality standards were surrounded by a rhetoric of quality improvements which was difficult for municipalities to ignore.

The Netherlands   In 1991, just a year after the actors involved in the Leidschendam conferences reached an agreement on the implementation of quality management systems, the National Association for Community Nursing and Home Help (LVT) started an experiment. This experiment was designed to ascertain the contents of a successful quality management system that would meet the standards of the International Organization for Standardization (ISO), and to explore which tools could facilitate the adoption of such a system. The LVT's reason to actively pursue the creation of quality standards was the introduction of competition in the health care market.

The LVT developed a blueprint for its members. This blueprint gave the Dutch home care sector a head start, offering tangible quality standards that allowed for proper quality measurement. The proactive attitude of the LVT, however, was not unique. Other branch organizations took similar actions (ZonMw, 2001: 37). But the LVT took a different path in one important respect. In 1994, it managed to convince its members of the need to stipulate compliance with the quality standards as a precondition of membership.[10] Though, in theory, it could suspend members that did not comply with the quality standards, in practice this was considered too strong a measure (Brandsen & Van Heffen, 2004a; 2004b). This raises the question as to why home care organizations were willing to adopt the quality standards, without the threat of punishment for non-compliance.

At the organizational level, the most important reason to comply with the quality standards was the prospect of increasing market competition. In 1994, commercial care providers were allowed to enter the home care market. The regular home care organizations felt a need for a quality mark to distinguish themselves from commercial providers (Sluijs & Wagner, 2003: 233). Since commercial providers did not receive public funding, they offered their services mainly to lucrative clients, burdening the regular providers with the less profitable clients. Consequently, traditional providers encountered financial problems. Pushed by market forces, some of them took a similar attitude (i.e. focussing on lucrative care provision) at the cost of public interest. Others started a private service branch, diminishing the transparency of the use of public funding (Trommel et al., 2004: 212). These unintended side effects generated enormous media coverage and gave regular providers a bad name. In order to counteract these negative effects, the LVT's quality mark became even more important.

---

10 Moreover, empirical research shows that the members experienced a high level of pressure from the LVT to work on (further) improving the quality management system (Van Heffen & Klok, 2004).

The increasing competition also made managers aware of the need to adopt a more businesslike style of management, including demonstrations of a clear relation between costs and products, a focus on output and performance, and maintaining financial validity (Van Hout & Brandsen, 2004). A powerful means of reducing costs is through structuring activities. This can be facilitated by introducing quality management systems, because it allows managers to govern internal processes and to control the quality of care in a systematic way. In contrast to other health sectors, such as hospitals and public health centres, the home care sector's activities can be clearly defined, which creates opportunities for managerial control over the performances (Van Herk, 1997).[11] The lack of complexity allows managers in home care organizations to hold a firm grip on their staff. As a consequence, the LVT quality standards could be transformed relatively easily into organizational procedures and protocols.

Lessons learned

In this chapter we explored the introduction of quality control systems in Denmark and the Netherlands. In the beginning of this chapter, we presented possible barriers to reform. In this section, we will confront these theoretical assumptions with the empirical data to determine how and to what extent they truly affected the reform processes in the long-term care sector of Denmark and the Netherlands.

Potential barriers

For both cases, we expected mutual dependency (which flows from the decision-making structure) to act as a barrier in both countries. In the Netherlands, mutual dependency pertains to the power balance between central government, on the one hand, and private healthcare providers and insurers, on the other hand. In Denmark, central government and municipalities are mutually dependent on one another, thereby causing tension between centralization and decentralization forces. The central government's need for a national quality policy is difficult to reconcile with the autonomous municipalities who have to execute the policy. The mutual dependency offers Dutch care providers and Danish municipalities a possible avenue to obstruct reform processes. We also expected paradigms to act as barriers hampering the introduction of quality standards. Specifically, these paradigms define the Danish disapproval of using quality standards in public service and the Dutch tradition to rely on professional self-regulation of the quality of care (i.e. the monitoring of quality by means of a peer review based on medical-professional quality norms).

---

11 Interestingly, an early study on the progress of implementing quality standards in the various health sectors has shown that the degree of competition and professional autonomy cannot explain differences on an organizational level (Wagner c.s., 1995: 58). Inter-organizational variation across the sectors is mainly explained by cultural characteristics and a preceding tradition of protocol usage (Wagner, 1995: 59; Sluijs & Wagner, 2000: 62).

Lastly, the introduction of a nationwide quality policy was expected to reduce local and professional autonomy, putting vested interests under pressure.

Explanation of reform

From a theoretical point of view, one would have expected much resistance to reform. Yet, the introduction of quality standards in the Danish and Dutch long-term care went rather smoothly. Several factors influenced this smooth reform. First, Danish and Dutch central governments opted for a strategy in which legal regulation provided a solid basis for a national quality policy, but did not impose top-down quality standards. The governments took notice of the formal and informal decision-making structures, making sure not to disrupt the existing structures too much, and incorporated the relevant actors in the reform process. In the Netherlands, this joint approach was even more important, since the introduction of the quality standards occurred in a period characterized by economic crises and the questioning of the legitimacy of strong state-interventions. Second, image problems and the introduction of market competition facilitated a change in paradigm and actors' preferences. Danish national and local governments were motivated to invest in the creation of quality standards because of the bad image of its eldercare. In the Netherlands, the introduction of market competition made managers of home care organizations more aware of the importance of quality standards. Based on the evidence presented in this chapter, we have come to the belief that institutional barriers to reform can be overcome if paradigms or preferences change.

References

Baumgartner, F.R., B.D. Jones (2002) *Policy Dynamics*, Chicago: University of Chicago Press.
Berkestijn, M.G. van, P.J.A. Colsen (1989) 'Kwaliteit van zorg: Een conferentie van de KNMG voor WVC' *Medisch Contact* vol. 44 (13) pp. 423–426.
Bouckaert, G., C. Pollitt (2000) *Public Management Reform: A Comparative Analysis,* New York: Oxford University Press.
Casparie, A.F., J. Legemaate, R.A.L. Rijkschroeff, M.J.E. Brugman,M.A.J.M. Buijsen, M.J. de gruijter, E.H. Hulst, D.G. Oudenampsen, A. van 't Riet (2001) *Evaluatie Kwaliteitswet zorginstellingen* Den Haag: ZonMw.
Day, P., R. Klein (1987) *Accountabilities in Five Public Services,* London: Tavistock Publications Ltd.
Dooren, W. van, S. van de Walle (2002) 'Self Promotion by Self Assessment? A Study of the Motives Underlying the Use of the Common Assessment Framework (CAF) in Belgium' Conference paper *NISPAcee* Cracow (Poland).
Driel, M. van (1989) Zelfregulering: Hoog opspelen of thuisblijven Deventer: Kluwer.
Finansministeriet (2002) Udfordringer og muligheder – Den kommunale økonomi mod 2010.

Finansministeriet (1995) *Budgetredegørelse 1995.*

Fokusgruppeinterviw –Ældreservice (2004). Interview made in groups of people from the administration of Eldercare in Græsted-Gilleleje. Conducted March 2004 by Bente Bjørnholt.

Grinten, T. van der, J.K. Helderman, K. Putters (2004) 'Een Stelsel van Stelsels' *B&M* vol. 31 (4) pp.201–210.

Heffen M.J. van, T. Brandsen (2004a) 'Brancheorganisaties en gedragscodes: De spagaat van zelfregulering' *Recht der Werkelijkheid* vol.2 pp. 31–50.

Heffen M.J. van, T. Brandsen (2004b) 'Codes of Conduct: Private Regulation of the Public Interest?' Conference paper *Conference of the Institute for Governance Studies* Enschede (the Netherlands).

Heffen M.J. van, P.J. Klok (2004) 'Explaining Progress in the Implementation of Quality Management Systems: Does Management-Based Regulation Matter?' Conference paper, *Annual Meeting of the Law and Society Association* Chicago (USA).

Herk, R. van (1997). *Artsen onder druk*, Utrecht: Elsevier.

Inspectie voor de Gezondheidszorg (2002) *Kwaliteitsborging in zorginstellingen: Intentie, wet en praktijk*, Staat van de Gezondheidszorg 2002, Retrieved May, 2005 from http://www.igz.nl.

Hout, E. van, T. Brandsen (2004) 'Hybridity in Dutch Domiciliary Care' Conference paper *European Group of Public Administration* Ljubljana (Slovenia).

Kasdorp, J. (2004) 'Rivaliserende waarden, eisen en wensen in de gezondheidszorg' *B&M*, vol. 31 (4) pp. 211–221.

Kasdorp, J.P. & T.E.D. van der Grinten (1999) 'Kwaliteit en doelmatigheid', *25 jaar sturing in de gezondheidszorg*, Den Haag: SCP, pp. 35–42.

Lovtidende (1997). Lov om social service, *Lov*, nr. 454 af 10/6.

March, J.G., J.P. Olsen (1983) 'Organizing Political Life: What Administrative Reorganization, Tells Us about Government' *The American Political Science Review*, vol. 77 (2) pp. 281–96.

Moe, T. M. (1989) 'The Politics of Bureaucratic Structure' John E., J.E. Chubb, P.E. Peterson (eds) *Can the Government Govern?*, Washington: The Brookings Institution pp. 267–331.

Okma, K.G.H. (2001) 'Health care, health policies and health care reforms in the Netherlands' *International Publication Series Health, Welfare and Sports*, nr.7, pp. 1–52.

Pollitt, C. (1993) *Managerialism and the Public Services. Cuts or Cultural Change in the 1990s?*, Great Britain: T.J. Press Ltd.

Pollitt C., G. Bourckaert (eds) (1995) *Quality Improvements in European Public Services. Concepts, Cases, and Commentary*, Biddles LTT: Guildford.

Putters, K., T.E.D. van der Grinten (2001) 'Schuivende verhoudingen in de besturing van de gezondheidszorg' Abma, T., R. in 't Veld (eds) *Handboek Beleidswetenschap*, Amsterdam: Boom, pp. 115–116.

Sluijs, E.M., C. Wagner (2003) 'Progress in the Implementation of Quality

Management in Dutch Health Care: 1995–2000' *International Journal for Quality in Health Care*, Vol.15 (3) pp. 223–234.

Sluijs, E.M., C. Wagner (2000) *Quality Systems in Health Care Organizations, The State of Affairs* (in Dutch), Utrecht: Nivel.

Sluijs, E.M., C. Wagner, M. Bennema-Broos (2000) *Samenvatting van twee nivel onderzoeken*, Utrecht: Nivel.

Socialministeriet (1998a) *Idekatelog, Kvalitets-standarder, Personlig og praktisk hjælp m.v Socialministeriet*, July 1998.

Socialministeriet (1998b) *Bekendtgørelse af 22. April 1998.*

Socialministeriet (2000a) *Kvalitetsstandarder i kommunerne. Personlig og praktisk hjælp m.v Lov om social service*, Status Udarbejdet af Socialministeiet Institut for offentlig økonomi og udvikling, April 2000.

Socialministeriet (2002) *Kvalitetsstandarder i hjemmeplejen – eksempler på god praksis* Socialministeriet institut for Pensions og Ældrepolitik 2002/01.

Socialministeiet (2003a). *Kvalitetsstandarder – Sammenhæng og synlighed på ældreområdet*, Udarbejdet af Socialministeriet Kontoret for ældre.

Socialministeriet (2003b) *Evaluering af ældreormrådet – Hvorfor kritik?*

Socialministeriet (2003c) *Kommunernes tilsyn med personlig og praktisk hjælp til hjemmeboende ældre borgere* (http://www.sm.dk/netpublikationer/2003/p3tilsyn3103/).

Treib, O., H. Bähr, G. Falkner (2005) 'Modes of Governance: A Note towards Conceptual Clarification' *European Governance Papers* (EUROGOV) No. N-05-02. Retrieved May, 2005 from http://www.connex-network.org/eurogov/pdf/egp-newgov-N-05-02.pdf.

Trommel, W., T. Brandsen, M. van Heffen-Oude Vrielink, M. Moulijn (2004) 'Performance Measurement in Public Governance: Successful Interpretations of Failure' *Society and Economy*, vol. 26 (2–3), pp. 195–221.

Verbeek, G. (1984) 'Het kwaliteitsbeleid van de overheid' *Tijdschrift voor Gezondheid en Politiek, Themanummer Kwaliteit van de zorg*, vol. 2 (4) pp. 16–21.

Wagner, C., D.H. de Bakker, E.M. Sluijs (1995) *Kwaliteitssystemen in instellingen, de stand van zaken in 1995*, Utrecht: Nivel.

Wilson, J.Q. (1989) *Bureaucracy – What Government Agencies Do and Why They Do It*, New York: Basic Books.

Winther, S. (1994). *Implementering og effektivitet.* Herning: Systime A/S.

Chapter 5

Reforming Germany's Constitutional Right to Asylum: A Shifting Paradigm

Fleur Alink[1]

A surprising reform in asylum policy

On 26 May 1993, a clear and required two-thirds majority of the German *Bundestag* (Federal Council) was in favour of changing Germany's constitution (Basic Law) regarding its asylum policy. The changes in Germany's constitution can be seen as a reform of the asylum policy because it was fundamental, intended, non-incremental, and enforced. After years of conflict and debate about the right to asylum, the two main political parties in Germany (Christian Democratic Union/Christian Social Union (CDU/CSU) and Social Democratic Party (SPD)) finally agreed on a stricter interpretation and reformed Article 16 of the constitution.

Article 16 stated that 'persons persecuted on political grounds shall enjoy the right to asylum'.[2] As a consequence of this broadly formulated article, every one who applied for asylum had to be taken into the asylum procedure. Though the new asylum article still upholds the right to asylum, three added restrictions make a fundamental difference in how to proceed with requests for asylum. First, the *rule of safe third countries* prohibits the entrance of Germany via a member state of the European Union. Refugees who reach Germany via another EU member state can be excluded from the asylum procedure. Second, the *rule of safe countries of origin* states that asylum seekers originating from so-called safe countries, i.e. countries in which supposedly no prosecution takes place, are excluded from the asylum procedure as well. The third added restriction is the *airport procedure*, which allows asylum requests to be processed at the airport. Asylum seekers whose application is rejected can be expelled more easily because airports are not technically German territory. As a result of these three restrictions, the opportunity to obtain asylum in Germany has become limited, as the possibilities for appealing for asylum have been reduced and expulsion has become easier.

---

1   This chapter is derived from a case study discussing the constitutional change in the right to asylum in Germany (Alink, F. ,forthcoming)
2   Politisch Verfolgte genieβën Asylrecht.

The changes in Article 16 show that the values and norms underlying German asylum policy have changed. At the same time, asylum procedures and organizational structures changed to enable the enforcement of the new asylum policy.

Interestingly, these changes happened despite opportunity and preference barriers. Three important barriers can be discerned. First, the rigidity of a constitution poses an obstacle to reform. Constitutions are designed for longevity and stability. Changes cannot be made by a whimsical *Bundestag*. Instead, a two-thirds majority of the members of the *Bundestag* and at least two-thirds of the votes of the *Bundesrat* are necessary to change the German constitution.[3] The second barrier is related to the first one: Germany's federal political system consists of numerous checks and balances that give substantial power to the sixteen states. The last fundamental barrier is Germany's inheritance of its Nazi past. Until the constitutional reform of 1993, Article 16 was unique in Europe because it allowed access to the asylum procedure without any restrictions. This generous policy was an immediate consequence of Germany's Nazi past, an inheritance whose presence still remains in German politics. After the Second World War, Germans felt morally obliged to act generously towards refugees. Consequently, a political majority viewed the right to asylum as inviolable. A taboo against discussions of changing Article 16 was thus created and perpetuated.

These barriers did not disappear. Yet, not only was it possible to reform Article 16 of the constitution, but this reform was also trendsetting. Germany's asylum policy was much more restrictive than European and national regulations existing at that time. Other countries soon followed Germany's example, spurred by sharp increases in the number of asylum seekers. The presence of barriers, as well as a trendsetting reform proposal, is usually considered factors blocking reform (see chapter 1). Yet reform did occur – implying that somehow existing barriers were overcome. This brings us to the question of how the different barriers were overcome. This chapter aims to examine the factors facilitating the constitutional reform of Germany's asylum policy. In the next section, it is argued why earlier attempts to change the right to asylum were not feasible. Section three describes the reform process and the role crisis played in this process. Section four addresses what happened to the barriers that previously barred reform and which factors facilitated this reform process. The last section links this chapter's findings to the terminology used in chapter 1.

Previous attempts to reform the right to asylum

Since the 1970s and especially the 1980s, the continuously expanding numbers of asylum seekers resulted in increasing societal and political pressure on Germany's generous asylum policy. Various rules and regulations changed. For example, in response to changing ideas about how to handle the asylum issue, new legislation

---

3   Although constitutional change is difficult to obtain in Germany, Busch (2000) shows that, when compared internationally, the legislature's amendment power is relatively large in Germany.

was implemented. Even though the asylum policy became more and more restrictive, the right to asylum remained the same. Article 16 was not open for discussion. This changed, however, when the taboo on changing – or even discussing – Article 16 was broken. The forbiddance was broken in the mid-1980s as a result of the sudden and massive influx of asylum seekers in West Berlin. At that time, Germany and its capital city Berlin were divided into East and West. The sudden and sharp rise in asylum seekers in West Berlin caused problems because appropriate housing and regulations were lacking.

Normally, people (travellers as well as asylum seekers) wishing to travel from East Germany to West Germany needed a valid visa for West Germany or any other country in Western Europe. If they did not have a visa, East German officials would not allow them to travel to West Germany. During the summer of 1986, however, East German administrators, in Berlin, refused to continue executing this visa policy. Their refusal was a result of a complex administrative and political relationships between East and West Germany and the Allied Powers.[4] Consequently, people who wanted to travel from East to West Berlin were not checked for (valid) visa documents. While East German administrators elsewhere in Germany continued to enforce the visa policy a 'hole in the Berlin Wall' was opened. This hole in the Wall became the only gateway for asylum seekers to enter West Germany and Western Europe. Consequently, thousands of asylum seekers came to West Berlin in the summer of 1986. This huge increase in asylum seekers resulted in problems as asylum procedures were not designed to deal with such large numbers of requests, and housing facilities were insufficient for the ever-increasing number of asylum seekers. At the same time, the influx created political and societal unrest.

As the situation in West Berlin grew out of control, discussing Article 16 of the constitution became possible. The CDU party in Berlin put the problematic refugee situation in West Berlin on the local agenda, and the situation was later adopted by the CDU/CSU at the federal level of the German Republic. The CDU/CSU claimed that a reduction in the number of asylum seekers could only be achieved if the right to asylum was restricted – which required a change in the constitution. Federal CDU/CSU Ministers advocating constitutional change included ministers such as the Minister of Internal Affairs Zimmermann, who was responsible for the asylum sector, and Chancellor Kohl. However, the suggestion to change Article 16 of the constitution faced tremendous resistance from other political parties as well from society. As the CDU/CSU was the only political party in favour of reforming the constitution, no majority in favour of constitutional reform – let alone a necessary two-thirds majority – existed in Parliament.

4　According to the East German government, the agreement on visa regulations between East and West Germany was only applicable to West Germany, not to West Berlin. The city of Berlin (East as well as West) was formally governed by the Allied Powers, not by the governments of East and West Germany.

Barriers to reform

The political system

The need for a two-thirds majority to change the constitution thus presents an important blocking veto-point in the decision-making structure of Germany. Another important barrier typical of German politics is its federal system of check and balances. Germany's federal system dates back to the end of World War II. The wide variety of government institutions fragments and disperses political power – the federal structure not only gives power to the *Bundesrat* (composed of state politicians), but also to interest groups and experts to influence the decision-making process on the federal level. Moreover, the federal system also results in numerous veto-points that a reform proposal has to go through. Even if a decision has been taken, a federal policy can be frustrated at the state level. Most states are governed by either CDU/CSU, or SPD. The federal government, however, rarely consists of a coalition of these two parties. Consequently, a federal CDU/CSU coalition without the SPD will need the support of the SPD at the state level if federal policy is to be implemented, and vice versa.

Policy inheritance

Constitutional revision, in itself, is a lengthy process characterized by numerous constraints. These constraints were exacerbated by cultural factors, most notably the policy inheritance of Germany's Nazi past, resulting in vested interests with regards to refugees and asylum policy. A moral obligation of tolerance towards asylum seekers compelled a majority of politicians to oppose the constitutional reform of Article 16; the right to asylum for everyone was inviolable and changing Article 16 was unacceptable, and remained a taboo.

Lacking support and urgency

Attempts to change the constitution failed because there was neither enough support nor a feeling of urgency in the political and societal arena to change the existing paradigm in the mid-1980s. The asylum issue was not a serious problem for German citizens, who were more concerned about environmental pollution.[5] Moreover, during the Cold War, the Germans (as well as other Western societies) were more sympathetic towards asylum seekers, especially when they came from communist countries. In addition, opponents of constitutional reform claimed that changing the constitution was not the solution for the kind of problems encountered in West Berlin and Germany at that time. Instead – and in spite of increasing numbers of asylum seekers – a majority in parliament searched for a solution within the framework of the constitution; i.e. the existing paradigm. The pressure on the policy sector disappeared after East Germany agreed (following diplomatic negotiations with West

---

5   The *Politbarometer* shows that environmental pollution was considered to be the most important problem for West Germans in 1989 (before the fall of the Iron Curtain).

German politicians) to enforce the visa policy for West Berlin again. This resulted in a drop in asylum seekers. Consequently, policy reform was no longer needed. As executing the already existing visa regulations did not change the existing paradigm, the crisis as well as the discussion on Article 16 ended without reform.

A combination of widespread resistance to reforming the established paradigm, lack of both urgency and support, and institutional constraints resulting from Germany's political system and decision-making structure, constitutes the most important reasons why Article 16 could not be reformed in the mid 1980s.

Crisis and reform

After the reunification of East and West Germany in 1990, the country experienced various problems. These included high costs due to the reunification, exceptional increases in the number of asylum seekers, and high rates of unemployment. Even though various problems were present at the same time, it was the asylum seekers issue that dominated political and social debates and newspaper headlines between the summer of 1991 and May 1993 (Schönwalder, 1999: 85; Marshall, 1996: 6; Koopmans, 1996).

Emerging crisis situation

A combination of rising numbers of asylum seekers and daylong riots against foreigners in the city of Hoyerswerda caused a crisis in the asylum sector.[6] Some experts call this crisis period the most controversial period in Germany's post war history (Marshall, 2000: 87; Schönwalder, 1999). Massive demonstrations and growing xenophobia spawned citizen's violence, resulting in large-scale societal turmoil. In 1992, West German citizens perceived the asylum seekers issue as the most important problem Germany's government faced – even more important than right-wing extremism, unemployment, and the problems in former East Germany.[7] During the crisis, the number of asylum seekers exploded. Germany had never before been confronted with such high numbers of asylum seekers (see table 5.1).

Table 5.1   **Asylum seekers in several European countries (BAFl, 2001: 39)**

Year	Germany	France	Netherlands	UK	Sweden
1990	193,100	54,800	21,200	26,200	29,400
1991	256,100	47,400	21,600	44,800	27,400
1992	438,200	28,900	20,300	24,600	84,000
1993	322,600	27,600	35,400	22,400	37,000

---

6   The riots in Hoyerswerda took place from 17–22 September 1991.

7   Based on *Politbarometer* West-Germany (1992). Former East German states considered other subjects, such as unemployment, to be more important.

At the same time, Germany experienced a sharp increase in violent acts by militant right-wing extremists (Koopmans, 1999). The rise in the number of asylum seekers was accompanied by a growing intolerance towards foreigners in general. This intolerance resulted in increasing violence towards asylum seekers and foreigners in general in the early 1990s (see table 5.2). Anti-foreigner violence reached its climax in 1992 and 1993.[8]

Table 5.2   Number of violent crimes against foreigners in East and West Germany (Ministry of the Interior, 1994)

Year	West	East	Total
1991	2031	395	2426
1992	5174	1162	6336
1993	6181	540	6721

Although violent acts were not exclusively aimed at asylum seekers but against foreigners in general, right-wing citizen's violence was an important issue during the crisis (Koopmans, 1996). Both proponents and opponents of changing Article 16 used these violent crimes as a justification for their arguments. Supporters of reform, like the governing party CDU/CSU, viewed violence as the result of the rising number of asylum seekers. Opponents such as the SPD believed that extreme-right violence was encouraged by CDU/CSU politicians who continued to emphasize the problems posed to Germany by asylum seekers and foreigners.

Political deadlock

During the crisis, the government consisted of the CDU/CSU and the Free Democratic Party (FDP). The seats in parliament were divided as follows: CDU/CSU (319), SPD (239), FDP (79), PDS (17) and the Greens (8).[9] All parties, except the CDU/CSU, opposed changing Article 16. Thus, coalition parties held contradictory views on the solution of the asylum issue. 'The issue was so divisive that a coalition agreement after the 1990 federal election could only be reached by excluding [the asylum issue] from the negotiations' (Marshall, 2000: 89). The conflict about the issue and – even more important – the solution for the escalating numbers of asylum seekers during this governing period, pushed the Federal Republic into a crisis.

The increase in the number of asylum seekers caused more and more problems in most of the states (*Länder*) and their municipalities, as well as in the policy sector. Reception centres were lacking, asylum procedures became clogged, logistical problems arose as, for instance, asylum seekers had to be spread across the different

---

8   The number of these crimes declined after 1993 but started to rise again after 1996, although they remained below the level of 1992 and 1993.

9   The crisis and reform of Article 16 took place during the so called twelfth *Wahlperiode*, between 1990 and 1994.

states, personnel was scarce, and handling requests for asylum took more time. The latter problem resulted in a backlog of more than 250,000 requests (Bierwirth, 1994: 256). Out of every 100 requests for asylum, around 7% were granted and 3% were refused and subsequently deported. However, as the number of deportations was low, 90% of the asylum seekers stayed longer than expected in reception centres. This, of course, resulted in more pressure on the hosting municipalities.

Interestingly, it was not the problems within the sector that became the focus of public discussion, but changing Article 16. Although the CDU/CSU was isolated in the political spectrum in its support of constitutional change, it framed the crisis in such a way that restricting the right to asylum seemed the only possible solution to decrease both the number of asylum seekers, and right-wing violence. The CDU/CSU perceived support in their stance from societal commotion and an increase in right wing attacks. Several surveys showed that foreigners were becoming unpopular among Germans. Even as early as 1991, a survey revealed that most Germans preferred a change in the constitution. A majority of 69% of the German population was convinced that asylum seekers were abusing the system (Marshall, 2000: 80). To tackle this problem, according to the CDU/CSU, a constitutional change was required.

Failing new law deepens the crisis

Though other political parties did feel the need for change, they preferred a solution within the existing framework of the constitution, i.e. the existing paradigm. Notwithstanding the different perspectives towards the asylum issue, the CDU/CSU continued negotiating with the SPD for a solution. Negotiations were inevitable for the CDU/CSU, as a consequence of Germany's political and decision-making structure. After several months of negotiations, party leaders from the CDU/CSU, FDP, and SPD reached an agreement on changing the asylum procedure without changing Article 16, meaning that their solution stayed well within the existing policy paradigm. This compromise of October 1991 contained a radical change of the asylum procedure, called the Asylum Procedure Acceleration Law (*Asylverfahrenbeschleunigungsgesetz*). It could only be successful with an effective implementation and cooperation from all the different states.

But even before an agreement was reached, it became clear that this new law would not succeed. Although FDP and SPD state politicians supported the Asylum Procedure Acceleration Law, it did not get any meaningful support from CDU/CSU state politicians. Prime Minister Teufel (CDU) of Baden-Württemberg and the Bavarian Minister of Internal Affairs, Stoiber (CSU), fiercely opposed the new law. Both state politicians made clear that, in their opinion, an acceleration of the asylum procedure was 'absolutely unrealistic, not to say ridiculous'.[10] According to Stoiber, the law was unfeasible.[11] However, Stoiber did agree with the law because he did not

10 Archiv der Gegenwart 11/12/1991, p. 36300.
11 Ibid.

want 'to disturb the process, in particular the process of a constitutional reform'.[12] Apparently, Stoiber was convinced of the inevitability of reforming Article 16. This view was shared by the CDU/CSU at the federal level who, in turn, were supported by experts such as professionals, judges, societal organizations, and scholars who thought the new law was pure illusion (Der Spiegel, 46/1992: 52). The managing director of the Immigration Service (*Bundesambt für die Anerkennung auländische Flüchtlingen, BAFI*), Von Niedling, even resigned because of the reformed asylum procedure.[13]

After the new asylum procedure's implementation, pressure on politicians and their asylum policy increased rather than decreased. This increase originated not only from the miserably failing new legislation but also from right wing attacks in the city of Rostock in August 1992. For four consecutive days, foreigners, asylum seekers, and their accommodations were attacked by right-wing extremists which, in turn, led to riots between the extremists and the police. These incidents led to anger among Germans, and to more attacks elsewhere in Germany. The city of Rostock dealt not only with right-wing attacks, but also with poor living conditions for asylum seekers (e.g. overcrowded reception areas) – a problem that plagued other cities, as well. Furthermore, the number of asylum seekers was even higher in 1992 than in 1991. In the first eight months of 1992 alone, around 274,000 asylum seekers arrived in Germany – a 94% increase compared to the first eight months of 1991 (BMI, 1994). Moreover, as the effect of the accelerating procedure turned out to be minimal, politicians' criticisms increased and civil protest actions expanded. Meanwhile, numerous municipalities set limits on the number of refugees they were prepared to accept, and local politicians demanded measures to deal with the influx of asylum seekers. While the crisis deepened, discussions about reforming the constitution continued. The implementation of the Asylum Procedure Acceleration Law had failed to stop the crisis.

Political breakthrough

As the crisis deepened during the summer of 1992, more and more states and a growing majority in society became in favour of reforming Article 16. The CDU/ CSU was no longer the only one proposing constitutional reform. The opponents of constitutional reform became under increasing pressure to change their position. FDP and SPD politicians gradually changed their opinion, though this change caused, especially for the SPD party, fierce and emotional party debates. In time, the SPD became divided between party members and municipality administrators, on the one hand, and members of the federal parliament, on the other. A majority of party members and state politicians were in favour of reform, while the federal politicians remained fiercely opposed. As the crisis deepened, SPD and FDP federal politicians started to fear a loss in voter support. Their fear was compounded by the

---

12 Gemeinschaftskommentar zum Asylverfahrengezets 35, Oktober 1993, p.39–40.
13 Gemeinschaftskommentar zum Asylverfahrengezets 35, Oktober 1993, p.42.

Asylum Procedure Acceleration Law – a law which the SPD and FDP had initiated – as this new law neither reduced the problems nor improved the situation. The combination of these factors resulted in both parties finally changing their stance toward constitutional reform. In the fall of 1992, the FDP decided that Article 16 could be reformed, but only if the individual right to asylum remained intact. During a special SPD party conference on 16 November 1992, a majority of party members voted in favour of a resolution that made negotiations for a constitutional reform possible.

As it became clear that a potential two-thirds majority of the *Bundestag* (CDU/CSU, FDP and SPD) supported constitutional reform, negotiations between political parties about a new asylum law commenced. During the so-called 'Nikolaus-Runde' meeting in December 1992, key politicians from the governing parties and the SPD met for days to debate how to reform Article 16 (Huber, 1994: 213). Only a relatively short period of time was needed to complete the negotiations because the Ministry of Internal Affairs had prepared for such an event long before Nikolaus-Runde actually took place.

In July 1992, even before the Asylum Procedure Acceleration Law had been implemented, the Minister of Internal Affairs and his civil servants had started to plan the whole reform process because they were convinced that only constitutional reform could solve the problems in the asylum sector.[14] Several options to restrict Article 16 were mapped out. According to a civil servant at the Ministry of Internal Affairs, 'It was very difficult to persist with these ideas at all (...). The Minister had serious doubts if it was possible. He therefore brought in a lot of expertise. But it was a lengthy and very difficult process'.[15] At the same time, key figures of the CDU/CSU party were informed about the Minister's plans. Although the party was unanimously convinced about the need to restrict the right to asylum, there was a difference of opinion as to what extent the right to asylum should be restricted.

While party chairman Schäuble looked for consensus within the CDU/CSU, people within the Internal Affairs Department were trying to formulate legislation that would be acceptable to the Supreme Court. During this process, civil servants visited commissions all over Germany to explain their ideas and find backing for their plans.[16] Hence, by the time the SPD changed its opinion about constitutional reform, a lot of the preparatory work had already been done, while at the same time unanimity had been achieved in the CDU/CSU party. Consequently, a relatively swift agreement and voting procedure was possible.

After the political parties had agreed on constitutional reform, the so-called *Asylkompromiß* (asylum compromise), the Ministry of Internal Affairs worked out all the details in the following months. Finally, on 26 May 1993 the *Bundestag* voted on the new asylum law. On that particular day, emotions ran high both inside and

---

14 Based on interviews with civil servants, 9 December 2002.

15 From an interview with a civil servant from the Ministry of Internal Affairs, 9 December 2002.

16 Based on interviews with civil servants, 9 December 2002.

outside the *Bundestag*. More than 10,000 people demonstrated against the planned reform of the constitution. During the voting session, 521 out of 654 representatives voted in favour, and 132 against the reform of Article 16. After the approval of the *Bundestag* and the *Bundesrat* the new policy became effective as of 1 July 1993.[17]

The acceptance of the reformed Article 16 in the *Bundestag* and *Bundesrat* resulted in a sudden ending of the crisis. The amount of attention, by both the media and parliament, given to the asylum issue dropped immediately, and emotional debates in parliament and mass demonstrations came to an end. The asylum issue had vanished from the policy agenda. On top of that, the number of asylum seekers diminished instantly once Article 16 and legislative changes were adopted. During the first six months of 1993, 224,099 asylum seekers submitted a request, while during the second six months of 1993 the number dropped with more than 50% to 98,500 requests. Moreover, in 1994 only 127,210 asylum requests were submitted.[18] Although these changes occurred after the enforcement of the new Basic Law, it is not clear if they stem solely from the constitutional reform. According to Bade (1994), it is possible that these improvements are the result of the Asylum Procedure Acceleration Law (1992) as well.

Facilitators for reform

Ever since the end of the World War II, West Germany's policy regarding asylum seekers had been dominated by the ethic and moral stance of generosity. No one was to be refused from the asylum seekers procedure. This stance was drastically altered in the 1990s. Values and norms regarding the permission for asylum seekers to enter Germany changed, denoting a shift in priorities. Generosity and guilt from the past no longer informed the asylum policy. To put it differently, protection of Germany against the influx of asylum seekers, as opposed to protection of refugees, became the basis of asylum policy. The restrictions of the right to asylum made it possible to exclude (groups of) asylum seekers from the asylum procedure and send them back to their country of origin, or to a safe country through which the asylum seekers had reached Germany. The opportunities for asylum seekers to gain asylum became limited. Moreover, restrictive legislation enabled government to pre-emptively exclude particular groups from the asylum procedure.

Considering the structural barriers, such as the federal system and the decision-making procedures, and preference barriers, such as the inheritance of the Nazi regime, still present in the early 1990s, the question arises as to how we can explain this constitutional reform. What facilitated the fundamental change of values and

17 On 28 May 1993, the *Bundesrat* voted in favour of reforming the asylum law. The states of Niedersachsen and Bremen, of which Bündnis 90/Grüne had a part in, voted against the reform. The states of Brandenburg and Hessen refrained from voting (Gemeinschaftskommentar zum Asylverfarhengezets 35, Oktober 1993: p. 35).

18 Asyl-Erfahrungsbericht, Bundesministerium des Innern, Bonn, 25 February 1994.

norms concerning the asylum issue? Why was changing Article 16 impossible in the late 1980s, but feasible during the early 1990s?

The ongoing crisis

An important factor that facilitated reform was not so much the occurrence of the crisis, but the fact that in the 1990s the crisis had been ongoing. In the 1980s, the crisis following the hole in the Wall was ended as East German officials agreed to enforce the visa policy for West Berlin again. In contrast, the 1990s crisis was not so easily solved. The number of asylum seekers and violent crimes committed against them continued to increase – thereby putting more and more pressure on existing policy procedures and paradigms – while the failed attempt to stop the crisis by introducing the Asylum Procedure Acceleration Law (1992) only confirmed CDU/CSU's point of view that reforming the constitution was needed in order to end the crisis.

Interestingly, and contrary to expectations expressed in existing reform literature (see chapter 1), the 1980s crisis did not result in diminished institutional barriers. The 1990s crisis, however, affected a number of preference barriers, if not structural barriers. Decision-making structures remained in place (a special majority was still needed to change the constitution), whereas the paradigm and policy inheritance barriers crumbled as the anti-reform coalition changed its opinion and became in favour of reforming the constitution.

Changing preferences: Gaining support for constitutional reform

The continuing crisis changed the opinion about the asylum issue in general, and Article 16 in particular. During the 1990s, the situation in Germany was completely different from that in the 1980s. The fall of the Iron Curtain had put the asylum issue in a new light. Although the communist enemy disappeared, and thus the need for people to flee from Eastern European countries, the number of asylum seekers from all over the world increased (UNHCR, 2000; BAFl, 2000: 22). The Germans, however, had become more reluctant to welcome asylum seekers. Gradually, society (including administrators at the state and local level) became in favour of reforming Article 16. In contrast to the mid 1980s, the early 1990s were characterized by a majority of the Germans favouring the reform of the Basic Law.

As the number of supporters for reforming Article 16 grew, federal politicians opposing reforming Article 16 became the minority. This incongruous situation caused trouble within the political parties of the FDP and especially within the SPD. In the SPD, party committee, local politicians, and party members felt they were not properly represented by federal SPD politicians who continued to oppose reforming Article 16 (Prantl, 1994: 141). During the crisis, the SPD and FDP at the federal level gradually – though grudgingly – changed their position on the asylum issue. This breakthrough in the taboo on changing Article 16 was possible because of the deeply felt and ongoing crisis.

Smart leadership by CDU/CDU politicians

The reformist attitude within the CDU/CSU, especially of the Minister of the Interior and his civil servants, was important to pave the road to accomplish reform. At a time when the CDU/CSU at the federal level was alone in its call for reform, the Minister of the Interior and his civil servants were already preparing for a constitutional reform. Because a two-thirds majority at the federal level was necessary to change the constitution, it was not possible for the CDU/CSU to adopt such a reform single-handedly. The opportunities for the governing politicians were limited because they had to obey institutional rules and decision-making procedures. Yet, this barrier did not stop the Minister of the Interior and his civil servants, who opted to prepare a plan for reform in the event a majority would become available. So by the time the SPD and FDP agreed on reforming Article 16, the Minister of the Interior was able to present a solid plan for reform which even included the constitutional feasibility of the reform proposal.

This case demonstrates how actors' preferences can and do change over time, for various reasons. Here, the impending loss of votes forced the SPD and FDP to ultimately change their preferences. Civil servants supported the constitutional reform because the asylum system was malfunctioning. For years, an enormous work load had clogged the system – a situation which only became worse during the crisis – while existing norms, rules, and routines resulted in havoc rather than stability. Although reform is sometimes considered upsetting and unsettling for people working in an institutionalized setting, it can be a solution to the problems that the policy sector faces.

Conclusion

By comparing the barriers and facilitators to reform presented in chapter 1 with the findings of this case study, it is possible to draw the following conclusions. The most important constraints to reform within this case stemmed both from calculus (opportunity/structure) as well as cultural (preference) constraints. The difficult procedures surrounding constitutional change and the numerous veto-players at the federal level can be seen as two important barriers within this case. Out of a moral duty flowing from its Nazi history, adaptations in asylum policy were only possible within the framework of Article 16. This historically grown situation is an example of a combination of path dependency, policy inheritance, and policy paradigm.

These barriers were present during the 1980s as well as the 1990s. Moreover, similar facilitators were present at both times: there was a crisis and CDU/CSU leadership can be characterized as reformist. The presence of similar barriers and similar facilitators makes it all the more intriguing that reforming Article 16 was possible in the 1990s but not in the 1980s.

Two important differences between the two periods stand out. First, during the early 1990s the support for reform was much more substantial compared to the mid 1980s.

As the crisis continued and the urgency to take measures became more apparent, the reform proposal gained more support. Party members and citizens, who previously had fiercely opposed constitutional reform, could only think of one solution to end the crisis: reforming Article 16. Civil servants working in the malfunctioning asylum sector wished to reform Article 16 as well. This change in support was brought about by a combination of severe problems within the asylum sector (such as deficient housing and clogged asylum procedures), and a changed Germany following the fall of the Iron Curtain. The latter refers to the second important difference between the 1980s and 1990s: the fall of the Iron Curtain which resulted in a dramatically changed German society where it was no longer a taboo to discuss the generous asylum policy. In the end, these changes in society changed the policy paradigm in the early 1990s, despite all the different barriers. Vested interests, norms, values, and preferences towards the asylum issue in general and asylum policy in particular changed. Finally, it is possible to conclude that the policy paradigm was the most formidable barrier to be overcome. It seems certain that other factors played a role in the outcome of the paradigm's ultimate defeat. Although decision-making structures remained in place, it was possible to overcome the policy paradigm-barrier through a combination of changing preferences, an ongoing crisis, leadership by CDU/CSU politicians, and reformist civil servants of the Ministry of the Interior. Combined, these factors facilitated the reform of Article 16.

References

Alink, F. (forthcoming) *Crisis als kans? Over de relatie tussen crises en hervormingen in het vreemdelingenbeleid van Nederland en Duitsland*, Dissertation, Leiden: Leiden University.

Bade, K.J. (1994) *Ausländer, Aussiedler, Asyl: Eine Bestandsaufname*, München: Verlag C.H. Beck.

Bierwirth, C. (1994) 'Zum neuen Asylrecht und zur Lage der Flüchtlinge in Deutschland aus der Sicht des UNHCR' Barwig, K. (ed), *Asyl nach der Änderung des Grundgesetzes*, Baden-Baden: Nomos Verlag pp. 256–265.

Bundesambt für die Anerkennung ausländischer Flüchtlinge (BAFl) (2000) *Zuwanderung und Asyl in Zahlen* 7. Auflage pp. 22.

Bundesambt für die Anerkennung ausländischer Flüchtlinge (BAFl) (2001) *Zuwanderung und Asyl in Zahlen* 8. Auflage pp. 39.

Bundesministerium des Inneren (BMI) (1994) *Verfassungsschutzbericht 1994* Bonn: BMI.

Bundesministerium des Inneren (BMI) (1994) *Asyl-Erfarhungsbericht 1994* Bonn: BMI.

Busch, A. (2000) 'The Grundgesetz after 50 Years: Analyzing Changes in the German Constitution' *German Politics* vol. 9 (1) pp. 41–60.

Der Spiegel (1992) *Wer will Menschen das Antun?* vol. 46.

Huber, B. (1994) 'Das Asylrecht in Deutschland' K. Barwig (ed.) *Asyl nach der Änderung des Grundgesetzes*, Baden-Baden: Nomos Verlag pp. 231–234.

Koopmans, R. (1996) 'Asyl: Die Karriere eines politischen Konflikts' Jahrbuch, WBZ (ed.) *Kommunikation und Entscheidung: Politische Funktionen öffentlicher Meinungsbildung und diskursiver Verfahren*, Berlin: Wissenschaftszentrum Berlin für Sozialforschung pp. 167–192.

Koopmans, R. (1999) 'Germany and its Immigrants: An Ambivalent Relationship' *Journal of Ethnic and Migration Studies*, vol. 25 (4) pp. 627–647.

Marshall, B. (1996) *British and German Refugee Policies in the European Context*, Great Britain: Chameleon Press Ltd.

Marshall, B. (2000) *Europe in Change: The new Germany and migration in Europe*, Manchester: Manchester University Press.

Prantl (1994) 'Asyl Debatte und Finale' Barwig, K. (ed.) *Asyl nach der Änderung des Grundgesetzes*, Baden-Baden: Nomos Verlag pp. 135–162.

Schönwalder, K. (1999) '"Persons persecuted on political grounds shall enjoy the right of asylum – but not in our country": Asylum policy and debates about refugees in the Federal Republic of Germany' Bloch, A., C. Levy (eds) *Refugees, Citizenship and Social Policy in Europe*, London: MacMillan Press Ltd. pp. 76–90.

UNHCR (2000) *The State of the World Refugees. Fifty Years of Humanitarian Action*, Oxford: Oxford University Press.

Chapter 6

The Republic of Ireland's Ban on Smoking in the Workplace: Reframing the Smoking Issue

Melvyn Read

A groundbreaking reform in Ireland

On 29 March 2004, the *Public Health (Tobacco)(Amendment) Act 2004 (Commencement) Order 2004* put into effect the controversial Section 47, which prohibited smoking tobacco products in all enclosed places or premises defined as a place of work, including licensed premises and registered clubs. Consequently, the Republic of Ireland became the first country in the world to implement comprehensive smoke-free legislation affecting all work places (with a few minor exceptions), including restaurants and pubs, with no allowance for designated smoking rooms on licensed premises (Fong et al., 2005). In the wake of this exacting tobacco control measure, other countries including Norway, Sweden, Italy, Cuba, Bhutan, New Zealand, and Uganda have adopted similarly strict laws.

In short, Ireland's smoking ban was ground breaking – a characteristic that typically makes it very difficult for a reform proposal to survive even the decision-making stage, let alone to actually be enforced (see chapter 1). This begs the question of why such a restrictive reform was possible at that time. Following a description of the smoking ban legislation, I will address the persistence of Irish smokers and how government actors started to think differently on how to deal with smoking in public places before and after the ban occurred. Following a description of the barriers that could have hampered the reform as well as a more thorough explanation of the opposition to the smoking ban, I will explain how the barriers crumbled, and which factors facilitated the process. In the conclusion, case findings will be linked to the concepts used in chapter 1.

Towards the smoking ban

Before the smoking ban was put into force, the Irish government had attempted to control smoking at various times. The government tried two general approaches. The first was control the smoking problem by means of legislation, whereas in the second approach the government opted for negotiating voluntary agreements.

However, neither method was successful. In the end, with the help of scientific evidence, politicians realized that only an anti-smoking act would result in a decline in smoking.

A history of smoking legislation

The genesis of the *Public Health (Tobacco)(Amendment) Act 2004* (from now on called the Anti-smoking Act (2004)) can be traced back to Section 2 of the *Tobacco (Health Promotion and Protection) Act 1988*, which furnished the Health Minister with the statutory framework to proscribe smoking in clearly defined public places including public transport, health premises, schools, and publicly owned buildings to which the public had access (for an overview of previous legislation, see table 6.1).[1] A year later, Section 6 of the *Safety, Health and Welfare at Work Act, 1989* imposed a 'duty [on] every employer to ensure, so far as is reasonably practicable, the safety, health and welfare at work of all his employees'. These Acts can be seen as efforts on the part of government to address the dangers associated with environmental tobacco smoke (or ETS, which refers to second hand smoke or passive smoke).

In the mid-1990s, the Irish legislative approach to anti-smoking policy-making slowed as the Irish government adopted the British government's style of negotiating voluntary agreements with stakeholders such as tobacco companies, trade unions, health groups and public (e.g. Department of Health, 1994). The non-governmental tobacco control community responded with a campaign aimed at lobbying politicians, public servants, and the trade unions on the question of ETS. Their aim was to keep the issue firmly within the political agenda of policy-makers in all sectors (Howell, 2004). The non-governmental campaign was a success. Consequently, the government dispensed with voluntary agreements and returned to its legislative approach by the end of the 1990s.

In 2000, *The Health (Miscellaneous Provision) Act* raised the legal age for buying tobacco products to 18 years. This was followed by the *Public Health (Tobacco) Act 2002*, which gave the Health Minister the authority to regulate where smoking is prohibited, including 'all or part of a licensed premises, registered club, or place of work or all or part of any other premises or place' (Section 47 (1f)). In the following year (2003), the *Tobacco Smoking (Prohibition) Regulations* specified licensed premises and registered clubs individually and set the date of 26 January 2004 for the 2002 Act to become operational. European Union (EU) technicalities, however, resulted in a series of legal challenges against the smoking ban in the Irish courts. Consequently, the Minister of Health abandoned the 2003 Regulations in favour of new legislation; the Anti-smoking Act (2004), which also specified licensed premises and registered clubs 'in so far as they are places of work' (Dáil Éireann, 20 November 2003, Vol. 575). The Commencement Order deemed 29 March 2004 the effective date.

---

1   The 1988 Act, specifying areas where smoking was forbidden, came into effect with the *Tobacco (Health Promotion and Protection) Regulations 1990*.

Table 6.1   Anti-smoking legislation in Ireland

Year	Title	Content
1988	Tobacco (Health Promotion and Protection) Act	Enables Minister of Health to proscribe smoking in public places (not at workplaces)
1989	Safety, Health, and Welfare at Work Act	Duty for employers to ensure safety, health, and welfare at work
2000	The Health (Miscellaneous Provision) Act	Raised legal age for buying tobacco products to 18 years
2002	Public Health (Tobacco) Act	Providing Minister of Health with powers to regulate where smoking is prohibited, including licensed premises and registered clubs, or place of work
2003	Tobacco Smoking (Prohibition) Regulations	Specified licensed premises and registered clubs individually, and sets 26 January 2004 for the 2002 Act to become operational. The Regulations were abandoned by the Minister of Health (because of EU technicalities) in favour of the 2004 Act
2004	Public Health (Tobacco) (Amendment) Act, i.e. Anti-smoking Act	Specified licensed premises and clubs in so far as they are places of work. As of 29 March 2004, smoking is forbidden in all work places

The problem of persistent smokers

Irish legislation to ban smoking in the workplace was the culmination of efforts on the part of the national government and health authorities dating back several decades to reduce consumption (McNicholas, 2004). Before the introduction of the Anti-smoking Act (2002), measures introduced by successive Irish Health Ministers emulated those of other countries, for example France, Germany, and the United Kingdom. The Irish government aimed at educating the public (especially children) about the inherent dangers associated with smoking by concentrating on reducing consumption with the help of a variety of information campaigns (Action on Smoking and Health, 2005). The information campaigns were based on the view that the longer children could be persuaded to delay their contact with tobacco and cigarettes, the greater the likelihood that they would resist the temptation to indulge in the practice of smoking and thereby avoid the smoking habit. Unfortunately for Ministers, although some reduction in smoking rates was achieved, smoking levels remained high amongst Ireland's smokers. A study of eight countries showed that while tobacco consumption was falling elsewhere, Ireland's pattern of tobacco consumption was sufficient to take that country from a sixth place ranking in 1961, to second in 1975 (Todd, 1978).

However, after 1975 this changed slightly. Annual adult consumption of cigarettes peaked in 1974, at 3,510 per capita, with a fairly rapid decline to approximately 2,304 cigarettes per capita in 2,000. Shaffey et al. (2003) propose that the decline in sales was due in part to the high cost of cigarettes. Since 1986, the underlying trend in smoking in Ireland was upward, evidenced by a slight overall increase in consumption. Smoking in Ireland remained a problem across all social classes and all age groups with a distinct bias towards young people with low incomes (Health Promotion Unit, 2003). The Study of Lifestyle, Attitudes and Nutrition (SLAN) Survey showed that 31% of adults were smokers (Health Promotion Unit, 2003). Further research found that Irish consumers are the third highest spenders on tobacco among comparative countries (Department of Health and Children, 2000: 31).

Shifting tides

Despite the evidence of some success, anti-smoking information campaigns were largely ineffective and inefficient in communicating the dangers of smoking. As the Irish government was returning to a legislative approach towards smoking from 2000 on, their decision to create a law to ban smoking in all workplaces was informed by increasing scientific evidence that smoking posed a serious health hazard. This scientific evidence was not only drawn from Irish experts, but also from international experts. Several US Surgeon General's Reports (Office of the Surgeon General, 1984, 1985 and 1986) were particularly influential, as was the work of Professor Repace, a leading US health physicist and veteran anti-smoking campaigner. Whilst in Dublin to speak at a seminar hosted by the Office to Tobacco Control, the Professor wrote in the *The Irish Times*, 'that approximately 150 bar workers a year in Ireland will die from ill health caused by ETS' (2002).

Following the scientific evidence on smoking, the Department of Health and Children published *Towards a Tobacco Free Society* (2000) in which they criticized the lack of information about tobacco and its use in Ireland, referring to the national health and lifestyle surveys. The report also argued that:

> The need to transpose European Union legislation combined with the new revelation about the marketing practices of the industry [the Committee had heard evidence of how the tobacco industry targets and promotes tobacco to children despite protests from representatives in the tobacco industry] presents us with a unique opportunity to review our arrangements (Department of Health and Children, 2000: 41).

Among the recommendations, the report called for 'tougher regulation of the tobacco industry' by government using a variety of EU directives to underpin the domestic regulations. These directives included; further protection for non-smokers, including prohibiting smoking in all enclosed work places (other than certain places of adult entertainment); the creation of a voluntary code of practice by which pubs and licensed facilities self-regulate smoking in bars; and improving compliance with the law by enhancing existing legislation and developing anti-smoking programmes (Department of Health and Children, 2000: 45).

A key report by an Independent Scientific Working Group confirmed that second-hand smoke was harmful and that employees need to be protected from it in their workplace (Allwright, 2002). In response to the Allwright report (2002), the Minister announced legislation on 30 January 2003, to ensure that all enclosed workplaces in Ireland would be smoke free by 1 January 2004 (Department of Health and Children, 2003a). Despite two false starts, several exemptions and finally, the notification to the European Union about these changes, the anti-smoking Act became operational on 29 March 2004.

Barriers to reform

Initially, opposition to the public smoking ban was muted. It was almost four months after the Minister announced his intentions that the anti-smoking ban lobby began to seriously oppose the ban (Gilmore, 2005: 5). Legislation to impose a smoking ban in almost all public places was not unexpected given the progressive nature of Ireland's anti-smoking legislation, but a smoking ban in all licensed premises was considered a step too far. In fact, it was presumed that existing barriers to tobacco control measures were sufficiently impregnable to prevent this controversial ban from coming into force. What, then, were the purported obstacles in the way of a ban on smoking in licensed premises?

Three broad barriers to reform can be identified: the pervading pro-smoking paradigm, the presence of an anti-reform coalition, and the opposition present in the Minister of Health's own party, Fianna Faíl. First, it is important to recognize the *cultural and social acceptability of smoking* in general, and in public houses in particular. These values are underpinned by both the hospitality industry and tobacco manufacturers. Given the high level of tobacco use in Ireland, the concept of a culture of smoking implies individuals smoking within a social environment without being questioned by non-smokers. In such a culture, non-smokers do not question the right to smoke even where such activity conflicts with their interests (e.g. health hazard) (Roper Organization, 1978).

Second, we observe *pro-active opposition on the part of individuals or organizations directly affected by a comprehensive smoking ban*. The anti-reform coalition consisted of three groups (see table 6.2). First of all this opposition came from traders selling alcohol which – like tobacco – requires a license that has to be applied for on annual basis. The licensed trade considered its position unassailable, having successfully resisted earlier legislative impositions on drinking and driving (International Herald Tribune, 26 July 1995). It was felt that publicans – keepers of pubs – had traditionally exercised a remarkable degree of influence over both local and national politicians. In particular, Fianna Faíl Deputies (TDs),[2] members of the Minister's own party, were perceived as being particularly close to the licensed trade.

---

2   Backbench members of the Irish Parliament are called Teachta Dála, (TD) and referred to as Deputies. The Taoiseach (at this time Ahern) is the Prime Minister. Ahern is also the leader of the Fianna Faíl Party, of which Martin was the Minister of Health and Children.

Second, lobby groups were representing the general interests of licensees; the Licensed Vintners' Association (LVA), representing Dublin publicans, and the Vintners' Federation of Ireland (VFI), serving the interests of 6,000 publicans outside the capital. To support their campaign, the VFI employed a major public relations company, Weber Shandwick FCC, a company with British American Tobacco, Brown and Williamson Tobacco and the Irish Hotels Federation (Centre for Media Democracy) on its client list.[3] Likewise, the LVA called upon the services of a company called Drury Communications, who conducted an economic impact study showing that job losses resulting from a smoking ban in licensed premises would be approximately 3,100 (Foley, 2003).

Third, the newly created Irish Hospitality Industry Alliance (IHIA), purporting to represent all parties associated with the hospitality industry, publicans, and all groups and individuals affected by the comprehensive smoking ban. This lobby group was created specifically to challenge the 2004 anti-smoking legislation, presenting itself as the principal representative to deal with the Irish government on behalf of all those opposed to the smoking ban. The IHIA chose to open its public relations campaign in New York, where a ban on smoking had been in force since 26 March 2003. IHIA delegates were accompanied by a founder member of one of the newest public relations agencies in Ireland, Mackin of Q4 Public Relations. Mackin was a former general-secretary of Fianna Fáil, who joined together with Gallagher, a former personal adviser to Prime Minister Ahern, and O'Sullivan, previously Director of Corporate Affairs with Telecom Eireann.[4] Surprisingly, the tobacco industry played a minor, almost non-existent role, in the campaign. Martin Mackin denied the accusation that the IHIA was representing the tobacco industry.

Table 6.2   Opposition by individuals and organisations directly affected by the smoking ban

Opposition organisations	Members
Unorganised team	Publicans
Lobby groups	The Licensed Vintners' Association (LVA) (represents Dublin publicans) The Vintners' Federation of Ireland (VFI) (represents non-Dublin publicans)
Peak organisation	Irish Hospitality Industry Alliance (IHIA) (represents everyone affected by the smoking ban)

Three of the four founder members of Q4 Public Relations, being closely associated with Fianna Fáil, offer the perfect link between the previous obstacle and the final barrier to reform: the vociferous political opposition from within the Minister's own

3   www.webershandwick.co.uk/Dublin (January 2006).

4   http://www.q4pr.ie/ (January 2006).

party, at both parliamentary and local government level. In contrast, opposition party members supported the measure. In fact, senior politicians of other parties criticized the Minister for his tardiness in putting the Act into operation by failing to be more unequivocal in specifying bars and public houses as areas where smoking was to be prohibited.

Opponents to the Anti-smoking Act (2004) viewed the bid to ban smoking in bars and restaurants as 'unworkable' on the grounds that the legislation was a challenge to a country devoted to pub culture. Turner, bartender at The Duke in Dublin, summed up the situation as perceived by many critics, 'It's a bad idea. Cigarettes and alcohol are synonymous, at least in Irish culture' (New York Times, 11 August 2003; cf. Helm, 2003; The Times, 29 March 2004; The Irish Examiner, 15 July 2004). This strong sense of pub culture combined with opposition by publicans and the Minister of Health's own party should have brought down the new act.

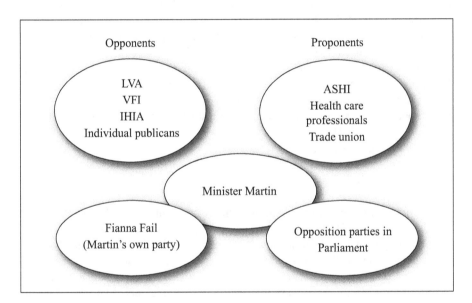

Figure 6.1   Actors involved in the reform process

Yet, these barriers did not block the reform. Despite a concerted effort on the part of the hospitality sector, which called for the smoking ban to be lifted, the Minister maintained the unequivocal support of Prime Minister Ahern, most of the government (some had buckled under pressure from the lobbyists (Howell, 2004)), and the opposition parties. In fact, after a year the measure could boast popular support as well. It highlights the fact that a prolonged public health campaign can succeed where evidence underpins the policy-making process (Howell, 2004). More importantly, however, it shows that politicians, civil servants, and non-governmental agencies can overcome vested economic interests in the pursuit of public health even if the opposition resists. The next section addresses how actors tried to oppose the new act.

Opposition at work

In the post-2003 legislation period, opposition to the ban on smoking in all enclosed workplaces grew and became more overt. First, public opinion seemed to be split on the smoking ban. Ministers had expected the proposed ban to be welcomed by the vast majority of the public (The Irish Times, 18 February 2003). A poll in the Irish Independent showed that 52% supported the measure while 42% opposed. More concerning was that just 37% supported the Minister's plan to bring the measure into operation on 1 January 2004; 33% wanted it phased in over few years, while 25% wanted the plans scrapped (The Irish Independent, 15 September 2003). These findings gave comfort to opponents of the ban and to some extent justified the expenditure of €250,000 by the IHIA on a campaign that focused on the loss of 65,000 jobs and massive revenues losses for the Exchequer, the department charged with the collection and management of the national revenue.

The Minister's announcement in January 2003 that smoking would be banned the following year caught interest groups off-guard (Gilmore, 2005). Although it did not take long for those involved to understand the potential impact of such legislation, there appeared to be no rush since the Minister's commitment was questioned (Gilmore, 2005: 15). By giving a warning of one-year, there seemed time enough to change the Minister's mind.

Publicans' opposition

The local campaign opposing the smoking ban began within hours of the announcement by the Department of Health and Children, when publicans and hoteliers announced their clashing views on the new regulations. Some landlords took unilateral action. Customers at Nevada Smiths, a public house – pub – in Limerick City, for instance, were allowed to smoke freely on the premises following the management's decision to erect posters stating: Smokers welcome. The leaseholders, Liam and Seamus Flannery, argued that some publicans had erected 'enclosed smoking rooms' which gave them advantage over those with insufficient space to follow suit (Limerick Leader, 10 July 2004).

In Kerry, publicans were more organized and they voted unanimously to defy the ban on smoking before it came into effect. Over 200 publicans said they would not enforce a full smoking ban but allow it to continue in designated areas. Publicans in Cork reached a similar decision (Condon, 2003a). Seventeen Waterford publicans, under the banner of European Smokers Against Discrimination, sought legal assistance from Europe's leading constitutional lawyers to mount a constitutional challenge to a blanket smoking ban in the workplace. Group members protested that while they saw merit in the smoking ban they felt that their civil rights had been affected. They proposed a compromise, the setting up of a designated smoking area with improved ventilation (Waterford News & Star, 16 July 2004).

Local protests were shored up by a variety of groups representing publicans in particular and the hospitality industry in general. The industry lobby groups offered the government a string of alternative solutions to the problem, including new ventilation systems, compulsory non-smoking areas, and no smoking at the bar. The LVA threatened legal action on the grounds that such a comprehensive blanket ban was unjustified based upon the available research. Yet at the same time, the LVA chose to advise its members to uphold the ban when it came into force (The Irish Examiner, 5 March 2004). O'Keefe, chief executive, warned publicans not to clash with anyone by flouting the law. Despite muted support for the Anti-smoking Act, the LVA continued to offer objections. In July 2004, it drew attention to the fact that '[r]esearch carried out by marketing research company Behaviour and Attitudes (2004) confirms the negative economic impact of the Smoking Ban on the Dublin licensed trade, with turnover down by as much as 16%, and overall employment levels cut by up to 14% since the introduction of the Smoking Ban' (Licensed Vintners' Association, 2004).[5]

The Vintners' Federation of Ireland (VFI) was less compliant, threatening to run Anti-smoking Ban candidates to challenge key seats in the forthcoming local elections. This threat followed after regional branches had voted to formally oppose the ban on smoking in the workplace. Kerry vintners were particularly vocal in their opposition. O'Sullivan, chair of Kerry VFI, stated that vintners around the country would follow suit if no compromise were achieved. Opposition was based on the view that the proposals were unworkable, unrealistic, and unenforceable. The preferred option was to invest in new air systems (see for example Breaking News, 2001). In 2003 it was stressed that the VFI was not pro-smoking but rather pro-choice (The Kingdom, 9 October 2003).

The two trade organizations adopted an approach designed to instil fear into the nation about the potential devastating economic effects of a ban on smoking. Dire warnings of massive losses to the Exchequer – pubs going out of business, the loss of 65,000 jobs, not to mention the possible collapse of Ireland's tourist industry – caused concern amongst the public. Moreover, the campaign was not to be seen as directed against the ban on smoking. The evidence was to be presented in such a way as to place campaigners in the best light, as reasonable people being responsible in highlighting the economic dangers that this smoking ban would provoke. They chose two tactics; first to lobby quietly and then to go public in order to discredit the scientific evidence marshalled in favour of a smoking ban.[6]

At the national level, the Irish Hospitality Industry Alliance was formed to represent pubs, hotels, and guesthouse owners and to negotiate with the Government on the Anti-smoking Act (The Irish Times, 15 August 2003). The role of the IHIA

---

5   Figures released in February 2005 by the Central Statistics Office of Ireland.

6   Figures released in February 2005, by the Central Statistic Office of Ireland, did not support the claims by the LVA.

was to present alternatives to the government. Murphy, spokesperson for the IHIA said it would be referring the regulations to its lawyers to seek their advice on a judicial review (The Irish Times, 24 October 2003). The creation of this organization raised suspicions about intervention by the tobacco industry, which previously had remained virtually absent from the campaign. Mackin, however, denied these allegations (The Irish Times, 18 February 2003). This did not prevent the Standards in Public Office Commission from requiring the IHIA to declare all donations of €127 or more (Standards in Public Office, 2004) – just to make sure that the tobacco industry did not influence the IHIA.

Political opposition

Interestingly, opposition parties in parliament did not oppose the anti-smoking legislation. If anything, they thought Martin, the Minister, did not go far or quickly enough. During the parliamentary debates on the previous version of the Anti-smoking Act (i.e. the 2002 version was later replaced by the 2004 version), the spokesperson for Health of the opposition party Fine Gael, Mitchell, accused Martin of not going far enough with his legislation to ban smoking. Mitchell claimed that Martin had not included public houses in the bill since they were not specifically mentioned in the bill (whereas other premises were expressly named). In response to this accusation, Martin introduced an amendment to the bill to include workplace, pubs, and licensed premises (Dáil Éireann, Vol. 546, 12 December 2001). The Labour opposition Party Deputy, McManus, interpreted the fact that publicans at that time were not yet expressing any concern about the new law as a sign that the government was not truly committed to the new law. In the words of the Select Committee on Children and Health, they were 'right not to be worried because there appears to be no serious commitment to deal with smoking in places of entertainment – pubs, indoor sporting facilities, etc.' (Joint Committee on Health and Children, 2001). Opposition party members also criticized members of the Minister's own Party Fianna Faíl for encouraging hospitality groups opposed to the ban to believe that they could exert sufficient pressure on government to reverse the policy position. Fine Gael Spokesperson Mitchell TD argued that by contradicting their own government's policy both Ministers and Backbenchers had undermined the Cabinet's health policy (Fine Geal press release, 30 October 2003).

Political opposition to the anti-smoking law was thus not generated by political opposition parties, but by the Minister's own party – Fianna Faíl. Minister Cullen (Minister for the Environment) suggested that 'small smoking areas' could be provided in pubs and restaurants. He also proposed that the ban should be phased in rather than being fully implemented in three months. His concern, in part, was that Ireland was following the 'political correctness of America' (Condon, 2003b). Former Junior Minster Davern referred to the smoking ban in pubs as 'too big a culture shock' and stated that such a ban would hit pubs and publicans very hard. He suggested that one-third of each pub should become a smoking-area with improved ventilation (Irish Examiner, 7 April 2003). However, his bid to have the legislation watered down failed to materialize. Cregan, (Fianna Fáil MP for Limerick West) broke ranks arguing that, 'Rightly or wrongly, this ban is perceived by the public as a police state action, and we have to listen to the public' (Limerick Leader, 11 October 2003). Interestingly, the Minister for Labour Affairs, Fahey, who was responsible for implementing the ban, sought an additional 20 inspectors to enforce the ban. For this, he received a rebuke from the Prime Minister for casting doubt on the government's ability to enforce the ban (Irish Examiner, 10 October 2003). In response, Fahey reiterated his full commitment to ensuring a safe and healthy work environment for all employees. At the local level of government, Galway's Fianna Fáil Councillor Hanley resigned his position as Chair of the Western Health Board after serving just a few months, on the grounds that the smoking ban was not open to consultation or compromise. The legislation, he argued, was sneaked into the Irish Parliament (Dáil), there was no debate, and he regarded it as an ill-thought-out piece of legislation.[7]

Crumbling barriers

In the case of Ireland's smoking ban, three barriers can be discerned: paradigm, anti-reform coalition, and opposition from within the minister's own party. In this section, I will address what happened to these barriers, followed by a description of additional factors that facilitated the reform process in the next section.

Shifting paradigm

The persistent Irish paradigm that smoking was always allowed and that non-smokers could not ask smokers to stop smoking in public places slowly crumbled as more and more scientific evidence showed the negative effects of smoking. This paradigm shift was aided by a growing awareness that as a basic human right, people should be treated equally, and people working in public areas could not be excluded from the right to work in a safe and healthy environment. One could not ban smoking in hospitals and offices, while continuing to allow smoking in other public places. As the paradigm shifted from life-style (ideological position) to health and safety (equity underpinned by human rights), it became easier to introduce an anti-smoking law. As the ideological component (free choice) was no longer part of the paradigm, one could no longer object to anti-smoking regulation based on freewill.

---

7   Hanley's position in the Western Health Board was somewhat questionable since he was both a publican and an executive member of the Vintner's Federation of Ireland. It is possible that his position was untenable without the added controversy of opposing the smoking ban.

Weak anti-reform coalition

Even though numerous interest groups and individual publicans opposed the Anti-smoking Act, this anti-reform coalition proved to be unsuccessful for a very simple reason: it was a weak coalition. Three factors contributed to this weakness. First the unilateral activity fell apart within days when individual publicans were warned that the renewal of liquor licences of those resisting the legislation would be challenged in the courts by regional Health Boards (Limerick Leader, 10 July 2004). Second, there was an ineffective public relations (PR)-tactic. Third, the anti-ban coalition failed to offer a united front towards the pro-ban lobby.

When the plan to introduce a smoking ban was announced, the anti-ban PR machine swung into action to influence public opinion by focusing on the impact the ban would have on Irish pubs and on the special place these pubs hold in Irish society (McNichols, 2004). It was the IHIA's campaign that played a significant role in opposing the smoking ban by presenting a series of scenarios demonstrating the detrimental effects of the ban; in particular the loss of 65,000 jobs, based, among others, on experiences in New York. These figures, reported by A & L Goodbody Consultancy, were used in such a way that they did not really match the more tentative findings found in the study 'Regularity Impact Assessment on Draft Ministerial regulations to ban Smoking in the Workplace', including hospitality venues (Foley, 2003: 2). The result of the misrepresentation was that:

> From the moment the IHIA emerged, it proved to be a millstone around the neck of the pro-choice, pro-compromise campaign. They created a situation in which the minister felt that his political career depended on him forcing the total ban through and effectively scuppered any chance of compromise (Gilmore, 2005: 40).

This would prove to be a major tactical blunder. The figures were proven to be wildly inaccurate. For example, figures provided to the Sunday Independent by New York City Hall suggested that the New York City's restaurants and bars had seen an increase of about 1,500 seasonally-adjusted jobs since the adoptation of the Smoke Free Air Act (Sunday Independent, 27 July 2003). In fact, the grim predictions had been rejected by American research that predicted a smoking ban would, in the mid-term, prove beneficial to the hospitality industry (Glantz & Charleswick, 1999; Americans for Non-smokers' Rights, 2003; cf. Sunday Tribune, 24 July 2004). To some extent this tactic lost the hospitality industry support it had within the media.

Moreover, the ISHA's public relations fiasco caused a rift between it and the publicans' associations. O'Sullivan of the VFI commented that:

The figures of 65,000 job losses was a disaster which still haunts us and haunts the pro-compromise campaign in Scotland, England, Wales and Northern Ireland. It is being held up as an example of how irresponsible the pro-choice, pro-compromise campaign can be (Gilmore, 2005: 34).

It was felt that the three organizations failed to speak with a unified voice as each looked to its own membership rather than considering the larger picture. Internal divisions and the lack of a common, overarching organization to direct the activities of the anti-ban campaigners created tensions and each of the anti-smoking ban groups acted on their own accord. The pro-ban group was permitted to keep abreast of and adapt to the opposition's activities (Gilmore, 2005).

Returning to the fold

The main political dissent came from within the Minister's own party, and newspaper headlines highlighted this rift (cf. The Independent, 11 October 2003). Kenney, leader of the main opposition party Fine Gael, asked the Prime Minister whether the new anti-smoking law would actually be implemented. Prime Minister Ahern answered unequivocally that the new law was an important public health initiative that would take effect from January, 2004 (Dáil Éireann, Vol. 571, 1 October 2003).

Thus the scene was set for a showdown between those Fianna Faíl ministers and its members of Parliament, who either opposed the measure or who had expressed dissatisfaction with the total ban, but instead preferred some form of compromise. It was clear that the Prime Minister was supporting the smoking ban, which made it difficult for members of the party to speak their concerns. However, many did – especially in the time leading up to the Party's congress. Many of these politicians had voiced their support for compromise merely to demonstrate that they recognized the concerns of their constituency publicans (Gilmore, 2005: 107). When it was made abundantly clear by Prime Minister Ahern that the smoking ban was going to be implemented, there was little else for the members of Parliament who opposed the measure to do but toe the party line once their objections had been publicly expressed.

Facilitators: An expanding pro-reform coalition and the actions of Minister Martin

Besides the crumbling barriers, two factors can be discerned that facilitated the reform process: a unified pro-reform coalition and Martin's actions (see figure 6.1 for an overview of the actors involved in the reform process).

An expanding pro-reform coalition

The Public Health Advocacy Campaign was a long-term affair that began with a small number of concerned organizations and grew into an expansive coalition incorporating a wide range of individual groups sharing an interest in achieving restrictive legislation on tobacco control. So developed, to stay within the framework presented in chapter 1, a pro-reform coalition.

Action on Smoking and Health Ireland (ASHI), founded in 1992 and jointly funded by the Irish Cancer Society and the Irish Heart Foundation, provided the driving force behind the crusade and the locus onto which the other pro-ban groups could attach themselves. Actors who became members of the pro-reform coalition included, for instance, health care professionals, the trade union movement, and the Irish Medical Organization (IMO). The trade union representing hospitality workers was instrumental in building support for a ban on smoking in the workplace. The pro-reform coalition's message that the issue was not about reducing tobacco consumption but rather about civil rights and that exempting pubs and bars would portray bar workers as 'second class workers' was well heard by both the public and politicians (Action on Smoking and Health, 2005: 3).

The pro-reform coalition used three tactics to promote its cause. First, it supported compliance with anti-smoking regulations. Second, it used its members to inform politicians that anti-smoking regulations were needed. For instance, Dr Michelle Egan, who represented the Irish College of General Practitioners (ICGP), told the Joint Committee on Health and Children that 'passive smoking clearly has a serious impact on public health' (Joint Committee on Health and Children, 1999). Third, the coalition used media to broadcast their message to the public. The pro-reform coalition's campaign was based on the understanding that, 'If you don't exist in the media, for all practical purposes you don't exist' (Howell, 2005: 18). The repeated message in the media was simple: it is a health and safety issue and, therefore, one of equality and equity. It was a message that few could oppose.

To test the feasibility of a comprehensive smoking ban, Minister for Health and Children Martin visited both New York and Boston. The visit served to strengthen his belief that a smoking ban was practicable. His stance was underpinned by research that showed a smoking ban would possibly increase pub takings (Glantz & Charlesworth, 1999). He acknowledged that the new measure would require some adjustment by the public, particularly in those workplaces which had not benefited from the existing legislation. The experience of previous legislative controls on smoking, introduced by the 1988 Act, convinced him that people adjust relatively easily to changes.[8]

---

8   Evidence to support this claim can be found in the way that public resistance to the Act faded away once it was in place. After a year of enforcement, compliance with the smoking ban was reported to be between 94% and 97% (Office of Tobacco Control, 2005), a success for a measure previously deemed unenforceable.

Martin was able to successfully support the anti-smoking law by using his resources, handling the situation in a tactical manner, and having a large support base. Martin's most important resource was scientific information. He used this information to rebuff any claims made by anti-reform actors. The Minister rebuffed, for instance, the tobacco industry's solution to the workplace predicament by improving ventilation. He was also able to prove false the hospitality industry's claim that the proposal would bring about the loss of up to 10,000 jobs. Research carried out on behalf of the bar owners and hoteliers to demonstrate that the ban was neither required nor wanted by the Irish public was said to be wanting (Department of Health and Children, 2003b).

Other tactics included, for instance, the development of a national public information campaign entitled *Smoke-Free at Work* to inform the public. Minister Martin and Cabinet proponents also made it abundantly clear to the publicans and the public that the law would be enforced (Breaking News, 8 July 2004; Breaking News, 9 July 2004; Department of Health and Children, 2004). Additionally, previously passed legislation entitled Martin to introduce the ban without consulting the Cabinet. He chose, however, to have the matter approved by Government rather than force the measure through, thereby giving it increased authority. In order to get it through the Cabinet, however, he had to use an additional tactic: threatening to resign if his fellow Cabinet ministers did not support him (Gilmore, 2005).

Martin could confidently utter this threat, knowing the large support base he had. This support base not only consisted of the pro-reform coalition, but also of important political actors. First, he could rely on the unswerving support of Taoiseach Ahern, who was adamantly in favour of securing a smoke-free environment for employees in the workplace, and was prepared to use his position as Prime Minister and leader of Fianna Fáil to bring dissenting party members into line. Second, Deputy Prime Minister Harney also backed the proposal. Third, the Minister could call on support from all the main opposition parties and his coalition colleague Progressive Democrat Minister of State for Health, O'Malley who, as a member of the coalition could ensure the minor party in government gave its full support to the proposed legislation (Howell, 2005: 20).

Conclusion

This chapter examined the introduction of a comprehensive, yet controversial, ban on smoking in all workplaces, including licensed premises. Reform was possible owing to the combination of several crucial factors. Interestingly, these factors did not interact causally, that is in a linear format – A leading to B – but rather they reinforced one another following the laying of firm foundations prior to the origination of the eventual legislation.

The foundations, which defined the reform preferences, served to increase the general awareness of the hazards associated with smoking. Whilst the public were aware of the inherent dangers of smoking, a sufficient number of them ignored the warnings, which brought about a plateau of smoking prevalence over which the health lobby had no effect. This necessitated the government to adopt a more pro-active strategy that required a new approach from those actors willing to take on the task of implementing tobacco control measures. The line of attack was to reframe the smoking issue in terms of equal rights and proper working conditions for all workers without exception. This was an argument favouring tobacco control that the Health Minister could present in the form of a new paradigm; a paradigm that not only attracted support from various quarters but also deflected criticism of the anti-ban opposition.

Acceptance of this new paradigm was accelerated by the existence of a strong pro-reform coalition that met little resistance from the anti-reform coalition owing to the latter's disorganization and the consequences of a major PR fiasco. We should not lose sight, however, of the strong agency of Minister of Health and Children Martin that underpinned the paradigm change. He drew upon an array of resources that included: the unconditional support of his party leader and Prime Minister, Ahern, the unequivocal acceptance of scientific data by influential politicians thereby allowing Minister Martin to successfully rebuff counter claims of opposition, the support of a wide ranging support base backing his proposals, and his tactical manoeuvring where his opponents were concerned. We should remain aware that the Anti-smoking Ban lobby could measure the Minister's commitment to the legislation on the smoking ban by his public pronouncements and his threat to resign if his Cabinet colleagues did not back him. Consequently, the Minister could demonstrate clear political will to achieve the passage and enforcement of the legislation.

Thus, we may see that Minister Martin's agency corresponds with current literature in that it characterizes the three components of reform. It highlights the need of strength and will while listening to potential opponents and incorporating their wishes as he did when specifying licensed premises and registered clubs in the anti-smoking legislation. It is clear that the Minister's agency was necessary though insufficient to achieve the reform. His agency was underpinned by changing preferences and shifting paradigms combined with a weak and disorganized anti-reform coalition – a combination which proved sufficiently robust to ensure that reform happened.

References

Action on Smoking and Health (2005) *Lessons Learned from Ireland's Smoke-free Law – The Case for Similar UK-wide Legislation*, London.

Allwright, S. (2002) *Report on the Health Effects of Environmental Tobacco Smoke (ETS) in the Workplace*, Dublin, Health and Safety Unit and Office of Tobacco Control.

Americans for Non-smokers' Rights (2003) *Economic impact of smoke-free ordinances: overview* http;//www.non-smoke.org/pdf/Economic-Impact.pdf (27 November 2003).

Breaking News (24 July 2001) *Vintners reject pub smoking bar proposal*, archives. tcm.ie/breakingnews/ 2001/07/24 (12 December 2005).

Breaking News (8 July 2004) *Galway pub backs down in smoking ban row*, archives. tcm.ie/breakingnews/2004/07/18 (12 December 2005).

Breaking News (9 July 2004) *Pub smoking rebellion stubbed out*, archives.tcm.ie/ breakingnews/2004/07/9 (12 December 2005).

Condon, D. (2003a) *Publicans vote to defy smoking ban* http://www.irishhealth. com/index.html?level=4&id=5298 (3 July 2005).

Condon, D. (2003b) *Minister opposed to pub smoking ban* http://www.irishhealth. com (3 January 2005).

Dáil Éireann Daily Report (12 December 2001) Vol. 546 col. 959, Dublin: Stationery Office.

Dáil Éireann Daily Report (1 October 2003) Vol. 571 col 821, Dublin: Stationery Office.

Dáil Éireann Daily Report (1 October 2003) Vol. 571 col 822, Dublin: Stationery Office.

Dáil Éireann Daily Report (20 November 2003) Vol. 575 col 786, Dublin: Stationery Office.

Department of Health (1994) *Working Together for Cleaner Air: DevelopingSsmoke-free Policies in the Workplaces*, Dublin: Health Promotion Unit.

Department of Health and Children (2000) *Towards a Tobacco Free Society: Report of the Tobacco Free Policy Review Group*, Dublin: Stationery Office.

Department of Health and Children (2003a) *Speech by Minister on the effects of Environmental Smoke in the Workplace* http://www.dohc.ie/press/ speeches/2003/2003130.html (23 November 2005).

Department of Health and Children (2003b) *Statement from the Minister for Health and Children, Micheál Martin TD, Regarding the proposed ban on smoking in the workplace* http://www.dohc.ie/press/release/2003/20030722a.html (8 February 2006).

Department of Health and Children (2004) *Speech by Micheál Martin TD, Minister for Health and Children at the announcement of the commencement date for the smoke-free workplace regulation* http://www.dohc.ie/press/speeches/2004/20040218. html (23 November 2005).

Fine Gael press release (30 October 2003) *Was it arrogance or incompetence that turned smoking ban into fiasco?*

Foley, S. (2003) *Regularity Impact Assessment on Draft Ministerial regulations to ban Smoking in the Workplace, including hospitality venues*, Prepared for the Irish Hospitality Industry Alliance, Dublin: Goodbody Consultancy.

Fong, G.T, Hyland, A., and Borland, R. (2005) 'Reduction in tobacco smoke pollution and increase in support for smoke-free places following the implementation of comprehensive smoke-free workplace legislation in Republic of Ireland' *Tobacco Control*, December, pp. 1–8.

Gilmore, N. (2005) *Clearing the Air: The Battle over the Smoking Ban*, Dublin: Libertaries Press.

Glantz, S.A. and Charlesworth, A. (1999) 'Tourism and Hotel Revenues before and after Passage of Smoke-free Restaurant Ordinances' *Journal of American Medical Association*, Vol. 281 (20), pp. 1911–18.

Health Promotion Unit (2003) *The National Health and Lifestyle Surveys 2002 Study of Lifestyle Attitudes and Nutrition* (SLAN) Dublin: Stationery Office.

Helm, J. (2003) *Ireland calls time on pub smoking* http://news.bbc.co.uk/go/pr/fr/-/2/hi/europe/3154207.stm (2 February 2006).

Howell, F. (2004) 'Ireland's Workplaces, Going Smoke Free' *British Medical Journal,* 328, pp. 847–848.

Howell, F. (21 April 2005) 'Public Health Policy: the smoking ban in Ireland' Conference paper, *Nursing for Public Health: Realising the Vision Conference,* Belfast, Ireland.

http://www.q4pr.ie/ (12 December 2005).

http://www.webershandwick.co.uk/Dublin (12 December 2005).

International Herald Tribune (26 July 1995) *European Topic: Around Europe.*

Joint Committee on Health and Children (1999) *A National Anti-Smoking Strategy: A Report on Smoking and Health,* Dublin: Houses of Oireachtas.

Joint Committee on Health and Children (2001) *Second Interim Report of the Subcommittee on Health and Smoking,* Dublin: Houses of Oireachtas.

Licensed Vintner's Association (9 July 2004) *Independent research shows impact of smoking ban among Dublin Publicans,* Dublin, Press Release.

Limerick Leader (11 October 2003) *Limerick TD comes out against smoking ban.*

Limerick Leader (10 July 2004) *Pub revolt on smoking ban ends.*

McNicholls, W.T. (2004) 'Controlling Passive Smoking through Legislation in Ireland: An Attack on Civil Liberty or Good Public Health Policy?' *European Respiratory Journal,* Vol. 24, pp. 337–338.

New York Times (11 August 2003) *Anti-tobacco trends has reached Europe.*

Office of the Surgeon General (1984) *The Health Consequences of Smoking – Chronic Obstructive Lung Disease,* Office on Smoking and Health, Washington: Public Health Service.

Office of the Surgeon General (1985) *The Health Consequences of Smoking – Cancer and Chronic Lung Disease in the Workplace,* Office on Smoking and Health, Washington: Public Health Service.

Office of the Surgeon General (1986) *The Health Consequences of Involuntary Smoking,* Office on Smoking and Health, Washington: Public Health Service.

Office of Tobacco Control (2005) *Smoke-Free Workplace in Ireland: A One-Year Review,* Dublin: OTC.

Public Health (Tobacco) Act 2002, Dublin: Stationery Office.

Public Health (Tobacco)(Amendment) Act 2004, Dublin: Stationery Office.

Public Health (Tobacco)(Amendment) Act 2004 (Commencement) Order 2004, Dublin: Stationery Office.

Roper Organization (1978) *A study of Public Attitudes toward cigarette smoking and the Tobacco Industry in 1978,* Vol. 1, Bates: 500070008–500070060.

Safety, Health and Welfare at Work Act 1989, Dublin: Stationery Office.

Shaffey, O., S. Dolwich, G.E. Guindon (2003) *Tobacco Control Country Policies,* Atlanta: American Cancer Society 2nd edition.

Standards in Public Office Commission (2004) *Annual Report, 2003,* Dublin: Stationery Office.

Sunday Independent (27 July 2003) *Cigarette ban job-loss myth up in smoke.*

Sunday Tribune (25 July 2004) *Study suggests pub sales will recover after smoking ban.*

The Health (Miscellaneous Provision) Act 2000, Dublin: Stationery Office.

The Independent (11 October 2003) *Proposed Irish ban on smoking in the work place enrages MPs and publicans.*

The Irish Independent (15 September 2003) *Public split on smoking ban-poll.*

The Irish Examiner (7 April 2003) *Irish Eyes on Smoking.*

The Irish Examiner (10 October 2003) *Fahey finally backs no-smoking ban.*

The Irish Examiner (5 March 2004) *Dublin publicans drop smoking ban challenge.*

The Irish Examiner (15 July 2004) *Smokers urged to back European legal challenge to smoke ban.*

The Irish Times (11 February 2002) *Right to Live Overrides Right to Smoke.*

The Irish Times (18 February 2003) *Almost 60% think Minister is right to impose smoking ban.*

The Irish Times (18 February 2003) *Minister faces battle over plans to ban smoking.*

The Irish Times (15 August 2003) *Employers urged to lobby against ban.*

The Irish Times (24 October 2003) *Hospitality alliance consults lawyers as smoking ban is signed into law.*

The Kingdom (9 October 2003) *Publicans warn minister they have more tactics at the ready.*

The Times (29 March 2004) *No fags, no fugs, no fun?*

Tobacco (Health Promotion and Protection) Act 1988, Dublin: Stationery Office.

Tobacco (Health Promotion and Protection) Regulations 1990, Dublin: Stationery Office.

Tobacco Smoking (Prohibition) Regulations 2003, Dublin: Stationery Office.

Todd, G. F. (1978) 'Cigarette Consumption per Adult of Each Sex in Various Countries', *Journal of Epidemiology Community Health*, Vol. 32, pp. 289–93.

Waterford News & Star (16 July 2004) *City publicans to challenge ban in High Court.*

Chapter 7

The Reform of Dutch Disability Insurance: A Crisis-induced Shift of Preferences and Possibilities

Duco Bannink, Sanneke Kuipers and Tineke Lantink

Innovative reform after decades of deadlock

From 1967 onwards the Dutch disability insurance act ensured income related benefits to every employee unable to work. Disability insurance was constituted by a benefit scheme that offered relatively generous protection. The benefit covered any employee unable to work as a consequence of sickness, accidents, and injuries. The benefit was granted to all those who could not continue their former occupation or a similar occupation, no matter what caused their impairment. In this system employers' representatives and trade unions (hereafter: social partners) had a strong position, because they were responsible for the implementation of benefits and had a two-third majority in the system's supervisory body, in which the government occupied only a one-third minority.

For a long time, this system of generous benefits and strong social partner involvement worked to the satisfaction of most actors involved. In the early 1990s, however, the Dutch social security system found itself in a deep crisis, because both the cost and number of people receiving disability insurance became higher and higher. As a result, and combined with the economic recession of the 1980s, a financial crisis was triggered. This was a turning point in the post-war history of the Dutch welfare state: 'Never before did a prolonged financial crisis of the Dutch state turn so directly into a political crisis, in which the political elite faced a massive rejection of its policy concerning welfare state arrangements' (Vlek, 1997: 280).

Reforms were set in motion in the summer of 1991. These resulted in unprecedented government cutbacks in social security.[1] Politicians pursued changes

---

1 The accumulated savings of 1992 and 1993, as a consequence of the proposals introduced since 1991, comprised more than the total savings of the austerity regimes in the six years prior (Vlek, 1997: 469). Though the benefit levels were already decreased from 80% to 70% of the prior income in 1985, the new cutbacks would cut the benefits even further

in both policy contents and implementation structures. First, disability insurance, the so-called jewel in the crown of the Dutch welfare state, was reformed on several benefit-policy aspects: the duration of benefits was limited, eligibility was restricted, the level of the benefits decreased, and the benefits became age-related. Second, taboos on the administration and implementation of social security were abolished. After decades of deadlock between the government and the social partners, a discussion of who would govern the social security administration became possible. The state enforced the introduction of market mechanisms to induce competition among the public organizations, which had been charged with the implementation of disability insurance. These privatization efforts served to make the administration of benefits more transparent and efficient.[2] In addition, government changed the system of benefit financing in order to address collective action problems.[3] Later, the disability benefit system was renationalized, because the strong position of social partners could continue in the privatized system. This was against the will of the Dutch Parliament.

These reforms followed decades of deadlock and were 'innovative' (Bonoli & Palier, 1998) since they resulted in a system that no longer complied with the corporatist regime logic that had characterized the Dutch social security system (Esping-Andersen, 1990). Theories on welfare states indicate that drastic change is very difficult to achieve (Mishra, 1990; Pierson, 1994; Esping-Andersen, 1999). The occurrence of drastic reform in such a highly institutionalized field as Dutch disability insurance is therefore surprising. The question for this chapter is why innovative reform on both dimensions (policy and administration) was possible after all those years of protracted stalemate.

The next section summarizes the long history of inertia and the barriers that obstructed previous reform attempts. In section three we dissect the disability reform efforts and results. Section four analyzes the factors that made these reforms possible. Finally, section five summarizes and discusses our case analysis, employing the analytical scheme presented in chapter 1.

(Kuipers, 2006). Both the duration of the 70%-benefit and the replacement rate thereafter became age dependent, 'a sharp break from a quarter of a century of disability entitlement to wage related benefits of unlimited duration' (Aarts & De Jong, 1996: 62). The new benefit to every chronically disabled employee would decrease at least another 10% after a few years (Advisory Committee Disability Insurance, report, May 2001: 108). Many people would loose more than 10%: a 40-year-old teacher would have a replacement rate of only 53% of her prior income (-17% compared to the old benefit level).

2   Later on, this administrative privatization was reversed because parliament feared negative effects of profit maximization on the lawful assessment of claims.

3   Employers would, in the future, directly feel the costs of disability claims among their employees. Hence, employers 'producing' many disability claims among their workers would pay a higher contribution.

Barriers to reform: The linkage of policy and administration

Before the 1990s, various attempts were made to reform the Dutch disability insurance system. However, these reform attempts never led to successful change. Several inter-related factors explain this inertia. First, the prevailing policy paradigm of the 1960s, 1970s, and beginning of the 1980s stabilized policy-making actors' preferences for years. Second, decision-making institutions enabled these actors to withstand pressures to reform the Dutch disability insurance system. The institutions could do so as a result of a tight connection between the disability benefits policy and the administrative system of disability insurance implementation. This connection placed persistent barriers to innovation and reform. The most prominent advocates of this tight coupling between policy formation and administration (the social partners) could veto reforms, reinforce their own strategic position, and rephrase policy initiatives as they saw fit to their paradigm.

A problematic policy inheritance

The 1967 Dutch Disability Insurance Act reflected an ambitious merger of two disability benefit programs which created a problematic policy heritage. It combined universal eligibility rights and the solidarity principle of the old residual disability act with generous income replacement and a low threshold of the Industrial Accidents Act. The latter was a publicly administered, but rather selective, insurance-based arrangement dating back to the first decade of the twentieth century.

The budget for the new disability act was based on estimates of 155,000 claimants, which soon appeared to be quite unrealistic. Soon after its inception, the popularity of the arrangement turned out to pale every estimate into insignificance: in 1980, more than 600,000 people depended on disability benefits. This number would continue to grow steadily during the 1980s (SCP, 1990). In 1970 there were 55 disability benefit recipients per 1000 workers, in 1980 this number increased to 130. In 1990 there were even 152 disability benefit recipients per 1000 workers. This meant that 15.2% of the workers received a disability benefit. In comparison to other European countries, this was a very large number. In Germany, for instance, the percentage of disability benefit recipients in 1980 was 5.9%, and this percentage decreased to 5.5% in 1990 (De Jong, 1999). Table 7.1 shows the development of disability recipients relative to employment in the Netherlands from 1975 to 1990.

Apart from the problematic policy inheritance that was produced by the 1967 merger, the organizational structure established by the 1967 Disability Act was also a legacy from the past. The Act was administered in the framework of the 1952 Social Security (Organization) Act that made the social partners responsible for the administration of the new benefit. The 1952 Act had institutionalized a powerful position of the social partners in the administrative system as well as in the supervision process.

Table 7.1   Disability benefit recipients in the Netherlands (De Jong, 1999: 253-271)

Disability recipients in the Netherlands				
	1975	1980	1985	1990
Employment (in 1000 FTE*)	4772	4950	4730	5664
Disability beneficiaries (in 1000 FTE)	311	611	703	790
Disability beneficiaries as % of employment	6.5 %	12.3 %	14.9 %	13.9 %

* FTE means full-time equivalents

The powerful position of social partners obstructs change

Already in 1967, the responsible minister, Gerard Veldkamp, doubted the efficiency of an administrative system in which social partners had so much power. He therefore asked the Social and Economic Council (SER) – an advisory body with representatives of government, employers, and unions – for advice on social insurance administration (Veldkamp, 1978; SER, 1984). The minister argued for a regional organization of administration under public rule. This would imply an important reform of the administrative system, since it was, until then, based on administration per sector by employers' and employees' representatives. The sector administration basically allowed the social partners full discretion in distributing benefits without government intervention. This structure had operated since the 1930s, and had been even more extended since then. Because they feared reform would bring with it more government involvement, the social partners considered the issue to be extremely delicate. They did not wish to give up their position in administration, because it contributed to their capacity to control the labour market (Bannink, 2004). The representatives of employers and trade unions delayed the legislative processes considerably by putting the required advice of the Social and Economic Council on hold (Klamer, 1990). The Council advised no earlier than in 1984. Not surprisingly, the Council (of which two-thirds of the members were representatives of labour unions and employers' organizations) advised that the existing administrative structure was to remain in place. The social partners argued that the benefit system should remain the responsibility of both employers and trade unions, since the benefits were deemed to be work-related. The social partners were thus able to withstand pressures to reform the administrative system by using their advisory power in the institution of the Social and Economic Council.

Alternative measures are taken: Cutbacks on sickness benefits

In January 1982, the centre-left coalition proposed cutbacks on another social security arrangement – the Sickness Insurance Act – in order to curb some of the ever-increasing costs of the social security system. The idea was that it was preferable to reduce short-term benefits, such as Sick Pay, rather than the long-term disability entitlements on which a more vulnerable group of people depended, e.g. the chronically ill and impaired (Aarts & De Jong, 1996). Nevertheless, this proposal drew a blaze of protest from the trade unions, since employees would receive a lower benefit. Therefore, the Minister of Social Affairs withdrew part of the cutback plan a few months later. The trade unions had been able to block the proposed reforms by putting pressure on MPs and Cabinet members. Voters punished the social democrats in the provincial elections, and the social partners in the Social and Economic Council rejected what was left of the proposed reforms in their advice on the matter (Vlek, 1997). In May 1982, the coalition split and although a centre-rightwing austerity government took office, the terms of the Sickness Insurance Act remained untouched.

The 'system revision' meets powerful professionals

Halfway the 1980s, however, both the administrative structure and the rather generous benefit came under pressure again. Because a growing number of people gained access to the disability system and almost none of the disabled ever 'recovered', the total number of disabled people increased steadily. It appeared that in the actual administrative process, virtually no activities were undertaken to reintegrate disability insurance beneficiaries into the labour market, while the entrance into the system was also not contained. The so-called 1987 system revision addressed these issues. In addition to an effort to simplify the system of social insurance benefits and administration, the benefit level was cut from 80% to 70% of the previous income. Also, employment chances would no longer be discounted in the assessment of disability, which would make eligibility criteria for benefits much stricter. These changes were expected to curb the growth of the disability population.

In practice, however, the doctors responsible for disability assessment continued to take employment chances into account (Van der Veen, 1990: 110). As argued in chapter 1, people within organizations have a strong preference to maintain and protect the status quo if it corresponds with their values and those of the dominant paradigm in the policy sector (Terry, 2003). In the case of disability insurance, the doctors continued to let their own sense of fairness (based on previous policy obligations to disability claimants) guide their assessment, even though the eligibility criteria had become much stricter by law. This was possible because the system allowed the doctors to decide quite autonomously about eligibility. As a result, the number of disability insurance beneficiaries continued to show an enormous increase.

Social partners defend their exclusive rights

Shortly after, in 1989, a Study Group on the Volume of the Disability Arrangements was established as an outcome of the yearly Fall Conference, during which government and social partners discussed upcoming socio-economic issues. The study group consisted of representatives of the government and the social partners and addressed the issue of rising claims and low re-employment once again. The study group advised the introduction of a so-called *volume policy*. This term refers to the idea that the policy reform does not primarily aim at the cost (i.e. the level of the benefit) of the system, but instead at the number, the volume, of disability insurance beneficiaries. Proposed measures included the introduction of various subsidies for the employment of disabled workers and additional measures supporting the employability of disabled workers in a company.

Again, the social partners used their powerful position in the system to withstand reform pressures (Bannink, 2004). The social partners argued that volume policies required the implementation of an administrative model that would place the responsibility for the administrative system entirely in the hands of social partners, thus restricting the government's role in the supervisory organ (Bannink, 2004). Anticipating the political rejection of the model, social partners argued that the implementation of volume policies (broadly supported in parliament) required the implementation of their preferred administrative model (rejected by parliamentary parties). The stricter claim assessment and focus on re-employment, according to the social partners, would benefit from a more streamlined administration that was no longer divided between social partners and government, but fully in the hands of the social partners. This strategy succeeded; although Parliament was reluctant, the Cabinet accepted the proposed combination of a limited role for the government in the administration system, and the implementation of the volume policy. Hence, the social partners were once again able to retain their powerful position in the system.

By the end of the 1980s, the development of cost reduction in disability policy appeared rather ineffective, because both costs and volume did not decrease (SCP, 1990). The inefficacy was partially caused by the fact that the restriction of benefit eligibility had been fiercely and successfully opposed by the social partners in the implementation process (Bannink, 2004; Kuipers, 2006).

To conclude, until the end of the 1980s, reforms were virtually absent. If anything, they were limited to first and second order changes (Hall, 1993), but reform did not affect the basis of the system. Indeed, social partners remained responsible for the administration of easily accessible workers' benefits. The social partners strongly preferred this system and were able to protect it from reform pressures by effectively using their position in the policy-making and implementation arena. They successfully argued that changing the benefit was problematic for the administration and, likewise, changing the administration would cause problems for the benefit. If anything, social partners were willing to allow an adjustment of benefit criteria, but their position as administrators of the social insurance system (without government involvement) was strongly defended. Social partners not only preferred to maintain the system of easily accessible workers' benefits (cultural approach), they also had strong institutional capacities to protect this system. Their strong position and the strategies they used to take advantage of their dominant position (calculus approach) were the barriers that caused decades of deadlock in the field of disability insurance. Table 7.2 gives an overview of previous attempts to reform disability administration.

Table 7.2   Chronological overview of previous failed attempts

Previous attempts to reform disability administration		
Year	**The attempt**	**Reasons for failure**
1967–1984	Attempt for changed administration through advice from Social Economic Council	Social partners' strong involvement in policy creation (they hold a two-third majority of the council).
1982	Centre left coalition proposes cutbacks. Content reform.	Social partners (especially trade-unions) organise massive protests, which ultimately led to withdrawal.
1987	System revision that is expected to curb the growth of the disability population. Content reform.	Medical professionals responsible for disability assessment continue taking the employment chances into account. This means that the system revision does not have the expected effect.
1989	Introduction of volume policy, aims at the number of disability insurance beneficiaries. Organizational reform.	Social partners use their power to implement an administrative model that limits the role of the central government and reinforces the position of the social partners in the administration of disability insurance benefit, considered necessary for volume policy.

Anatomy of innovative reform

Despite all previously failed efforts, a large-scale government intervention in both the disability insurance benefit policy and the administration took place in the beginning of the 1990s. At that time, Prime Minister Lubbers recognized the seriousness of the crisis and underscored this by making his famous declaration that 'the Netherlands are sick'. The emerging crisis caused the centre-leftwing (CDA and PvdA) government to propose cutbacks in the costs of the disability system by means of the Disability Benefit Schemes (Entitlement) Act. This act severely limited eligibility rights and introduced regular medical (re)assessments.[4] The reform

---

4   The definition of employment was adjusted to include all generally accepted occupations instead of only the work one had before the impairment. In addition, regular assessment of disability was introduced: all beneficiaries younger than 50 would be re-examined according to the new criteria. For those who could claim disability benefits, the duration of their entitlement to a full benefit (70% of previous income) would be restricted. After a few years, depending on the claimant's age, the benefit would be reduced considerably (the extent of the reduction again dependent on age and employment record). Particularly the

proposals evoked dismissive reactions by left-wing opposition parties, the left-wing coalition member and labour unions. These parties started to look for alternative reform trajectories in order to prevent the proposed policy change from materializing. Their search resulted in a parliamentary anti-corporatist coalition that, instead of cutting back benefits, aimed at limiting social partners' autonomy in administration. In other words, they did no longer perceive the problems in disability insurance to be caused by the contents of the policies, but instead saw the administrative system as the major cause of high costs.

Parliament steps in

The Social Democrats in Parliament were outraged that their representatives in the Cabinet had agreed on the Disability Benefit Schemes (Entitlement) Act. Together with the left-wing opposition parties, Social Democrat members of Parliament argued that social partners' unwillingness to support administrative reform proposals caused disability claims to rise (Official Reports, 1991–1992: 6338).

Meanwhile, the National Court of Audit published an investigative report about the lack of supervision on the administrative bodies responsible for the implementation of the disability and unemployment insurances (Court of Audit Report, TK 22555, no. 1-2, 1991). Commotion rose in parliament, since growing irritation about the social partners' rule of the administration coincided with the draft bill for the new Social Security (Organization) Act. This draft had been heavily influenced by the social partners' views on administration. Most importantly, the draft proposed that a coordination agency representing only the social partners would be established; the agency would acquire some of the tasks of the current supervisory body in which government was also represented. The Court of Audit report, together with the Social Democratic wish to curb the policy reforms, strengthened the belief of many Social Democrats that the corporatist structure of the social security sector was a problem that needed to be addressed first (NRC Handelsblad, 14 January 1992; Trouw, 17 January 1992).

Hence, the Social Democrat members of Parliament deemed stricter disability criteria unnecessary and proposed, instead, administrative reform as the appropriate means to curb volume growth. Buurmeijer, a Social Democrat member of Parliament, submitted a motion asking State Secretary Ter Veld to establish a structure of supervision over administration in which social partners did not have a majority (TK 22011, no. 7, 1991). This motion was supported by all left-wing parties and also, surprisingly, by the liberal party. The liberal party supported administrative reform, because, in its opinion, the current administrative structure interfered too much with the market logic. Nevertheless, Secretary Ter Veld was unwilling to implement the motion. This was because she did not want to disrupt the social partners' ongoing efforts to implement the - previously agreed upon - proposals to reduce the number of

benefit level of younger claimants (for instance around 30 years old) would be more than halved (Aarts & De Jong, 1996).

disability recipients (in combination with the new model that fully handed power in administration to the social partners). Her unwillingness frustrated reform-oriented politicians to such an extent that they demanded a Parliamentary Enquiry into social insurance administration. A committee to perform this enquiry was formed in May, 1992, and the report of the Parliamentary Enquiry was published in 1993.

A Parliamentary Enquiry further induces reform

The Enquiry concluded that there had been virtually no systematic legislative or ministerial control on the administration of social insurance. In particular, the Enquiry found that: the aims of the social policies were unspecified, the output criteria for supervision of administrative bodies were not operationalized, the responsibilities of the Social Security council (which supervised the administration and implementation of social law) were unclear, the surveys of this council among administrative bodies were infrequent, unsystematic and ill-guided and, finally, the Ministry of Social Affairs seemed to have no idea of what was going on (Committee Report, TK 22730, no. 7–8, 1993). The picture that emerged from the daily-televized hearings of the parliamentary enquiry committee was that of a tacit conspiracy between the social partners to abuse the disability insurance arrangement through their role in the administration of the system. This devastated the image of all organizations that represented employers and workers (Aarts & De Jong, 1996: 65).

The Parliamentary Enquiry induced a reform of the disability insurance system in a way that had been inconceivable before the 1990s. The Dutch employers' organization and the trade unions were (in their own words) thrown out of the institutional structure (Kuipers, 2006). Independent supervision by a newly established governmental authority replaced the supervision by the former Social Insurance Council, in which the representatives of labour and capital together had a majority (Bannink, 2004). The new organization law was temporary, and stipulated that benefit administration would in the future become market-driven. The previously responsible administrative organizations governed by the social partners were now to compete for assignments of companies and branch representatives in their own region (Van der Veen et al., 1996: 28). This competition was predicted to increase the quality, efficiency, and effectiveness of benefit administration.

Social partners change their preferences

Benefit reform took another direction from the mid-1990s and onward: the emphasis was no longer on the level of protection, but on the financial responsibilities for protection. Therefore, in 1994, employers became responsible for income coverage in the first six weeks of sickness/impairment. Later on, in 1996, their financial responsibility was extended to the entire first year. In 1998, reforms were introduced that shifted financial responsibilities for the disability benefits to employers and differentiated the contributions among them.

The effects of these reform measures were less costly than expected by the social partners: it appeared that approximately 80% of the Dutch employees were not directly affected by those benefit cuts. Most collective labour agreements reinsured the gap between the old and the new benefit levels. As a result, the level of protection that the system offered to employees did not decrease. Because it proved possible to reinsure decreased benefits through collective labour agreements, the trade unions no longer opposed these cutbacks (Van Schendelen & Pauw, 1998; Bannink, 2004). Furthermore, benefit privatization shifted part of the financial burden of social insurance from the public to the private domain, so that the involvement of the social partners in the administration of benefits was not contained. On the contrary, their involvement seemed to grow (Caminada & Goudswaard, 2003). The social partners, therefore, no longer resisted government proposals for further privatization. De-collectivization of benefit contributory obligations, coupled with the introduction of market incentives in the administrative system, now became serious options for the social partners. Therefore, the Social and Economic Council did not reject the underlying logic of privatization and de-collectivization, although they rejected the specific design of government proposals (SER, 1995).

Paradoxically, the social partners embraced policy proposals that were actually aimed to diminish their strategic position in administration. When the political support for benefit privatization grew, the social partners also came to support the privatization of administration. A privatized administrative system, they argued, would nicely fit a privatized benefit system. Therefore, in 1998, two leading women in industrial negotiations, Jongerius (labour union FNV) and Snelders (employers' organization VNO/NCW), made the so-called Ladies' Accord. In the Accord, labour union FNV and employers' organization VNO/NCW agreed to support market liberalization of social insurance administration, including claim assessment, on the condition that the social partners would become the purchasers of administrative services by privatized agencies. In such a privatized administrative system, the social partners could operate as the autonomous, private demanders of privatized administrative services. Instead of introducing market incentives in order to contain social partners' freedom to move, this agreement between the largest labour union and the largest employers' organization redefined privatization as a reform trajectory that increased social partners' autonomy in administration.

Parliament steps in again

In reaction to the Ladies' Accord, parliamentary parties withdrew their support to the further privatization of administration. Political parties feared that full privatization of the system under rule of the social partners would effectively reinstall the old system, in which social partners enjoyed a strong, virtually autonomous, position vis-à-vis the state. In the first place, parliament rejected that claim assessment was to become a competency executed by the social partners. Claim assessment was to remain independent from the parties involved. As a result, in the second place, further privatization of the system became a difficult issue. It had appeared difficult to separate claim assessment and other administrative tasks before. Therefore, instead of the full privatization of the system – as in the Ladies' Accord – parliament proposed to reverse the reform trajectory and fully re-nationalize the social insurance administration (retaining public claim assessment and bringing under public rule the other administrative tasks). In order to keep the incumbent pro-privatization liberal party satisfied, the re-employment services for disabled and unemployed beneficiary recipients should be completely privatized. By applying for re-nationalization of the social insurance administration, parliament obstructed the further market liberalization of disability insurance administration. Forced by parliament, the government subsequently changed its plans drastically, and opted for the re-nationalization of the administrative system, leaving intact the privatized nature of the worker re-employment services.

The new administrative structure was enacted in 2002, and included some remarkable changes compared to the earlier plans. Instead of independent competing administrative institutions with both public and private tasks, one single public institution would be established for the administration of employees' insurances, the UWV (Caminada & Goudswaard, 2003). The government decided that the administration of the unemployment benefit and the disability benefit was a public affair, and necessarily the responsibility of a public institution, in this case the UWV. Competition was no longer considered desirable. The politicians became responsible for the policy and the supervision; the decisions in individual cases were to be made by the UWV (TK 26448, no. 7, 2000: 14). To guarantee independency, supervision became a task of the newly created agency the Inspection on Work and Income that fell under the Ministry for Social Affairs and Employment (TK 27588, no. 3, 2001: 6).

From corporatism to 'marketization' to public control

In sum, major shifts occurred in a couple of years, from a corporatist system of administration and implementation of disability benefits, to plans for competition in the administrative system, to the re-nationalization of the system. Alongside these changes, the benefit was de-collectivized and privatized. Instead of the main policy objective in former decades – to financially compensate people who were not able to work – the main goal had now become to re-employ benefit recipients. With the new administrative structure and privatized benefits, government wished to prevent long-term unemployment and disability by placing emphasis on reintegration efforts.

All in all, the changes amounted to a shift of policy paradigm. The privatization of the benefit, the liberalization, and later re-nationalization of the administrative system, each reflect a strong shift away from the corporatist paradigm. Instead, responsibilities were replaced from organized actors to, on the one hand, individual citizens and, on the other, the state. In terms of Esping-Andersen's (1990) typology, we see a shift away from the conservative-corporatist regime in the directions of *both* the liberal (market-oriented) and the social-democratic (state-oriented) regimes. Table 7.3 presents a chronological overview of events in social insurance administration, as described above.

Table 7.3   Chronological overview of events in social insurance administration in the 1990s

Anatomy of disability administration reform		
Year	The attempt	Outcome
1992–1993	Parliament wants to stall benefit cutbacks and submits a motion to decrease the role of social partners in the supervision of administration. Mainly content reform attempts.	The State Secretary is unwilling to implement the motion, in order to prevent disruption of social partners' efforts to reduce the number of disability recipients. As a consequence, parliament demands a Parliamentary Enquiry.
1993	Parliamentary Enquiry induces an administrative reform of the disability insurance system.	The Parliamentary Enquiry shows the abusive use of the insurance system by social partners. Social partners are then thrown out of the institutional structure by a new temporary organizational law, which will ultimately lead toward a market-driven benefit administration.
1994–1998	Several changes in financial responsibilities of employers, which diminish the strategic position of the social partners. Content reforms.	Employers become financially responsible for the income coverage in the first six weeks and, later, the whole first year of impairment. Social partners agree because they believe they will become the purchasers of administrative services in a privatized administration system.
1998–2002	After a period of further increasing the power of social partners, the implementation of new administrative structure in 2002.	Parliamentary parties withdraw support for further privatization of administration out of fear for reinstallation of the old system. Social insurance administration is re-nationalized, and the re-employment services are fully privatised.

Explaining reform: Changing preferences precede structural change

With this reform, the government was able to overrule the social partners, with whom they had been in a tug-of-war regarding the administration ever since the introduction of the Social Security (Organization) Act in 1952 (Bannink, 2004). In addition, changes in the insurance policy were introduced that marked a watershed in the policy's history (Aarts et al, 2002: 3; Jaspers, 2001: 39). What changed the willingness and ability of actors within the Dutch policy-making system to push for reform of both disability insurance policy and administration? How is it possible to explain this surprising shift? The calculus approach – such as presented in chapter 1 – instructs us to look at changed decision-making procedures, structures, and actors' institutional capacities that affected the ability to reform. The cultural approach directs attention to the changed preferences of policy-making actors: the social partners and the political parties.

Crisis creation by leadership

It is argued that large-scale reforms are often preceded by a crisis that underlines a sense of urgency and severity of the situation (Boin & 't Hart, 2000). In this case, the crisis was evoked by the Dutch prime minister in 1990 when he publicly stated that 'the Netherlands are sick,' in referring to the unprecedented number of nearly one million people receiving disability benefits. Prime Minister Lubbers tied his political faith to the limit of one million: if the number of disability claims passed this limit, he would resign. His statements firmly placed the issue on the political agenda and drew a blaze of publicity (Kuipers, 2006; Bos, 1999). In reaction, the Social Economic Council – including representatives of both employers and trade unions – unanimously recommended that more efforts should be directed to curb the growth of the disability program (Van Wijnbergen, 2000), probably in an effort to retain the initiative in the debate on disability insurance (Bannink, 2004).

The Cabinet decided to seize this opportunity and proposed a reform package targeted at saving 3.75 billion Dutch guilders (1.7 billion euro) during its incumbency (Vlek, 1997: 568). With a prime minister who wished to finish his job (Lubbers was governing his third term, and had pursued a long-term agenda of sound budgetary strictness) and a Minister of Finance who wished to show that even Social Democrats could pursue austerity policies, there was little room for mercy. The Ministry of Social Affairs was one of the largest spending departments and therefore also faced the largest cutbacks (Kuipers, 2006). Apart from saving money through cutbacks, the Cabinet attempted to curb the benefit dependency growth by making the benefits less attractive and the claimants less eligible.

Changing preferences in Parliament

Lubbers's crisis narrative coincided with changing preferences in Parliament. In Parliament, attention shifted from the adjustment of benefits to the issue of administration. The Social Democrats found an unlikely ally in the right wing opposition party, who strongly advocated a minimal role for social partners in policymaking and implementation. For the Social Democrats, this alliance was a means to stall the cutbacks on benefits that the Cabinet had agreed to (Bannink, 2004; Kuipers, 2006). Together, the Social Democrats and the Liberals issued a Parliamentary Enquiry into social insurance administration. The conclusions of the enquiry were strongly dismissive regarding the social partners' role in the administrative system. The ad hoc parliamentary alliance that initiated the Enquiry clearly rejected the social partners' emphasis on the interconnected benefit policy and its administration. The parliamentary enquiry committee showed that not so much the policy, but the administration, was the cause of disability insurance volume growth. Now the political discussion on benefits and administration became separated: the social partners were blamed for serious flaws in the administration, and were therefore denied their traditional role in policy-making. As a result, social partners lost some of their veto power. This impotence became abundantly clear when the proposed 1989 administrative model, in which the social partners would become fully responsible for the administrative system, and which was strongly supported by the social partners, was rejected in Parliament. Instead, Parliament followed the lead of the parliamentary enquiry committee and reduced social partners' influence in administration.

A reform window opens, agents step in

In sum, the window of reform opened by the public statements of the Prime Minister and the social partners' own indicated willingness to curb further volume growth had produced a joint proposal to drastically change the disability benefits policy. In reaction, an ad hoc coalition was formed that triggered substantial reform of the administrative structure. The trade unions and employers' organizations, traditionally able to bar such changes, were compromised by the outcomes of the Parliamentary Enquiry. The social partners' expertise and influence was now seen as incriminating evidence of their ongoing abuse of undemocratic power. They were no longer able to oppose administrative reform as they had done in the decades before.

In chapter 1, it was argued that reform-oriented actors that use such a *window of opportunity* need to go with the flow and make their reforms compatible with current national and international trends. This was clearly the case for Dutch policy makers on disability insurance, because the institutional sclerosis of corporatism was severely disputed in the early 1990s (Therborn, 1986; Visser & Hemerijck, 1997; Hendriks & Toonen, 2001). The propositions to reform social insurance administration made in the first half of the 1990s explicitly addressed the corporatist nature of the system.

Later on, the flow was followed again when market-oriented reforms of the system were proposed. What is more, however, some parliamentary actors actually *designed* the flow in Dutch politics. Social Democratic MPs rejecting benefit cutbacks, together with Liberal MPs rejecting the corporatist administrative monopoly, took the initiative to start the Parliamentary Enquiry procedure. Subsequently, the enquiry conclusions strongly affected political debate. The Cabinet indeed followed this flow, but only after pressure to do so by Parliament. The Assistant Secretary was only willing to adjust his draft for a new Social Security (Organization) Act after parliament accepted a number of motions that were submitted in the debate on the Parliamentary Enquiry conclusions (TK 23141, no. 12, 1993; TK 22730, no. 18, 20, 24, 1993; see also Bannink, 2004: 155–9). Here we see an instance of *agency* overruling institutional barriers. Social partners fought to protect their powerful position in the administration of disability insurance benefits. In the beginning, they linked changes in the benefit policy (i.e. the assessment criteria, the level of the benefit) in order to retain their powerful position in administration. Changes to the financial structures of the system, which entailed a partial privatization, did not result in the expected problems for the trade unions. Hence, the social partners no longer saw a problem in further privatizing the system, and came to support the further privatization of administration.

Consequently, but unintended, the privatization of parts of the administration of benefits had brought the social partners back to the centre stage of social insurance administration. Until the Ladies' Accord – the agreement between social partners to support the privatization of benefit administration – Parliament had accepted the resurfacing and expanding role (as market players) of social partners in the administrative system, possibly to facilitate social partners' acceptance of the shift of the disability risk from collective to private 'shoulders'. The Ladies' Accord made Parliament realize that old players regained their old positions in a new form, as the social partners had again provided themselves substantial autonomy vis-à-vis the state. Therefore Parliament opted for the re-nationalization of the social insurance administration, without changing its views on the privatization of benefits policy. This, eventually, led to the implementation of another new act of social insurance administration, the Work and Income (Implementation Structure) Act of 2002.

Conclusion

In this chapter the reform of Dutch disability insurance benefits and administration has been analyzed. A reform, according to the definition in chapter 1, is a fundamental, intended, and enforced change of the policy paradigm and the organizational structure of a policy sector. The reform in our case study complies with this description. It was surprising because it took place after years of deadlock, and because the changes produced a system that no longer complied with the corporatist regime logic.

The most important barriers to reform in this case can be attributed to institutional and cultural constraints (see Table 7.4). The organizational structure was a legacy from the past. The Netherlands is known for the corporatist organization of policies. Social security, and more specifically the disability insurance, epitomized this kind of organization. Social partners' prominent role in that structure supported their strength in decision-making. Social partners had, for a long time, been able to block reform by emphasising and using the interconnection between the disability insurance benefit and the administration.

Table 7.4   Barriers and facilitators reform Dutch disability insurance

Barriers		Facilitators	
The position of the social partners in policy making and administration (policy inheritance)		Focus on rising costs made it possible for actors to change their preferences (diminished barriers, preferences remain the same)	
Barriers	**Type of barrier**	**Facilitators**	**Type of facilitator**
The strong involvement of social partners in policy creation (SER) as well as implementation	Opportunities: Decision-making structure	Public statements Prime Minister ('The Netherlands are sick')	Agency: Leadership
		Willingness social partners to curb further growth (in order to keep control over the debate)	Agency: Go with the flow/Find support
Social partners' focus on the volume and bipartite organization	Preferences: Vested Interests	Ad hoc coalition between left and right wing parties to trigger substantial reform of administrative structure	Agency: Find support
High sensitivity of cutbacks in level of provision	Preferences: Internalised goals	Parliamentary Enquiry into social insurance administration that compromised the trade unions and employers' organizations	Agency: Find support
		Awareness that cutbacks in insurance do not have to hurt the employees, due to collective labour agreements	Agency: Change of preference

A crisis in the early 1990s made it possible to introduce and implement new social security legislation: the social partners were cast aside when the Parliamentary Enquiry revealed their role in the abuse of the insurance system. Public blame on the social partners was an important facilitator for the separation of administration and policy on the political agenda. As a result, alternative reform directions became more acceptable and social partners lost much of their veto power. In other words, the changing preferences of parliamentary actors on the corporatist administration of benefits (cultural approach) affected the veto powers and influence of social partners in policy-making (calculus approach). This facilitated the initial step of drastic reform. Government strongly limited the role of social partners in administration and partially privatized the benefit system. This reform was initially marked by a strong shift away from the prevailing corporatist policy paradigm.

In the Ladies' Accord (1998), however, the social partners seized the opportunity to become the autonomous purchasers of social insurance services. They found a new way to pursue their ever-present preference to protect their roles in administration. In reaction to the Accord, as we have seen, parliamentary parties and government actors realized they rejected giving social partners a strong position in administration. The Ladies' Accord 're-politicized' the issue and turned the administrative structure into a highly disputed issue. As a result, parliament finally re-nationalized the administrative system.

This reform in the disability insurance is an example of what Leemans (1976: 88–9) called 'upsetting and unsettling' for individuals and especially organized actors. There were some strong forces in favour of the status quo, but the crisis in the disability insurance in the early 1990s made clear that changes had to be made. Now, more than a decade later, we can conclude that reform indeed took place. The new social insurance legislation as well as the administrative reforms and changes in Dutch disability benefits policy, were remarkable. However, the question remains how long they will last. In 2006, the new social insurance legislation will be evaluated. It is very well possible that a new government will change social security legislation again. However, the paradigm shift and changed preferences we witnessed during this reform process make it more likely that new adjustments will include forms of privatization and competition again. Though it is impossible to tell which reforms of the past decade will continue and which will be reversed, new marks are set for the decade to come.

References

Aarts, L.J.M., Ph.R. de Jong (1996) 'The Dutch Disability Program and How it Grew' Aarts, L.J.M., R.V. Burkhauser, Ph.R. De Jong (eds), *Curing the Dutch Disease*, Aldershot: Avebury, pp. 21–46.

Aarts, L.J.M., Ph.R. de Jong, R. van der Veen (2002) *Met de beste bedoelingen. WAO 1975-1999: trends, onderzoek en beleid*, Den Haag: Elsevier bedrijfsinformatie.

Advisory Committee Disability Insurance (2001) *Werk maken van Arbeidsgeschiktheid*, The Hague: Sdu.

Algemene Rekenkamer (Court of Audit) (1992) *Toezicht door de Sociale Verzekeringsraad*, 31 March 1992, Kamerstuk 22555, #2.

Bannink, D. (2004) *The Reform of Dutch Disability Insurance: A Confrontation of a Policy Learning and a Policy Feedback Approach to Welfare State Change*, Dissertation, Enschede: University of Twente.

Boin, A., P. 't Hart (2000) 'Institutional Crises and Reforms in Policy Sectors'

Wagenaar, H. (ed.) *Government Institutions: Effects, Changes and Normative Foundations*, Dordrecht: Kluwer Academic Publishers, pp. 9–32.

Bonoli, G., B. Palier (1998) 'Changing the Politics of Social Programmes: Innovative Change in British and French Welfare Reforms' *Journal of European Social Policy* vol. 8 (4) pp. 317–330.

Bos, C. (1999) *De Institutionele crisis in het WAO-beleid. Fictie of feit?* MA Thesis, Leiden: Leiden University.

Caminada, C.L.J., K.P. Goudswaard (2003) *Verdeelde zekerheid: De verdeling van baten en lasten van sociale zekerheid en pensioenen*, Den Haag: Sdu Uitgevers.

De Jong, Ph.R. (1999) 'Reforming Social Policy: Learning from the Dutch Experience' *Swiss Journal of Economics and Statistics*, vol. 135 (3) pp. 253–271.

Esping-Andersen, G. (1990) *The Three Worlds of Welfare Capitalism*, Princeton: Princeton University Press.

Esping-Andersen, G. (1999) *Social Foundations of Postindustrial Economies*, Oxford: Oxford University Press.

Jaspers, A.Ph.C.M. (2001) *De gemeenschap is aansprakelijk: honderd jaar sociale verzekering 1901–2001*, Lelystad: Vermande.

Hall, P.A. (1993) 'Policy Paradigms, Social Learning, and the State: The Case of Economic Policymaking in Britain' *Comparative Politics* vol. 25 (3) pp. 275–296.

Hendriks, F., T.A.J. Toonen (2001) 'Introduction: Towards an Institutional Analysis of Dutch Consensualism' Toonen, T.A.J, F. Hendriks (eds), *Polder Politics*, Aldershot: Ashgate pp. 3–20.

Klamer, A. (1990) *Verzuilde dromen: 40 jaar SER*, Amsterdam: Balans.

Kuipers, S.L. (2006) *The Crisis Imperative: Crisis Rhetoric and Welfare State Reform in Belgium and the Netherlands in the Early 1990s*, Amsterdam: Amsterdam University Press.

Leemans, A.F. (1976) 'A Conceptual Framework for the Study of Reform of Central Government' Leemans, A.F. (ed.) *The Management of Change in Government*, The Hague: Martinus Nijhoff pp. 65–98.

Mishra, R. (1990) *The Welfare State in Capitalist Society: Policies of Retrenchment and Maintenance in Europe, North America and Australia*, New York: Harvester Wheatsheaf.

NRC Handelsblad (14 January 1992) *Het belangrijkst is de aanpak van de harde kern werklozen*.

Official Reports of the House of Representatives, 1991–1992.

Pierson, P. (1994) *Dismantling the Welfare State? Reagan, Thatcher, and the Politics of Retrenchment*, Cambridge: Cambridge University Press.

Schendelen, M.P.C.M. van, B.M.J. Pauw (1998) *Lobbyen in Nederland: Professie en profijt*, Den Haag: Sdu Uitgevers.

Social Economic Council (1984) Advies hoofdlijnen gewijzigd stelsel van sociale zekerheid bij werkloosheid en arbeidsongeschiktheid, nr.84/16, The Hague: SER.

Social Economic Council (1995) Kabinetsvoornemens ZW, AAW en WAO, nr.95/05, The Hague: SER.

Sociaal en Cultureel Rapport (1990) Rijswijk/Den Haag: Sociaal en Cultureel Planbureau/VUGA.

Terry, L.D. (2003) *Leadership of Public Bureaucracies. The Administrator as Conservator*, New York: M.E. Sharpe 2nd edition.

Therborn, G. (1986) *Why Some People Are More Unemployed Than Others*, London: Verso.

TK 22011, no. 7, Hoofdlijnen van een nieuwe uitvoeringsorganisatie sociale verzekeringen; Motie van het lid Buurmeijer c.s., 1991.

TK 22555, no. 1-2, Toezicht door de Sociale Verzekeringsraad; Brief van de Algemene Rekenkamer; Rapport, 1991.

TK 22730, no. 7-8, Parlementaire enquête uitvoeringsorganen sociale verzekeringen; Brief van de enquêtecommissie; Rapport van de commissie, 1993.

TK 22730, no. 18, Parlementaire enquête uitvoeringsorganen sociale verzekeringen; Motie van het lid Brouwer, 1993.

TK 22730, no. 20, Parlementaire enquête uitvoeringsorganen sociale verzekeringen; Motie van het lid Van Mierlo, 1993.

TK 22730, no. 24, Parlementaire enquête uitvoeringsorganen sociale verzekeringen; Gewijzigde motie van het lid Wöltgens c.s. ter vervanging van die gedrukt onder nr. 22, 1993.

TK 23141, no. 12, De aanpassing van de uitvoeringsorganisatie sociale verzekeringen (nieuwe Organisatiewet sociale verzekeringen); Tweede nota van wijziging, 1993.

TK 26448, no. 7, Structuur van de uitvoering werk en inkomen (SUWI); Brief minister en staatssecretaris met het nader kabinetsstandpunt over de toekomstige Structuur Werk en Inkomen, 2000.

TK 27588, no. 3, Wet structuur uitvoeringsorganisatie werk en inkomen; Memorie van toelichting, 2001.

Trouw (17 January 1992) *Snijden in uitkeringen de gemakkelijkste weg.*

Veen, R.J. van der (1990) *De sociale grenzen van beleid: Een onderzoek naar de uitvoering en effecten van het stelsel van sociale zekerheid*, Leiden: Stenfert Kroese.

Veen, R.J. van der, D. Bannink, R. Pierik, W. Trommel (1996) *De toekomst van de Sociale Zekerheid*, Amsterdam: Welboom.

Veldkamp, G.M.J. (1978) *Inleiding tot de sociale zekerheid en de toepassing ervan in Nederland en België*, Dl. 1: Karakter en geschiedenis, Deventer: Kluwer.

Visser, J., A.C. Hemerijck (1997) *'A Dutch Miracle': Job growth, welfare reform and corporatism in the Netherlands,* Amsterdam: Amsterdam University Press.

Vlek, R.J.J. (1997) *Inactieven in Actie: Belangenstrijd en belangenbehartiging van uitkeringsgerechtigden in de Nederlandse politiek 1974–1994*, Groningen: Wolters Noordhoff.

Wijnbergen, C. van (2000). *Co-opting the Opposition: The Role of Party Competition and Coalition-Making in Curing the Dutch Welfare State.* New Haven, Yale University: Paper for the graduate student training retreat in comparative research.

Chapter 8

Modernizing English Local Government: Voice, Loyalty, and Exit in the Demise of the Committee System

Francesca Gains

Introduction

This chapter examines how the New Labour Government in the UK reformed the long-established committee system of political management in English local government and introduced a separation of powers in all but the smallest authorities. The Local Government Act 2000 was the central plank in New Labour's local government modernization agenda.[1] The New Labour modernizers' critique of existing local government structures was that they were inefficient, obscured that the real power lay with party elites, and also did not encourage outward looking decision-making. The aims of the Act were to enhance the efficiency, transparency, and accountability of decision-making, and to improve trust in the conduct of local decision-making.

The reforms ensured that all councils with populations over 85,000 had to move from a committee system, whereby (in theory) all of a council's decisions were made by the whole council but could be delegated to politically balanced committees, to the creation of a separate political executive holding decision-making powers. Three different executive options were possible: a leader cabinet system, a mayor cabinet system, and a mayor working in tandem with a council manager. The mayoral options represented the most radical change as a mayor is elected on a separate mandate. However, most local authorities (i.e. councils) adopted the leader cabinet executive form whereby the leader of the majority group or of a coalition is supported by a small cabinet of executive councillors with a portfolio responsibility. The remaining non-executive councillors were to have new roles as community champions, freed up from endless committee debating, and now able to spend time

---

1   In the English system of local government there are 388 local authorities or councils each covering a defined geographical area. The council is made up of locally elected representatives or councillors who represent their locality. This chapter draws on an evaluation of the Local Government 2000 Act, which changed the political management arrangements in these authorities, for the Office of the Deputy Prime Minister conducted by the Evaluating Local Governance (ELG) research team (see www.elgnce.org.uk for details).

in their communities. Non-executives were also given new powers of overview and scrutiny of the executive.

The Local Government Act 2000 fundamentally changed the governance arrangements, requiring a huge institutional and cultural change in decision-making processes and in the roles played by both local bureaucrats (from hereon referred to as officers) and councillors. Yet the legislation permitted an extraordinary degree of flexibility in how it could be adopted: local authorities could choose which executive option to operate. An examination of the adoption of the Local Government Act 2000 provides a helpful case study for this volume as various barriers were present – both at the national and the local level.

The following section of this chapter will provide background on the local government sector in the UK and the guiding formal and informal rules of the game, namely a committee system of decision-making and strong party control. The section concludes with a brief discussion of previous reform attempts and the barriers that blocked these attempts. Section three describes the Act; its contents as well as how it was created. Section four addresses how national barriers were overcome. Local barriers are explained in section five, whereas how these local barriers were overcome is described in section six. The chapter concludes by suggesting that reform was driven by a strong government with a window of opportunity to enforce mandatory change overcoming local veto. Despite the possibility for local lock-in in adopting the provisions of the Act, fundamental change was realized as the reforms incentivized executive councillors and officers offering an enhanced decision-making role or *voice*. This driver for change was joined by the public service motivation or *loyalty* of officers recognizing the legitimacy of central government policy choices. Finally the *exit* of many non-executive councillors permitted new entrants, better able to adopt the new standard operating procedures (cf. Hirschman, 1970).

Traditional decision-making in English local government

The local government sector in England is made up of 388 separate principal local authorities responsible for the management and delivery of public services across a wide range of functions: education, social care, housing, the collection and removal of waste, libraries, roads, street lighting. The rural areas of England have a two-tier system with large county authorities with responsibility for education and social services sitting over smaller district authorities who provide more local services like housing and waste management. In the rest of England, there is a single tier system, with metropolitan-authorities in the large urban areas and unitary authorities centred around large market towns (Wilson & Game, 2002). Although with the introduction of New Public Management ideas of privatization, out-sourcing and a greater focus on partnership, less and less services are delivered in-house, it is still the job of local councillors to ensure the provision of services and make political decisions about how that provision is delivered (Sullivan & Skelcher, 2002). Locally elected councillors can point to their electoral mandate in providing legitimacy for their activities.

Yet despite this vast sphere of competence, comparatively speaking, English local government has far less autonomy than its continental or American counterpart (Denters & Rose, 2005). English local government is answerable to the national government, which has legislative and financial power over the sector. Local authorities only raise one quarter of the taxes needed to provide services, with the remainder coming from central government in the form of grants. Due to this set-up, the local government sector has historically been limited in the extent it could depart from national policy directives (Wilson & Game, 2002) – especially since in recent years, the provision of central grants has been increasingly tied to achieving specific performance goals agreed upon with the Treasury (Stoker, 2004a).

Since the nineteenth century, the political management of local government has been organized under the committee system where the decision-making power of the full council is delegated to politically balanced committees, and in turn sub-committees, with functional responsibilities such as education, housing, social services, and waste disposal (Stoker et al., 2003; Stoker 2004a; Stewart, 2003). Each committee had representatives of all the political parties on the council and as each committee deliberated and passed recommendations up to the next tier. In theory every elected member of the authority played a role in decision-making. The advantages of this system were its inclusiveness as well as the opportunities it afforded for interested parties to become involved in the various decision-making stages.

However, the virtues of this system also provided the basis for weaknesses. The very nature of the committee system led critics to argue that the slow and protracted decision-making was very inefficient and inflexible. This was partly due to elected members becoming too involved in detailed matters which should have been decided by officers (Stoker et al., 2003). A second major criticism was that the ostensible openness of the committee-style decision-making belied the fact that in recent years decision-making in local government was undertaken by the party in power (Bulpitt, 1976; Copus, 1999). For critics of the system, this strong party control of decision-making meant that the party in power dominated committees, and decisions were actually made in private party meetings that were not publicly accountable (Stoker, 2004a).

Previous attempts had been made to reform the system (for a more detailed history, see Stoker et al., 2003, and Stewart, 2003). The Maud Committee sought to introduce management boards made up of five to nine leading councillors to set the policy direction (Maud, 1967). The Maud-proposals, which were not statutory, were comprehensively rejected by the local government community, unwilling to alter the traditional style of committee decision-making (Stewart, 2003: 56). As Leach, Stewart and Walsh point out, 'it challenged the committee system, and therefore the role of the councillor. It lay beyond the boundaries set by the dominant organizational assumptions' (1994: 29). In 1987, the Widdecombe Committee re-examined the arguments of the Maud Committee and concluded that the Maud Committee's recommendations would improve efficiency but would have a detrimental effect on the officer role in asking them to serve the management board made up of executive councillors and backbench councillors at the same time (1986). Although the Widdecombe Report led to some changes (for example on the ability of senior officers to be active politically), the Report concluded that the committee system was the most suitable way of allocating decision-making powers (Stoker et al., 2003). In the early 1990s, the then Secretary of State Heseltine brought forward proposals for local authorities to organize on the basis of a cabinet system of decision-making, and for the possibilities of an elected mayor. But the legislation was again lenient and local authorities did not respond (Stewart, 2003: 57). By 1993, Heseltine had moved and further encouragement for experimentation was not taken up.

Three previous attempts at reform had floundered and the explanation is threefold. First, both elected councillors and officers were normatively and institutionally committed to a traditional policy paradigm (March & Olsen, 1984; Hall, 1993). In this policy paradigm, decision-making in local government was linked to the ideas and practices of the committee system underpinned by the realities of effective party control of decision-making. Change to that policy paradigm and the principle that decision-making was collective was so deeply ingrained in cultural and institutional practices that change seemed unthinkable. Second, as a consequence of the UK party system, successive national governments were unwilling to impose reform that would be unwelcome to their supporters in local government. Many Members of Parliament (MPs) have held office in local government and local parties provide financial, campaigning, and organizational support for national representatives. Finally, previous attempts to introduce reform had failed because these reforms had not been mandatory. Consequently, local authorities could refuse to implement these reforms (i.e. they had a veto-point). The fourth and finally successful attempt is described in the following section.

Introducing a separation of powers in English local government

In the run up to the 1997 general election the then opposition New Labour party, lead by Blair, gained ascendancy in the polls and formulated serious policy proposals for government. Their 'Third Way' approach married an acknowledgement of the financial and managerial realities of New Public Management for the public sector with an understanding of the need for networked governance and the desire for an active and accountable state (Gains, 2003: 14; Stoker, 2004a). Proposals for local government modernization were influenced by an independent review of local democracy by the Commission for Local Democracy whose report called for more accountability and transparency in local decision-making (1995). The Commission called for options for elected mayors and this idea was taken up in pre-election campaigning. Once elected, Blair wrote a pamphlet that made the case for reform (Blair, 1998), and in establishing a new Greater London Authority, the idea of a mayor and assembly was enacted. Alongside this development in London's arrangements, the case for a wider reform of local government was expressed in two White Papers (DETR 1998, 1999).

The White Papers criticized the existing system for its lack of transparency, accountability, and efficiency. The proposed solution was to reorganize the decision-making to introduce a separation of power with a smaller executive group of councillors proposing and implementing policies to speed up decision-making and encourage more responsive and outward facing policy-making. With more clearly defined responsibility for decisions, it was argued the system would be more transparent and encourage more public interest in the activities of the executive. The remaining majority of non-executive councillors would have more time to represent their local constituents and to play a new role in scrutinizing the work of the executive through overview and scrutiny committees.

The Government published a draft Local Government (Organization and Standards) Bill 1999, which contained three models, all of which suggested a separation of executive and non-executive roles: a directly elected mayor with a cabinet; a directly elected mayor and council manager; and a cabinet with a leader. A directly elected mayor would serve as the political leader for that community, supported by a cabinet drawn from among the council members chosen by the mayor. Depending on local political circumstances and choices, the cabinet may be formed from a single party or from a coalition of parties, and cabinet members could hold their own portfolios and were empowered to take executive decisions. In the mayor and council manager model, the mayor's role would be primarily one of influence, guidance, and leadership, defining strategic policy with day-to-day decision-making delegated to the council manager.

The third model, a cabinet with a leader, came closest to existing practice in majority controlled authorities. Under this form the leader is decided by the council, while the cabinet is made up of councillors, either appointed by the leader, or elected by the council. As with a directly elected mayor, the cabinet could be drawn from a single party or a coalition. The leader might define the portfolios of the cabinet. The cabinet can take decisions collectively, but decision-making power could also be given to individual cabinet members or the leader.

In July 2000, following the standing committee discussions, the Bill moved back and forth between the Commons and Lords with two significant amendments eventually changing the original proposals. In the Commons, for the Bills report stage and third reading, the government brought forward an amendment to address the concerns of local authority associations and pressure groups who argued that private executive decision-making undermined the transparency and accountability of the reforms. The Amendment required that executives publish a forward plan of forthcoming key decisions so the public could be aware of what decisions would be made and on what basis. The provision also permitted scrutiny committees to call in executive decisions for scrutiny before they were implemented. In response to pressures from opposition parties, the government accepted a final concession and allowed smaller authorities a wider set of choices. The key argument was that these authorities would have perhaps neither the political nor administrative resources to implement one of the three main models under the Act. Therefore a fourth option was offered, of adopting alternative arrangements based on adaptations of the existing committee system and the introduction of scrutiny systems. This is available only to authorities with a population under 85,000 and as a fall-back in the case of a no-vote in a mayoral referendum. The Bill finally passed through its parliamentary stages on 25 July 2000.

The Act passed responsibility for decision-making in most areas to an executive, and the new constitutions permitted greater delegation of decision-making to officers and individual cabinet members. The centrality of party politics in local government was acknowledged in that single party executives were permitted, and also within the role parties played in setting a policy and budget framework. However guidance on the Act stressed that party politics were to play no part in the new scrutiny arrangements. In adopting the provisions of the reform, each authority could choose which model to adopt, what kind of powers to give to executive councillors, and how this power was to be checked by non-executive councillors in their constitutions. In theory at least, the old policy paradigm was to be displaced by the idea of a separation of powers in local government decision-making.

Barriers and facilitators at the national level

During previous attempts, the barrier at the national level had consisted of the UK party system, which had made national governments unwilling to impose reform unwelcome to their supporters at the local level whose preferences were to maintain the existing policy paradigm. These barriers were overcome by a combination of three facilitators. First, a *window of opportunity* was created by a revitalized and confident Labour party returning to power after eighteen years. The authority of the Labour leadership was strong, enabling national government to push the Act through. Second, the level of personal support by *Blair* for modernization of local government was strong as well. His support, helped the Act on its way (Stoker, 2004b). Third, the national government's *preferences* had shifted. New Labour's Third Way (i.e. the new preference) combined New Public Management (NPM), the need for accountability, and the need for networked governance – the new Act was just one of many expressions of the national government's new preference.

This preference for a reformed local authority was so strong, that Labour decided the reform should be mandatory, thereby robbing local authorities of their veto-point. Nevertheless, local authorities' power to choose between the various models of governance remained intact. Consequently, many decisions still had to be taken at the local level before the new Act could be adopted. As it turned out, barriers present during previous attempts still played a role in this reform process: actors at the local level still harboured a strong preference for maintaining the status quo, as they were committed to the traditional policy paradigm. The next section discusses the nature of the remaining local barriers to reform.

Identifying barriers to reform at the local level

Path dependency in institutional arrangements – sticking with a committee structure

It is clear that in writing their new constitutions many local authorities showed a path dependent approach to change in creating new institutional rules and roles for councillors and officers. The path dependency arose firstly from the effects due to the sunken investment committed to previous administrative and organizational arrangements (Pierson, 2000). So, for example, even though the legislation aimed to cut the number of meetings and to encourage scrutiny activities in order to work in a different way (possibly spending time outside town halls), it is clear that many authorities simply established their scrutiny meetings in place of the former committee and sub-committee meetings (Stoker et al., 2004). Similarly, although the new Act permitted individual executive members to take decisions alone as an efficiency measure, some authorities chose to establish advisory panels to sit in the room at the same time as executive members made their decisions, thereby effectively replicating committee-style decision-making (Stoker, et al., 2004).

Path dependency in the informal rules – strong party control

Strong party control was a feature of the informal rules of the pre-reform policy paradigm (Dryzek, 1996). Strong party allegiances presented a barrier in local adoption of the Act. First, the party effect is apparent when looking at which authorities have moved to a strong executive model. Labour-run authorities are more likely to have weaker leadership structures reflecting their more collectivist party traditions and ethos (Stoker, et al., 2003). A party effect is also observable when looking at the degree to which impartial scrutiny has been realized. For example, despite guidelines stating that party meetings should be discouraged and party whipping is not permitted, whipping still occurs regularly at scrutiny meetings, showing the strong policy paradigm of party management accepted by many actors at the local level (Stoker, et al., 2003).

Resistance to change amongst local actors

As pointed out in chapter 1, reform is upsetting. Interviews highlight that the introduction of the new system has impacted the *feelings* of participants. One theme that is mentioned time and time again by both elected members and officers is that non-executives have experienced a form of bereavement. For example, one officer said 'they mourn for the old system', and a non-executive councillor explained they 'mourned the loss of committees' (interviews conducted for Evaluating Local Governance (ELG) research). It is argued here that to understand the responses of individuals towards change, it is necessary to acknowledge their emotive or affective response to institutional arrangements. Marris argues that actors operate within structures of meaning that help to make sense of their actions (1974). Uninitiated change challenges those structures of meaning and invokes a response to change that is ambivalent. 'The will to adapt to change has to overcome an impulse to restore the past' (Marris, 1974: 5). Those subject to uninitiated change need to overcome the conservative impulse and find new structures of meaning for themselves in the changed circumstance they are operating in. This transition is an emotional adjustment and involves a temporal element. For many actors at the local level it will take time to change the way they act and operate to reflect the new decision-making processes.

Facilitators of reform at the local level

A number of local barriers to reform have been identified. In summary, these reflect a strong existing policy paradigm in local government centred around the committee system of decision-making, underpinned by strong party control with local councillors and bureaucrats normatively and institutionally committed to this policy paradigm. This is particularly the case for non-executive councillors for whom the changes were unwelcome and unsettling. While deciding which model to choose, local authorities not only faced local barriers, but also dwindling support from the national level for the mayoral option. Following electoral difficulties for New Labour in the election of a mayor for London and in devolution for Scotland and Wales, support by the New Labour leadership for the mayoral option ebbed away, and there was minimal central pressure on Labour authorities to take the most radical option (Pimlott & Rao, 2002; Stoker, 2004b). Yet, eleven authorities (3%) managed to overcome the tough referendum criteria set out in the Act and adopt the mayoral option (with only one adopting the mayor and council manager option). Most authorities (81%) took the leader cabinet form, with the remaining 16% of small authorities opting to operate a streamlined committee system (Stoker, et al., 2003).

Despite local barriers and dwindling support from national government for the mayoral option, three out of four authorities choosing the leader cabinet model made significant changes introducing either constitutional arrangements suggesting strong leadership or strong scrutiny functions or both, in line with the aims of the policy makers (Gains, John & Stoker, 2005). How were these barriers overcome?

New standard operating procedures created benefits

There is strong evidence that benefits played a major role in encouraging the adoption of radically new standard operating procedures (Ostrom, 1997). Two groups of actors stood to benefit most from the reforms. First, executive councillors could receive higher remuneration and hold all the executive authority in the Council. One leader of a large county authority operating a leader cabinet system explained, 'The Act makes it easier to get things done rather than [being] lost in committees'. A chief officer in an urban area also with a leader cabinet system commented that under the new system, 'politicians are less hands-on and more strategic' (Interviews for the ELG research). In a survey of officers and councillors in a sample group of forty authorities, almost half of executive councillors reported that the new arrangements were an improvement (for full results see Stoker, et al., 2004).

Second, officers also stood to benefit from the reforms through an increase in delegated decision-making powers. Officers have gained significant autonomy from the changes with 46% indicating increased delegated decision-making powers stemming from the reforms. The extent to which they voiced approval for the reform is correlated to experiencing increased delegated powers (Stoker, et al., 2004). Officers also benefited from the reform because working patterns changed to provide a much more focussed and less bureaucratic working relationship with executive councillors similar to that between ministers and senior civil servants (Gains, 2004). As one chief executive of an urban area with a leader cabinet system explained, 'Officers see the strength of the system. It is good for joined-up work and there is less danger of a *silo approach*'. Another chief officer in a mayoral authority argued that the new system 'is more holistic and a much better decision-making process. There is no scope for incoherence' (interviews for the ELG research). For both these actors there is a strong incentive to changing practices and roles in line with the aims of the policy makers in order to gain those benefits.

Public service ethos

Pratchett and Wingfield identified some shared public service values in local government including the need for accountability, adherence to political authority, and sense of community (1996). These values were apparent in relation to the constitutional reform process. The ELG data highlights that these values may have acted to support the reform process. The ELG survey showed local bureaucrats' support for strong scrutiny and their dislike of party domination – aspects closely associated with a public service ethos in local government (Stoker, et al., 2004). This shared informal value system in relation to accountability would suggest why new standard operating procedures were adopted despite, in the case of the development of scrutiny, creating less than optimal operating conditions for officers, as they face the difficult role of serving both executive and non-executive councillors. A keen awareness of the legitimacy and political authority of central government to impose reform was indicated by ELG interview data. Officers drove the reform process in part to respond to the legislative imperative emanating from central government. One chief finance officer said, 'We respond to the national framework and have to play to the rules of the game' (ELG research). The final feature of a public service ethos is a concern for the wider community and this was also indicated in interview data. One chief executive, for instance, saw the reform as 'another opportunity to push things forward to improve the lot of the people of Tocksville' (Stoker, et al., 2004). The data suggests some support for the idea that even in authorities where the likely benefits of reform did not incentivize councillors and political resistance to adoption was high, officers still acted as a driving force in adopting the 2000 Act. They did this because of their public service motivation with its emphasis on adherence to political authority, stress on the value of accountability, and sense of community.

Overcoming resistance – taking the exit option

It is clear that for many non-executive councillors, one option in response to the degree of change required was to take the exit option and leave local government altogether. In some authorities the turnover of councillors means that as many as a quarter of the elected members are new and therefore have no institutional or normative commitment to the old policy paradigm (Stoker, et al., forthcoming). In some authorities anecdotal evidence suggests this churning is even higher (Stoker, et al., 2004).

Conclusion

The Local Government Act 2000 radically altered the institutional arrangements for political management in local government in England, introducing a separation of powers into local government and the end of the committee-style of decision-making, which had existed since the nineteenth century. Elite support for the committee system policy paradigm had been gradually eroded over the previous thirty years, under the influence of managerialist ideas, which first found expression in the 1960s. When New Labour came to power in 1997, these managerialist ideas were joined by a concern to enhance democratic legitimacy at the local level and the new government was influenced by reformist ideas emanating from an independent commission for local democracy. The reform benefited by being introduced by a strong government at the beginning of its first term of office. It was the first time for 18 years that Labour was in office again. The party accepted the need for changes in policy. This, combined with its strong electoral victory provided a window of opportunity for reform. The leadership of the party were enthused by modernization and such was their confidence following a strong electoral mandate that they were able to ensure change was mandatory – effectively overcoming the previous veto point of local adoption. Two significant concessions offered during the Bill's legislative stages bolstered support from the local government associations and pressure groups and gave a coherent new alternative to the committee system offering checks and balances to the increased executive power.

The most radical option, namely the mayoral authorities, suffered from a lack of political drive once the legislation was in place. Nevertheless, most authorities adopted a leader cabinet system ensuring significant change. In adopting the leader cabinet system variations were possible and there were opportunities for barriers in local adoption. Barriers included path dependency of the previous institutional arrangements and informal values around party loyalties and party traditions. Also noticeable was the impact of affective responses of non-executives to the reform involving feelings of loss and nostalgia and adding to a reluctance to adopt new standard operating procedures.

However three facilitators assisted in overcoming these barriers, ensuring the reform was fundamental. First, and most obviously, reform was driven by executive councillors and officers who could see benefits in terms of their access to decision-making power. Second, and perhaps less obvious, it is argued that the strong public service motivation of officers acted to drive reform. Finally, resistance from non-executive councillors for whom the reform required the biggest change in role and responsibilities was minimized because of the turnover of councillors.

References

Blair, T. (1998) *Leading the Way: A New Vision for Local Government*, London: IPPR.

Bulpitt, J.G. (1976) *Party Politics in English Local Government*, London: Longman.

Commission for Local Democracy (1995) *Taking Ccharge: The Rebirth of Local Democracy*, London: Commission for Local Democracy.

Copus, C. (1999) 'The Party Group: A Barrier to Democratic Renewal' *Local Government Studies*, vol. 25 (4), pp. 77–98.

Denters, B., L. Rose (2005) *Comparing Local Governance*, Basingstoke: Palgrave Macmillan.

DETR (1998) *Modern Local Government: In touch with the People*, London: Department of the Environment, Transport and the Regions.

DETR (1999) *Local Leadership, Local Choice*, London: Department of the Environment, Transport and the Regions.

Dryzek, J. (1996) 'The Informal Logic of Institutional Design' Goodin, R (ed.) *The Theory of Institutional Design*, Cambridge: Cambridge University Press, pp. 103–125.

Gains, F. (2004) 'The Local Bureaucrat? A Block to Reform or a Key to Unlocking Change?' Stoker, G., D. Wilson (eds), *Local Government in a New Century*, Houndmills: Palgrave, pp. 91–106.

Gains, F. (2003) 'Surveying the Landscape of Modernisation: Executive Agencies under New Labour' *Public Policy and Administration* 18 (2) pp. 4–20.

Gains, F., P. John, P. Stoker (2005) 'Path Dependency and the Reform of English Local Government' *Public Administration* vol. 83 (1), pp. 25–46.

Hall, P. (1993) 'Policy Paradigms, Social learning and the State' *Comparative Politics*, vol. 25 (3), pp. 275–296.

Hirschman, A.O. (1970) *Exit, Voice and Loyalty: Responses to decline in Firms, Organizations, and States*, Cambridge: Harvard University Press.

Leach, S., J. Stewart, K. Walsh (1994) *The Changing Organisation and Management of Local Government*, Basingstoke: Macmillian.

March, J., J. Olsen (1984) 'The New Institutionalism: Organisational Factors in Political Life' *American Political Science Review*, vol. 78, pp.743–749.

Marris, P. (1974) *Loss and Change*, London: Routledge and Kegan Paul.

Maud (1967), *Volume 2: The Local Government Councillor, Report of the Committee on the Management of Local Government*, London: HMSO.

Ostrom, E. (1997) 'Investing in Capital, Institutions and Incentives' Clague, C. (ed) *Institutions and Economic Development*. Baltimore: John Hopkins University Press.

Pierson, P. (2000) 'Increasing Returns, Path Dependence, and the Study of Politics' *American Political Science Review*, vol. 94, pp.251–267.

Pimlott, B., N. Rao (2002) *Governing London*, Oxford: OUP.

Pratchett, L., M. Wingfield (1996) 'Petty Bureaucracy and Woolly-minded Liberalism? The Changing Ethos of Local Government Officers' *Public Administration*, 74 (4) 639–656.

Stewart, J. (2003) *Modernising British Local Government*, Basingstoke: Palgrave Macmillan

Stoker, G. (2004a) *Transforming Local Governance*, Basingstoke: Palgrave Macmillan.

Stoker, G. (2004b) *How are Mayors Measuring Up*, London: ODPM, www.elgnce. org.uk.

Stoker, G. F. Gains, A. Harding, P. John, N. Rao (2003) *Implementing the 2000 Act with respect to New Council Constitutions and the Ethical Framework: First Report and Executive Summary*, London: ODPM, www.elgnce.org.uk.

Stoker, G., F. Gains, S. Greasley, P. John, N. Rao, A. Harding (2004) *Operating the New Council Constitutions in English Local Authorities: A Process Report*, London: ODPM www.elgnce.og.uk.

Stoker, G., F. Gains, S. Greasley, P. John, N. Rao (forthcoming) *Report of the 2005 Councillor, Officer and Stakeholder Survey*, www.elgnce.org.uk, London: Office of the Deputy Prime Minister.

Sullivan, H., C. Skelcher (2002) *Working across boundaries*. Basingstoke: Palgrave Macmillian.

Widdecombe Committee, (1986) *The Report of the Inquiry into the Conduct of Local Authority Business*, London: HMSO.

Wilson, D., C. Game (2002) *Local Government in the UK*, London: Palgrave.

Chapter 9

District Development Planning in Heidelberg: Realizing Change through Political Leadership and Community Involvement

Michael Haus[1]

The successful introduction of participatory policy-making in urban planning

Heidelberg is a German city of approximately 140,000 inhabitants, located in the Land (state) of Baden-Wuerttemberg. In 1990, at the beginning of the first term as a directly elected mayor, Mayor Weber started the initiative of so-called *district development planning* (*Stadtteilrahmenplanung*, hereafter: DDP) in order to meet three main objectives: to improve and enrich the knowledge base for a decentralized form of city planning, to integrate various branches of municipal administration and policy fields, and to address and foster the identification of citizens with their district. Besides the fact that this (among other initiatives) was a way of realizing participatory and post-materialist ideas which the mayor had stressed during her election campaign, DDP was motivated by the fact that city planning had focused on the overall city without having detailed information available on the district level. Furthermore, the famous old inner city part had dominated restructuring efforts, whereas the mayor held and promulgated the concept that the districts outside of the old inner city, in which citizens led their daily lives, could also be involved.

The plan was to carry out individual planning processes for each of the city's 14 districts, while at the same time maintaining a common design in every process. In a first step, this meant taking stock of the history, current situation, and future options of each district. In a second step, proposals for policy measures were to be worked

1 The following account stems from an international research project, financed by the European Commission, which focused on the interplay between political leadership and community involvement in different European cities. Empirical analysis is primarily based on document analysis, interviews with key actors and participatory observation. The results of the German findings from this PLUS (*Participation, Leadership and Urban Sustainability*) project were published in an English research report (Egner et al., 2004, for a summary see Haus et al., 2006; Egner et al., 2006) and as book in German language (Haus et al., 2006). The author is grateful to Hubert Heinelt, Björn Egner and especially Christine König.

out together with citizens. For the city of Heidelberg, this was the first time that a decentralized structure of city settlement was acknowledged in the city's planning procedures.

Participatory processes are often bound to fail completely or lead to dissatisfying results, starting with enthusiastic promises and ending with cynical disillusionment. This does not seem to have been the case in DDP. Whereas, on the political side, central actors like deputy heads and local politicians have come to accept DDP as a regular element in urban planning, participation in single districts has been widened over the years. That is why DDP has gained national attention in comparative analyses of city planning and administrative reform policies (Schneider, 1997; Jaedicke, et al., 2000; Egner et al., 2006; Haus, et al., 2006). The fate of DDP in Heidelberg is remarkable because it required a long-term effort of the whole administration, which is rarely known to be achieved in city administrations of comparable size (2,200 employees in 2002). Although the directly elected mayor in Baden-Wuerttemberg is head of the entire administration, basic decisions must be taken by the city council. The three deputy mayors, who had different political affiliations, had led their directorates quite autonomously. In addition, there had been no stable majority in the council for the mayor to rely on. Against the background of this volume, the central question with respect to the Heidelberg case, then, is: why did Heidelberg succeed in carrying out an alternative approach to urban planning in a period of 15 years?

In the next section, the DDP process and its political context shall be presented in a more detailed way. This will highlight several barriers to reform, as well as challenges connected with the initiative. The astonishing element in the Heidelberg case, however, is not that fierce resistance had to be overcome by powerful political majorities. The main challenge was in upholding a long-term effort to carry out urban planning in a decentralized and participatory way. At the same time, this should not be confused with classical issues of effective implementation (which is not the focus of this volume). There was no once-and-for-all authoritative decision taken which was then to be implemented. This reform has to be understood less as a decision to be executed by the executive and the administrative brands of the city, and more as a commitment to a different way of doing politics. What is found in the Heidelberg case is the establishment of a *reiterative policy-making process*, which can fail every time it proceeds. Here, though, it did not fail.

In the following section, the idea behind DDP is described. Then, insights into the barriers that hampered reform are divulged, followed by a discussion of the facilitators which made it work. Attention is directed especially at the question of how political leadership and practices of community involvement helped to overcome barriers located within the formal institutions of local government. In a final section, general conclusions about barriers and facilitators are discussed by relating the case of DDP to the conceptual framework of this book.

District development framework planning in Heidelberg

Like most of the bigger cities in Germany, Heidelberg functions with two administrative units at the local level, i.e. municipality and county. It is thus responsible for cultural institutions, schools, municipal roads, fire protection, water supply and sewerage, garbage collection and disposal, and urban planning including land utilization, social support and welfare services. Besides the realm of local self-administration, the city also operates the lowest tier of state administration (here, the city council has no authority, but the mayor is the administrative head in charge). In the South German model of local government, both the mayor and the municipal council hold genuine democratic legitimacy and legal competence (dualism) (cf. Wollman 2003, 2004).

It was not before the 1980s that participatory initiatives began in Heidelberg's district politics. This was accomplished through the introduction of district councils, albeit they have only advisory functions to the city council. According to §65 of the municipal code of Baden-Wuerttemberg, the members of the district councils (Bezirksbeiräte) are districts' inhabitants appointed by the city council. Appointments correspond to the share of votes in the respective district. This means that party proportions vary from district to district. The municipal code stipulates that the district councils must be heard in all important matters affecting the district. For this, they formulate a statement and send a representative to meetings of council committees discussing the matter. The mayor is chair of all council committees and, thus, also of the district councils.

From all this, it becomes clear that the district councils can only gain influence by finding an internal consensus which can be powerfully presented to the city council, the administration, and/or the public. District councils can, however, also have an important function when disagreement prevails, because in this case differences in interest or problem perception become more transparent. Obviously, the district councils as such cannot provide for a decentralized policy approach because they cannot develop coherent concepts to this end.

From 1990 onwards, DDP was the leading district development concept in Heidelberg. DDP constitutes various institutional arenas of citizen participation linked with the formal bodies of local government (see figure 9.1). Roughly, two stages can be distinguished. In the first stage, information about the district is gathered in a systematic way and basic problems of the district's development are identified. In the second stage, proposals for developmental aims and policy measures are identified. The result is a fairly comprehensive documentation of knowledge and opinions about one of the city's districts, covering all policy sectors that engage any given city district. In this way, urban planning changes into integrative social development planning, in which construction and land use issues are discussed within broader policy questions, such as the question of housing and social services for different target groups. This stands in contrast to many German municipalities, where planning factually never transcended construction policy, and where more ambitious understandings of urban planning experienced a disillusionment after being fashionable in the 1970s (Albers, 1998: 572).

The DDP process contains specific practices of citizen participation: district meetings, future workshops, and thematic workshops with invited stakeholders. These institutional arenas of citizen participation are linked with the formal bodies of local government, i.e. the city council (including its committee for urban development) and the district councils.[2] In addition, there is an intra-administrative arena with two levels: the level of the top executives (the mayor and deputy mayors), and a working group with those offices giving inputs to the thematic workshops. This group will vary from district to district with the Office for Urban Development and Statistics as a core organizational unit. Almost all offices have participated in a workshop at least once, and since a framework plan covers practically all (urban) policy fields the number of participants will be quite high. For example, in the district framework plan for the district Emmertsgrund, there have been eighteen different expert inputs to the thematic workshops in 1998. They have come from many from city offices (urban development, citizens' office, public order, culture, schools, housing etc.) and institutions (e.g. the public library), but also from city-owned enterprises (for public transport, economic development, housing) and a housing co-op.

This institutional design (see figure 9.1) actually puts emphasis on the interaction of citizens/stakeholders, on the one hand, and administrative actors, on the other. The interaction between civil servants and citizens becomes especially clear in how the thematic workshops are designed. Here, representatives of the administration (sometimes senior officials or even deputy mayors) present ideas or projects currently under consideration in the administrative realm. Participants in the thematic workshops (assigned to specific working groups, e.g. social issues, traffic, urban planning) do not only meet the representatives of the city administration and put their own proposals on the agenda, but they are also entitled to give a vote on what they think are the most important and urgent measures. The employees can also give a vote. The opinions are thoroughly documented and then it is made public who (citizens/administration) has favoured which proposals. Consequently, citizens are more than just discussants, whereas the political and active role of the administration also becomes visible – quite contrary to a lot of New Public Management thinking, which wants administrators to manage and compete, and politicians to define goals (see Hood, 1991; Pollitt & Bouckaert, 2000).

---

2   The committee for urban development and traffic is an advisory committee of the city council headed (as all council committees) by the mayor. It is important for preparing decisions taken by the council and its meetings are public.

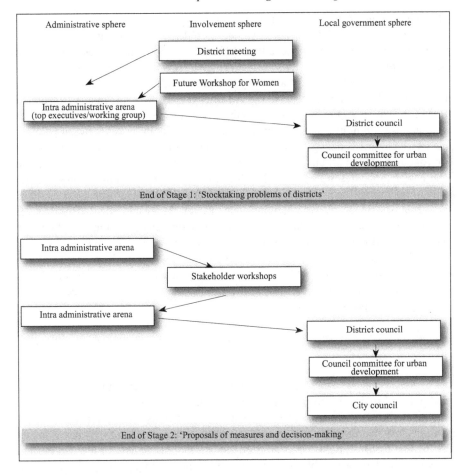

Figure 9.1   Arenas in District Development

The DDP reform: A case of potential failure

Participatory planning practices could not be found in Heidelberg before Mayor Weber took over office in 1990, despite the existence of vivid social movements (feminist, environmental etc.), as in most university cities, demanding more participation and having criticism on growth policies. The strength of new social movements was manifest in the electoral success of the Heidelbergian Green party, or better *Grüne Alternative Liste* (GAL), in 1984, when it was elected to eight seats in the council (out of 40). The GAL is formally independent from the national party organization, but shares, for example, the internet homepage. The rise of the Green Party and Green lists in Germany in the early 1980s was intimately connected to the new social movements. It is still reflected in the self-understanding of the GAL in

Heidelberg which calls itself 'the reservoir of ecologically and alternatively oriented forces in Heidelberg' (http://www.gruen-stark-heidelberg.de/30.0.html).

However, the city – and especially the (former) mayor – did not respond to these demands for changes in the city's political culture. Two factors can be pointed out as barriers to the development of a more participatory culture in Heidelberg. The first one is located in the power constellation in cities organized by the municipal code of Baden-Wuerttemberg in general, and in the city of Heidelberg in particular: various veto points within the municipal institutions require compromise between political actors which can be endangered by outsiders. Second, the leadership style of the former mayor obstructed a participative policy-making culture. Both the power constellation and leadership styles are connected with challenges in the administration's internal way of operating: the problem with initiating administrative reforms is to establish new routines which reflect changing demands of the environment (Brunsson & Olsen, 1993). For the city administration, participatory city planning would involve a new way of doing things which was an enormous challenge to established routines: city offices had to change from a sector way of thinking to a spatial way of thinking. To these factors, one may add the observation that there are many general sources of failures for citizen participation in local policy-making. The next sections will discuss these aspects more in detail.

A potentially obstructive power constellation and a non-participatory leadership style

As in presidential systems, the direct election of mayors brings with it the possibility that political majorities in the council may deviate from the party affiliation of the central political leadership. The fact that city politicians were reluctant to adopt participatory instruments and decentralized ways of planning can firstly be explained by the fact that uncertain power constellations – like in the case of directly elected mayors who lack a reliable majority in the council – imply the probability that mayors concentrate on their administrative powers and avoid conflicts over more 'political' questions (cf. Gissendanner, 2005). This was the case in Heidelberg. The former mayor (Zundel) concentrated on his administrative and budgetary powers in order to realize big infrastructure projects, which were economically and socially important according to a logic of urban growth and a functionalist view of social integration (constructing a city along considerations of functionally specified areas), but also brought prestige to his person. Examples are the construction of new city quarters 'from scratch', new university areas on the green field, and also the attempt to restore the old inner city part (Schneider, 1997). The mayor stuck to a more technocratic style of policy-making and held parties and citizens at a distance, and finally in 1981 even split with his party, the Social Democrats, and was thus without his own majority in city council. From the council elections in 1984 onward, he even faced a majority of opposing political forces in the council (comprised of Social Democrats, Greens and left Liberals).

Nevertheless, the old mayor was in office from 1966 to 1990 (re-elected twice).[3] There were no pressing financial problems or intractable societal actors that made fundamental change unavoidable. This changed in the last years of his tenure, when the majority of Green party and Social Democrats were heavily opposing what they considered to be an unlimited policy of growth. This led to severe conflicts and finally the decision of the mayor not to run for office again. The difficulty of realizing a participatory, decentralized way of urban planning was thus located in the *power centre* of city politics in Heidelberg and the policies produced by local decision-making.[4]

The mayor, the city council, and the deputy mayors were clear veto players in this decision-making process. According to the regulations laid down in the municipal code, *deputy mayors* are appointed by the council according to the strength of the parties. Furthermore, decisions about their respective portfolio must be decided by the mayor and the council in a consensual way, and so must decisions about important posts in the administration. However, once the deputy mayors have been elected, it is rather impossible to move them out of office before their tenure of eight years ends (the same with the directly elected mayor). Thus, it seems appropriate to consider the deputy mayors as veto players, at least when it comes to decisions which affect their responsibilities. Because of this strong interdependence between the mayor, the city council, and the deputy mayors, administrative objectives and political interests have to be accommodated if only to prevent that the deputy mayors resist policy proposals. These dynamics are often found in the analysis of municipal politics: regulations on the appointment and legal position of the deputy mayors characteristically leads to a kind of *administrative pluralism* which brings about the need for re-integration if policy-making shall not end in deadlock (Wehling, 2003: 27).

The same holds true for the *city council*: the main problem is not that councillors, in general, are resistant to citizen participation and urban districts as the focus for city planning. It is rather about political power and the distributions of accountability. Here, the role of district politics also has to be taken into consideration. District councils did not gain real importance until DDP started. Within DDP, district councillors are invited together with other key actors of the district to take part in planning workshops. In these workshops, proposals for measures are discussed and evaluated with votes by the participating key actors and members of the city administration. The district councils then decide whether they are in favour of the resultant plans, but they can comment on it in the city council. Thus, DDP also relies on the cooperation of the district councils, giving them also some kind of veto

---

3 Incumbents of the *mayoral position* in the South West of Germany, in general, have a very high chance of being re-elected, which together with the long tenure of eight years leads to experienced incumbents. Their power position within their party, however, is comparatively low (see Haus & Heinelt, 2002).

4 Characterized by Rolf-Richard Grauhan as a form of executive leadership (Grauhan, 1970).

power. Since district councils gain importance through the whole process they will likely support it – but at the same time, this can be considered as problematic by the city council that might fear losing importance.

Problems with the effectiveness of citizen participation

The robustness of DDP as a long-term endeavour, aiming to change the routines of public administration and urban politics, is also dependent upon the legitimacy of such attempts. In these cases, reflections on why participatory processes often fail are helpful to understand a possible reluctance towards DDP. Holtkamp (2005) summarized the reasons for re-occurring failure by stating that practices of citizen participation are often based on citizens discussing ambitious *visions*, that do not result in decisions about concrete measures; the implementation of visions is very uncertain and difficult to observe. Citizen participation is often introduced in combination with far-reaching promises of direct democracy – leading to disappointment when it becomes clear that local democracy is still to a large degree representative. In addition, citizen participation is embedded in comprehensive approaches to urban planning, suggesting that planning is a highly rational process, which conflicts with the incremental logic of most urban politics. Citizen participation sometimes also coincides with already existing crises, or failure due to budget pressure. Moreover, citizen participation may have to deal with veto power of societal actors that either leaves no room for creative processes, or results in changes in power positions of actors who can threaten to make use of their exit option. Finally, citizen participation runs the risk of creating problems with negative externalities because participants do not consider how others are affected by a decision, not least because participation in interactive policy-making is itself most often socially biased.

This list of sources of failure serves to elucidate why participation in urban politics is a risky endeavour and needs careful consideration of decent institutional design as well as intelligent network management. Less (with respect to rhetoric) can be more (with respect to satisfying processes), if participatory planning is to be more than a flash in the pan.

The DDP reform process

Due to the barriers mentioned above, the social movements in favour of more citizen participation did not gain ground within Heidelberg politics and the larger part of local society for a long time. As mentioned, this changed in the last years of Mayor Zundel's tenure, when the city council majority of the Green party and the Social Democrats (i.e. his originally own party) heavily opposed an unlimited policy of growth. The dismal state of the participation culture came more and more in conflict with growing expectations on the part of the population, leading to fierce struggles between the old mayor and the council majority that demanded urban policies that focused on quality of life issues instead of urban growth. In 1990, this led to the decision of the mayor to resign from office (cf. Schneider, 1997). A new candidate stepped forward: Weber.

A new mayor in town

With a policy background as a Member of European Parliament on environmentalist and feminist issues, but no experience in leading a municipal administration, Weber could not hope for gaining authority as a policy expert for the most important fields. Nevertheless, she was prudent in constructing an agenda which fitted her personality and her skills.[5] She presented herself in the election campaign as a candidate committed to the values of the *New Political Culture* (see Clark & Hoffmann-Martinot, 1998) and of communitarian ideas – a policy paradigm she referred to through her whole tenure as a mayor (see Weber, 1997). She stressed values of citizen participation, gender equality and quality of life and thus promised to promote post-material values in urban politics.

Weber was elected in 1990. At the beginning of her tenure, when the portfolios of the different directorates were to be settled anew to some extent, the Mayor made her organizational priorities very clear – reflecting the promise of citizen participation made in her election campaign (Schneider, 1997; Haus et al., 2006). She realized the founding of a new administrative unit, the Office for Urban Development and Statistics, as part of her own portfolio. In addition, she assured that the DDP process was developed by qualified civil servants. She searched for new employees with a multi-professional profile. In principle, the mayors and city council supported the idea of DDP. Open opposition against increased citizen participation would have been a very unpopular position. Who would oppose the fashionable idea of more citizen participation? The deputy mayors and city councillors may have hoped that they could step outside the shadow of the previous mayor's dominance in public discussions, if processes would become more open. Although there was no fierce opposition against the agenda of the mayor, there was scepticism on the part of local media and sections of the council, according to interview partners in the Office for Urban Development and Statistic. Both waited, backstage, the outcome of her agenda. This scepticism became more manifest in later stages of the process.

The start of DDP

DDP was the mayor's idea, but the concrete design of the initiative was worked out together with the Office for Urban Development and Statistics, in cooperation

---

5   One may wonder whether this engagement for participation and networking must be explained by referring to ideas and norms (cultural approach) or to strategic action (calculus approach). The general clause is that politicians must always think in terms of power and strategic action, as could also be the case within promoting citizen participation. If one has a look at Weber's rhetoric, there is no indication to think that her plans are something she would not actually believe in.

with a private consultant. At its meeting on 4 March 1992, the city council's committee for urban development approved the DDP concept as having the status of 'a self-commitment of the city' concerning implications for construction plans and infrastructural measures, as well as setting fiscal priorities (Drucksache, 267/92). As mentioned above, DDP for all the 14 districts took 15 years, which was more time than originally intended. However, in average, actually one DDP was finished per year, which can be considered as a respectable outcome, probably without parallel in the world of German municipal politics.[6] The first DDP project was carried out in the district of Kirchheim at the early time of 1991, and the first thematic workshops for this district were held in 1995. The involvement of city actors followed a coherent line. The workshops were not simply an open forum to talk about the future of the district, since there were representatives from a broad range of city offices. These representatives presented concrete plans, thus carrying responsibility for at least a part of the agenda discussed at the workshops. All proposals were discussed within an informal group of administrative leaders, and another group of city employees was occupied with the concrete preparation and realization of policies.

Increasing resistance to DDP in action

The mayor was confronted with the problem of power politics already within the first DDP. The city council, as well as those at the top of the administration, interpreted DDP as a decrease in their authority. The straightforwardness of the mayor in promoting the participatory agenda (which, besides DDP, comprised several other projects, especially in the realm of hotly debated traffic policy) irritated the council and induced the pressure to redefine its role. The council, for example, did not agree with the political status of measures mentioned in the district plans. In 1991, already, the first DDP – which concerned a plan for a new tram line – was not formally confirmed by the city council. Other DDP plans also contained conflictive topics, mainly touching infrastructural projects and questions of settlement. Furthermore, the council interpreted the definition of DDP ('a framework for further decisions') as a decrease of their authority. Councillors wanted to be in charge of measures proposed by the participating citizens, especially in times of budget pressure. But they also disliked the procedure that with affirming one plan they were also affirming all the small proposals made within it. As a consequence very small measures, like a new bicycle track, put a serious threat to the plans as a whole (interview with the head of the Office for Urban Development and Planning, in: Haus et al, 2006).

The city treasurer and other top administrators responded in the same defensive manner. Although, in 1994, the council's committee for urban development had accepted formulation that proposals were to be made 'in a standardized form', including 'costs and time horizons for financing', and should be included in middle-

---

6   There is no complete empirical overview on planning processes in all German cities. Judging from available literature and information given by practitioners, however, no other example with an exhaustive decentralized urban developmental planning is known.

term financial planning (Drucksache, 794/94), they resisted it later on. This was because such operating procedures would have reduced flexibility and influence in decision-making in a time of higher fiscal pressure.

DDP is adjusted

Since Weber expected the objection of the first district plan by the councillors and wanted to prevent the whole process from failure due to single conflicts, she decided that the highly controversial issues of the new tramline should be discussed in a special planning forum. An effect of learning from this early experience was that certain topics (not least implying difficult NIMBY problems)[7] could not be decided by DDP. Another outreach to the council was made after the fourth DDP in 1997. The city council representatives (the so-called Ältestenrat), the mayor, as well as other representatives of the administration, tried to settle a reinterpretation of the rules. These rules included that measures mentioned in a DDP would not automatically be implemented but should involve agreement within the city council. Hence, the character of the plans was changing, which made the top administrators and councillors more cooperative. DDP changed from a hard planning tool to a sketch of sensible measures within the districts that could be used to hold administration and council accountable. As a result of these changes, all other DDP-proposals were accepted within the city council.

DDP is adjourned

In 1993, the Mayor wrote a letter to all councillors informing that DDP would take seven years longer than originally intended. The local media proclaimed the slow death of the whole project: 'What a mammoth undertaking! A project certainly well-intended, but unfortunately a project whose final failure can well be foreknown by now' (Rhein-Neckar Zeitung, 29 October 1993). More and more actors (chamber of architects, local politicians) criticized a lacking cohesiveness of the district planning with overall objectives of city and regional planning. They proclaimed that a framework for the city and the region was needed before going into the districts. The campaign for council elections in spring 1994 also offered a forum to raise criticism of a too narrow planning approach (Schneider, 1997: 124–5). The mayor quite surprisingly reacted to this criticism with an initiative for a complex city development plan in 1994, which led to three years of discussion, preparation and decision-making. Steps taken were, among others, public discussions with experts and politicians, as well as an analysis of strengths and weaknesses made by a consultant agency. In February of 1997, the *Urban Development Plan 2010* was adopted by a council majority. It set the comprehensive and integrative scope of action for the whole city by putting emphasis on social issues, a robust and innovative economy, and the preservation of the environment.

---

7   Not In My Back Yard problems.

Towards a successful reform

Despite the sceptical voices and criticism of various actors, the DDP process did not end. In the course of events, more and more citizens were invited and actually did take part in the process. The willingness of citizens to participate in the planning workshops has not decreased throughout the years (see table 9.1). The workshops themselves made it possible to present different opinions about controversial issues.[8]

In addition, the Heidelberg approach comprised each of the city's districts, thereby treating them procedurally in an equal way. Hence, it would not be possible to stop until all the districts were part of the DDP process. Such an approach sidestepped from the common approach of federal and Länder governments, in which programmes were launched that combined a participatory approach with area-based social policy objectives of targeting disadvantaged neighbourhoods. In this approach, state funding has often been the most important incentive for launching area initiatives, which means that area-targeted programmes are in danger of vanishing once financial support from the state has ended (Zimmermann, 2005: 175).

Table 9.1   Attendance at thematic workshops

District	Kirchheim (1995)			Emmertsgrund (1998)			Handschuhsheim (2002)		
	total	male	Female	total	male	female	total	male	female
Key persons	55	36	19	71	38	33	96	65	31
City representatives	42	29	13	35	24	11	32	18	14

Although the discussions in Heidelberg often led rather to more transparent conflicts than consensus, participation did witness clear results.[9] There was a growing awareness of the different living conditions in the various districts. Participatory

8   However, this citizen involvement in the case of DDP was certainly biased. For example, there was hardly any representation of immigrants (although they were regularly invited and sometimes appeared). One could discuss how much this affects the legitimacy of the initiative.

9   There is no official documentation of measures implemented. It is possible to examine the list of proposals for one district and determine if measures had been executed. Fifty-two different proposals can be identified (most of them still further differentiated into sub-proposals). Out of these, only nine were not put into practice in at least some way. Moreover, of these failed proposals, only three have a relatively high ranking in the plenum of the workshops (interestingly, also by votes of the administration). Nevertheless, the great majority of proposals have led to concrete measures, sometimes in cooperation with societal organizations. Participation of the key persons in the workshop seems to have an impact on the city's policies.

observation brought to light how city officials referred to these differences in order to argue for the appropriateness of proposals made by citizens (e.g. more playing fields in a districts were children were already quite privileged in terms of private facilities).

The re-election of the mayor in 1998 made the continuation of the DDP initiative possible. As a result an average of one DDP was finished per year until now, which is a respectable outcome, probably without parallel in the world of German municipal politics.[10] In fact, it is rather exceptional that a policy agenda with an implementation endurance of 15 years was realized.

The DDP reform explained: Facilitators of reform

How can this reform be explained? Personal continuity, a strong position of leadership comprising administrative and political functions seem to be a precondition for such success. It was also crucial that the mayor took important decisions at the very beginning of her tenure, thereby creating the organizational basis for the DDP and focusing political attention, from the beginning, toward a new policy style.

Creating a supportive organizational environment

At the very beginning of the DDP process, the mayor ensured a firm basis in the administration. She used the initial impetus of her being directly elected in order to demonstrate capacity to act. In addition, the mayor could rely on an *organizational environment,* which comprised the administrative units and personnel necessary for fostering cooperation between the different departments and offices. In order to realize this, she used the windows of opportunity at the beginning of her tenure when the portfolios of the different directorates were, to some extent, to be settled anew. Besides creating the Office for Urban Development and Statistics as the organizational core for the new planning approach, this meant for example that the Office for the Equality of Man and Woman (later organizing the *future workshops for women*) was formed within her portfolio. In addition, the mayor cared for a suitable professional background of the new employees in the Office for Urban Development and Statistics, and with this she gained the necessary commitment for her plans. This was also important in order to develop a *common language* with the other offices, but also to construct win-win constellations (see Haus et al., 2006). Within the administrative side, a certain consensus grew about appropriate and inappropriate demands of citizens, which made the discussions with participants quite feasible and clear.

---

10 There is no complete empirical overview on planning processes in all German cities. Judging from available literature and information given by practitioners, however, no other example with an exhaustive decentralized urban developmental planning is known.

Preventing pitfalls and disillusionment

Also important is that the pitfalls of participatory approaches, as described above, were circumvented in DDP. Contrary to much of the rhetoric in German urban politics, participation in DDP has never been presented as a comprehensive transformation of representative democracy and public administration, but instead is presented as one way of complementing it. In fact, unrealistic expectations were headed off not only by telling citizens that the councillors, in the end, make binding decisions, but also by deploying several filters in the workshops by which participants are asked to make up their minds whether certain measures are urgent and feasible. DDP participants could discuss concrete objectives and measures within their sphere of living or working, thus questions of implementation were not far away from their overview. The workshops gave representatives from a broad range of city offices responsibility for at least a part of the agenda discussed at the workshops.

Another characteristic of special importance for policy-making in local governance was that DDP was not part of a *state* policy, demanding participation and the construction of networks/partnerships in order to gain subsidies from central government, but that it relied completely on the will and initiative of local authorities.[11]

Managing resistance: Go with the flow politics

The mayor was able to overcome several problems stemming from the fear for loss of power and influence on districts plans within the city. Here we can see facilitating processes such as *go with the flow* and *coalition building*.

Despite the fact that the first DDP was never formally passed in the council, it turned out to be an important guideline for following decisions. Weber decided that highly controversial issues, which could lead to failure of the whole process, should be discussed in a special planning forum. This learning from early experiences, and stepping aside from pushing plans, relieved the process from immediate rejection by the city council. Furthermore, the mayor tried to handle the sensitivity of certain rules of DDP by announcing a process of reinterpretation of the rules. One can also notice this type of leadership towards other actors in the course of DDP (chamber of architects, council parties).

With the *Urban Development Plan 2010* the arena of political decision-making (council) and the deliberative arenas of the workshops were linked. Since the councillors were practically absent from the interactive arenas of DDP, citizens put their trust in the effectiveness of their participation primarily in the person of the mayor, and also in the members of city administration. The members foster this attitude by promising to consider and discuss proposed measures and ideas in the political arena. DDP had thus become more dependent on permanent leadership (and

---

11 One of the districts got into the federal program 'Socially Integrated City' (*Soziale Stadt*), but that was after DDP had been realized.

community involvement): political leaders, besides the mayor, have to permanently link the different arenas.

The end product: A dynamic of self-commitment

Although it is not possible to give an account of all DDP processes, some general insights can be given into the success of the participatory design: actual participation, broad representation of visions and opinions, clear results, and commitment of participants. Citizens actually took part in the process and/or were represented by public officials in the workshops. So, DDP has led to a more pluralized voice of the (private) districts where formerly the district associations were dominant actors. At the same time, many measures proposed within the workshops were actually realized – not only those gaining many votes. Participation did have clear results and the proposals generally seem to have some substance. In addition, the Heidelberg approach comprised each of the city's districts and created a *dynamic of self-commitment* that reinforced the DDP process along the way.

Conclusions

It should have become clear that barriers in the Heidelberg case can be connected to the complex decision-making structure with a relatively high number of veto players, the legacy of policy inheritance (no previous culture of participation) and the prevailing paradigm in municipal politics and administration (administration and politicians were not used to interacting with local community). However, the dismal state of a working participation culture resulted in more and more conflict with growing expectations on the part of the population, which made the time ripe for change.

Creating mechanisms of self-enforcement or dynamic commitment were ways to deal with the barriers to lasting change in the internal routines of city administration.[12] The first step for this was the explicit commitment of the new mayor in her election campaign. It was clear that establishing new ways for community involvement was to be considered a standard by which her political work would be measured. With the direct election, this agenda gained democratic legitimacy that could not be ignored by other actors. Self-enforcement was then realized by creating a situation where all districts (including their representatives, the district councils) could legitimately expect decentralized planning after this had been done for the first districts. Stopping

---

12 The concept of self-enforcement is often used by rational choice and historical institutionalists to explain why institutions are *stable*, because actors have no incentive to change them (Weingast, 1996: 175). I am adding the expression dynamic commitment to point to the fact that also particular decisions or acts within an institutional frame sustained by a logic of appropriateness can lead to processes of self-enforcement (cf. March & Olsen, 1989).

this process would not only have been a failure of the mayor and her personal agenda, but also of the whole city administration. What can be observed is a combination of political leadership and community involvement that opened up the political system to new arenas (Haus & Heinelt, 2005).

It could be argued that the barriers located in the political power centre were not really overcome, since councillors and deputy mayors succeeded in obstructing plans with a stricter binding force for future decisions. At the same time, this resistance was somehow made handle-able, because the plans were an important point of departure for actual planning processes, with no governing coalition in the council being able to counteract them with a political program. Facilitators would thus be leaders successful in finding support (not least by early measures in organizational questions, but also by ongoing participation and *good plans*), a situation of policy change (there was a clear mandate resulting from direct elections), and a change of preference and decline in support for the policy inheritance.

For overcoming the several crises and avoiding the outburst of potential crises respectively, it was, however, important that DDP was not something decided upon and then simply enforced, but embedded in a broader kind of leadership. As the executive and political leader of the city, the mayor created and maintained institutional settings that supported the different actors' willingness to cooperate and create change. This was connected to a new paradigm of urban planning which could be roughly characterized as communitarian, stressing the value of citizen participation.

References

Albers, G. (1998) 'Stadtentwicklung/Bauleitplanung' Wollmann, H., Roth, R. (eds) *Kommunalpolitik. Politisches Handeln in den Gemeinden*, Bonn: Bundeszentrale für politische Bildung pp. 572–585.

Brunsson, N., J.P. Olsen (1993) *The Reforming Organization*, London: Routledge.

Clark, T.N., V. Hoffmann-Martinot (1998) (eds) *The New Political Culture*, Boulder: Westview Press.

Egner, B., M. Haus, H. Heinelt, C. König (2004) *Participation, Leadership and Urban Sustainability*, Country Report Germany, Darmstadt (http://www.plus eura.org/public%20pdf%20files/german_country_report%20.pdf).

Egner, B., M. Haus, C. König (2006) 'Strong Mayors and Policy Innovations: Lessons from two German Cities' Heinelt, H., D. Sweeting, P. Getimis (eds) *Legitimacy and Urban Governance: A Cross-national Comparative Study*, London: Routledge, 144–160.

Gissendanner, S. (2005) 'Rekrutierung, Wahl und Wirkung direkt gewählter Bürgermeister in Niedersachsen' Haus, M. (ed.) *Institutionenwandel lokaler Politik in Deutschland. Zwischen Innovation und Beharrung*, Wiesbaden: VS Verlag pp. 85–109.

Grauhan, R.-R. (1970) *Politische Verwaltung. Auswahl und Stellung der*

Oberbürgermeister als Verwaltungschefs deutscher Großstädte, Freiburg: Rombach.

Haus, M., H. Heinelt (2002) 'Modernisierungstrends in lokaler Politik und Verwaltung aus der Sicht leitender Kommunalbediensteter. Eine vergleichende Analyse' Bogumil, J. (ed.) *Kommunale Entscheidungsprozesse im Wandel: Theoretische und empirische Analysen*, Opladen: Leske+Budrich pp. 111–136.

Haus, M., H. Heinelt (2005) 'How to Achieve Governability at the Local Level? Theoretical and Conceptual Considerations on a Complementarity of Urban Leadership and Community Involvement' Haus, M., H. Heinelt, M. Stewart (eds) *Urban Governance and Democracy: Leadership and Community Involvement*, London: Routledge pp. 12–39.

Haus, M., H. Heinelt, B. Egner, C. König (2006) *Partizipation und Führung in der lokalen Politik*, Baden-Baden: Nomos.

Holtkamp, L. (2005) 'Neue Formen kommunaler Bürgerbeteiligung – Netzwerkeuphorie und Beteiligungsrealität' Oebbecke, J. (ed.) *Nicht-Normative Steuerung in dezentralen Systemen*, Stuttgart (forthcoming).

Hood, C. (1991) 'A Public Management for All Seasons?' *Public Administration* vol. 69, pp. 3–19.

Jaedicke, W., T. Thrun, H. Wollmann, (2000) *Modernisierung der Kommunalverwaltung. Evaluierungsstudie zur Verwaltungsmodernisierung im Bereich Planen, Bauen, Umwelt*, Stuttgart et al: Wüstenrot Stiftung.

Pollitt, C., G. Bouckaert, (2000) *Public Management Reform: An international comparison*, Oxford: University Press.

Rhein-Neckar Zeitung (29 October 1993) *Gescheitert...*

Schneider, H. (1997) *Stadtentwicklung als politischer Prozeß. Stadtentwicklungstrategien in Heidelberg, Wuppertal, Dresden und Trier*, Opladen: Leske+Budrich.

Weber, B. (1997) 'Stadtentwicklung mit den Bürgerinnen und Bürgern – Entwicklungspotentiale der Zivilgesellschaft am Beispiel Heidelberg' Schmals, K. M., H. Heinelt (eds) *Zivile Gesellschaft. Entwicklung, Defizite und Potentiale*, Opladen: Leske+Budrich pp. 59–79.

Wehling, H.-G. (2003) 'Kommunalpolitik in Baden-Württemberg' Kost, A., H.-G. Wehling (eds) *Kommunalpolitik in den deutschen Ländern. Eine Einführung*, Wiesbaden: VS Verlag pp. 23–40.

Weingast, B. R. (1996) 'Political Institutions: Rational Choice Perspectives' Goodin, R. E., H.-D. Klingemann (eds) *A New Handbook of Political Science*, Oxford: University Press pp. 167–190.

Wollmann, H. (2003) 'The Directly Elected (Chief Executive) Mayor and Local Leadership in German Local Government: in Comparative Perspective' *Kunnallistieteellinen aikakauskirja (Finnish Local Government Studies)* no. 2, pp. 126–143.

Wollmann, H. (2004) 'Urban Leadership in German Local Politics: The Rise, Role and Performance of the Directly Elected (Chief Executive) Mayor' *International Journal for Urban and Regional Research* vol. 28, no. 1, pp. 150–165.

Zimmermann, K. (2005) 'Das Programm Soziale Stadt als Versuch einer lokalen Institutionenpolitik?' Haus, M. (ed.) *Institutionenwandel lokaler Politik in Deutschland. Zwischen Innovation und Beharrung*, Wiesbaden: VS Verlag pp. 156–176.

Chapter 10

Safety Policy Reform in Rotterdam: Changing Priorities in Big City Governance

Julien van Ostaaijen and Frank Hendriks[1]

Introduction

Policy priorities in the Dutch city of Rotterdam experienced a fundamental transformation at the end of the 1990s. A culture of fragmented safety policies with different projects on different levels was replaced by a uniform approach with central coordination.

This transformation is remarkable, as two major barriers had to be overcome to establish this change. First, there was a barrier in terms of policy inheritance, since safety had never been a priority in a city where economic development, especially the harbour and related policy areas, dominated the political agenda.[2] And second, in order to create a coherent safety policy, coordination between various actors at different levels had to be established (The Netherlands School of Public Administration, 2001; Hendriks & Tops, 2005).

The presence of these barriers begs the question how an encompassing safety policy became possible in Rotterdam. To answer this question, we will first give some information about what preceded this reform and elaborate on the obstacles that blocked earlier attempts to reform safety policy. Following a description of the reform, we will analyse how the barriers were overcome. In our conclusion, we link our findings to the theoretical framework introduced in chapter 1.

---

1   The case described in this chapter is derived from research that is currently being conducted in the city of Rotterdam (November, 2005). This research is not in its final stage, but the already finished Hendriks, F. & P.W. Tops (2005)-document is an important source of information for this chapter.

2   The municipality's policy towards running the city and its harbour remained largely constant until 1970. From the 1970s onwards, the city focused more on housing policy and dealing with the harbour's side effects, such as environmental pollution (Kreukels & Wever, 1996: 299). For more information about the development of Rotterdam in the 20th century, see Van de Laar (2000). For the emergence of the attention on safety, see Hendriks & Tops (2005).

Barriers to the reform

By the end of the twentieth century, two major – and linked – barriers prevented an encompassing safety approach in Rotterdam. A policy inheritance, in this case a lack of attention towards safety issues, created the first barrier. The second was the lack of coordination between various organizations due to cultural constraints and specific decision-making structures. Consequently, existing policy was fragmented and uncoordinated. These barriers are discussed below.

Policy inheritance

Rotterdam has always been a city where economic development, especially that of the harbour and harbour-related activities, was the most important political priority (Kreukels & Wever, 1996). However, the municipal executive (mayor and aldermen) was forced to change its focus in the 1980s and 1990s when crime increased and citizens started to feel unsafe (Van der Leun, Snel & Engbersen, 2001: 239). These problems became especially pressing by the end of the 1990s (Stichting Intraval, 2000), but response to growing crime and the public's feelings of distress was rather slow. By the end of the 1990s, the only target that had been introduced was the need to improve citizen's feelings regarding safety from a six to a seven. A monitoring device – which was actually used to come up with these numbers in the first place – was used to poll citizens to determine their 'level of safeness' (Stichting Intraval, 2000, Stichting Intraval, 2001).

In order to reach seven, the municipal executive's agenda for 1998–2002 included dealing with public safety. The safety program addressed issues relating to safety and consisted of thirty projects. Looking back, participants in the program considered the program to be a merry-go-round: different safety projects from organizations all over Rotterdam came together in the program without an encompassing policy. Even though the projects covered numerous safety-related topics, there was no common ground (City of Rotterdam, 2001; Hendriks & Tops, 2005: 9). The participants' view on the incoherent structure was supported by research conducted by students of the Netherlands School of Public Administration. They concluded that:

> The city dealt with its problems by introducing an overload of initiatives and projects both at the central as well as decentralized level (…). In numerous cases, it was unclear whether the projects had been implemented, whether the projects were backed by financial resources, what the target exactly was, and how the projects cooperated with existing activities (The Netherlands School of Public Administration, 2001: 36).

The lack of coordination was apparent, for instance, in the city's drugs policy. Chasing away drug addicts in one area only made them reappear somewhere else in the city, resulting in the so-called waterbed effect. As the alderman responsible for safety commented:

> In the time of Bram Peper [mayor of Rotterdam from 1982 until 1998, JvO/ FH] we hoped that a lot of small projects would achieve success, in the spirit of letting a thousand flowers blossom (…). But despite everything we still have not managed to get government and citizens to develop a common approach towards safety (Rotterdams Dagblad, 25 May 2000).

Decision-making structures and cultural constraints

An overall safety approach needs the cooperation of the key Rotterdam actors: the municipal executive (mayor and aldermen), the city districts, and the municipal service departments. Rotterdam has eleven city districts, with their own (elected) council and civil servants. The municipal service departments, such as the Rotterdam City Development Corporation, the Rotterdam Department for Urban Planning and Housing, and the Rotterdam Municipal Port Management, provide the services to implement policies from both the municipal executive and the district executives.

The police and the district attorney are equally important when it comes to safety. Cooperation between these non-governmental actors is difficult in itself, as each institution implements its own projects (City of Rotterdam, 2001: 6), but their cooperation with the governmental actors is even more difficult. Each governmental actor has its own tasks and responsibilities. The municipal executive makes plans for the entire city, but each district has its own elected city council and district executive that implements their own policies. In some districts, political coalitions do not correspond with the political coalition at the municipal level. Both the municipal executive and the district executives are dependent on the municipal service departments for the enforcement of their policy. The most important municipal service departments for safety policy are Social Affairs, Health, City Cleaning, City Repairs, Housing and Planning, City Development, and City Supervisors. Most of them are large and autonomous organizations that have their own professional staff and priorities. Sometimes their planned efforts are written down more than one year in advance, so it is hard to change them according to rapidly changing political wishes.

The coordination between these actors proved difficult. It was almost impossible to come to 'fruitful ways of cooperation' because the three main actors in the Rotterdam safety policy perceived each other quite negatively: the city districts were considered to be 'amateuristic', the central city 'arrogant', and the municipal service departments 'internally focused monopolists' (The Netherlands School of Public Administration, 2001: 8, 33).

In short, two connected barriers obstructed reform: on the one hand, the policy inheritance (safety was not top priority) made it difficult for safety to get a more prominent place on the city's agenda. On the other hand, cultural differences had created an atmosphere in which it was difficult for actors to cooperate. Therefore, the safety policy that did exist was fragmented and incoherent.

Towards a coordinated safety policy

A new mayor

1999 saw the beginning of the safety reform, as Opstelten became the first Liberal mayor of Rotterdam since the end of World War II. Once appointed, he visited various places in Rotterdam to get acquainted with the city. During these visits, he was surprised to learn about the severe safety problems that the city had to deal with. He discovered that hardly any measures had been taken to improve citizen's feeling of safety and reach the level of safeness target of seven. On a more organizational front, he was surprised that the Rotterdam safety policy lacked an overall coordinated structure; something that did exist in Utrecht, a smaller city where Opstelten had previously been mayor.[3] The new mayor declared that he would personally be involved in solving the safety problems: 'In my opinion, we have to solve this problem integrally and with a long-term focus. This will require a lot of managerial and judicial negotiation' (Rotterdams Dagblad, 15 April 1999). Due to two major issues that needed his attention in his first year (a scandal with the former mayor about misuse of municipal funds and the European football championship in the summer of 2000) his focus was more or less shifted away from safety until after the summer of 2000.

Citizens' protests

At the same time Opstelten was appointed, citizens started to voice their discomfort about the safety approach. In 1999, citizens, influenced by the *waterbed effect* occupied the city hall for a short period of time.[4] Independent research (ordered by the municipal executive) confirmed citizens' unsafe feelings; it concluded that the actual amount of criminal activities in Rotterdam had increased. Almost 50% of the citizens of Rotterdam felt unsafe at times – 20% higher than the national average and about 10% higher than in the other three big Dutch cities of Amsterdam, The Hague, and Utrecht (Stichting Intraval, 2000).

An important demonstration occurred at City Hall on 27 March 2001, when representatives of sixty neighbourhood organizations expressed their growing unease with the level of safety in the city. Their criticism was harsh: 'Crime is

---

3   Personal interview, January 2004.

4   Growing problems with drug addicts in one part of the city because they have been chased away elsewhere.

increasing and citizens feel more and more unsafe (...). The police [have] lost authority' (Rotterdams Dagblad, 28 March 2001). 'Everyday, we, the citizens of Rotterdam, feel more unsafe in this city – on the streets, in public areas, and in our own homes. This cannot go on like this. Those who are responsible for our safety should be addressed' (Rotterdams Dagblad, 27 March 2001). After the speeches, the representatives offered the mayor a petition in which their worries were expressed. In this document, they asked all political parties in the city council, as well as the city government, the police, and the city districts to work together with citizens to 'deal with the problem that more and more people feel unsafe and not to accept the current unacceptable situation'.[5]

The safety conference

Together with his personal advisor and the safety manager, Mayor Opstelten organized a large safety conference in the beginning of 2001. The first step in making safety policy a higher priority was having all the important players present at this conference. This difficult task was delegated to the safety manager, who had just been appointed to lead the Safety Project Bureau, the bureau that enforced many of the then active safety projects in Rotterdam. With the help of the mayor's backing, the safety manager succeeded in getting the important players together. The meeting was held in Kaatsheuvel and was attended by the mayor and aldermen, some members of the city council, top police officers, district attorney officials, chairmen of the 11 city districts, and the heads of the municipal service departments. The mayor's intention with this conference was clear from the start. Once he had listed a number of individual projects of the police, justice, and municipal executive, he asked the following rhetorical questions: 'Are we on the right track regarding *integral* safety policies? Is it not too much a project machine and should there not be more structure?' (City of Rotterdam, 2001: 6).

During the conference most actors gave presentations on safety problems within the city. The mayor stressed that citizens were expressing their growing unease with the problems. The aforementioned petition of 27 March 2001 had been presented by the public just two days before the Kaatsheuvel conference. At the end of the conference, it was the mayor who summarized everything and initiated a Five Year Action Program. This program would make neighbourhood safety a priority. In accordance with this program, the final declaration of the conference states: 'Safety is the guiding theme for the policy in Rotterdam neighbourhoods. All parties involved in the Rotterdam safety policy totally agree on this' (City of Rotterdam, 2001: 69). Apart from the Five Year Action Program, the city districts would write neighbourhood safety action programs for each of the neighbourhoods within their borders. The Five Year Action Program would be the leading document on safety for the entire city. The Project Bureau Safety (now named Program Bureau Safety

---

5   The text of the petition can be found on www.sbr-rotterdam.nl (as seen on 4 May 2005).

to stress that the time of initiating projects without an overall structure was over) would coordinate on an administrative level, develop the Five Year Action Program, and assist the city districts in writing the neighbourhood action programs. The Safety Committee (*Stuurgroep Veilig*) – a gathering of the major actors (mayor, chief of police, district attorney, safety manager, and the alderman for safety) with the mayor as chairman – would coordinate the safety approach from a central level.[6]

Leefbaar Rotterdam and Fortuyn

A year after the conference, most measures had not yet been realized. The Five Year Action Program and the neighbourhood action programs were still being developed. At the same time, the citizens made it clear they still wanted change by voting en masse for a new party – *Leefbaar* ('liveable/viable') *Rotterdam* (LR) – during the municipal elections on 6 March 2002. During the election campaign, Leefbaar Rotterdam had continuously campaigned for a safer and cleaner Rotterdam. This strategy paid off: Leefbaar Rotterdam became the biggest party in the city council. Leefbaar Rotterdam won 17 out of the 45 seats at the expense of the social democrats and liberals. Leefbaar Rotterdam, together with the Christian Democrats (CDA) and Liberals (VVD), formed the new municipal executive; excluding the social democrats from the governing coalition for the first time since World War II.

Fortuyn (Leefbaar Rotterdam leader since the beginning of 2002) had led Leefbaar Rotterdam to its election victory. Before Fortuyn became the leader of Leefbaar Rotterdam, he had already been known as an outsider who challenged the national government for the national elections of May 2002. His national electorate was growing when he announced he would also lead Leefbaar Rotterdam for the municipal elections. Fortuyn and Leefbaar Rotterdam emphasized subjects such as safety and immigrants. In his first speech he said: 'We lead the wrong lists. Rotterdam is the New York of the Netherlands before Giuliani. We have the highest crime rate and the most unsolved murders' (Rotterdams Dagblad, 20 January 2002). Further, Fortuyn disassociated himself from other politicians, especially those from the Social Democratic party (PvdA), that – in his eyes – had caused the problems in the first place: 'Leefbaar Rotterdam should break with the elitist (regent) culture of the PvdA. The PvdA should be in opposition' (Rotterdams Dagblad, 20 January 2002).

The municipal elections created a political landslide: Leefbaar Rotterdam became the big winner. Fortuyn's presence in Rotterdam politics was nevertheless short lived. On 6 May 2002, a left-wing activist who believed that Fortuyn was a danger for Dutch society assassinated Fortuyn. A wave of consternation swept through the Netherlands, especially Rotterdam. For many Rotterdam citizens, Fortuyn was the only politician who could relate to how they felt. The new political coalition that formed a new municipal executive shortly after Fortuyn's death did not want to let

---

6   In August 2002, the mayor proposed to make this a weekly gathering – which it still is (September 2005).

his heritage be forgotten. The executive emphasized that it understood the message from the electorate and promised that Rotterdam would become a much safer city.

The new municipal executive

In September 2002, the new coalition of Leefbaar Rotterdam, CDA, and VVD presented its political agenda, which consisted of five priorities – safety being the top priority, followed by housing, education and youth, economic development, and integration. The coalition announced to strive for the goal of 'no more unsafe neighbourhoods in 2006' (Municipal Executive of Rotterdam, 2002: 11). The concept of safety, already broadly defined in the neighbourhood safety action programs to include issues such as a clean and intact environment, was further broadened by the coalition. According to the new coalition, the meaning of safety included public cleanliness, restoration of public spaces, neighbourhood supervision, and annoyance caused by traffic problems. Initially, the new coalition more or less ignored the soft sectors, because it wanted to focus more on repression and other more visible aspects of safety, such as putting more police on the streets. Eventually, when the coalition came to accept that social cohesion was a condition for safe neighbourhoods, this was included in safety policy as well.[7]

The new municipal executive emphasized that it would focus on implementation and action, instead of just planning. It acknowledged that numerous safety plans had been made by the previous executive, but now it was time to implement them – quickly. Implementation was mainly focused on the Five Year Action Program and the neighbourhood safety action programs initiated during the safety conference in Kaatsheuvel. In addition, for the period of 2003–2006, the municipal executive directed over €100 million to safety measures – more than half of the budget available to the executive. Finally, measurable targets and indicators were formulated to enable the monitoring of the implementation progress.

The safety index

The most important instrument to measure the implementation progress is the safety index (on a scale from 1 to 10) based on objective data collected in neighbourhoods. A higher rating meant a safer neighbourhood.[8] The 2003 safety index did not

---

7   The city government for instance started a project called People Make the City (*Mensen Maken de Stad*) where in parts of the city, civil servants try to achieve a street-agenda for residents. Examples of this agenda can be that people should start greeting each other or organize street activities together. The desired goal was to create more social cohesion among the neighbourhood residents and thereby decrease feelings of unsafety.

8   Rotterdam has about 80 neighbourhoods. Civil servants and independent researchers measure the safety in 62 of them. The others are too small to gather statistically reliable data. Once a year, the municipal executive of Rotterdam publishes the safety index, a combined number of objective data (number of crimes committed, number of people that reported crime to the police, etc.) and subjective data (research about the citizens feeling of safety in the

remarkably differ from previous safety indexes (5.64 versus 5.61 in 2002 or 5.63 in 2001). However, the 2004 safety index showed that the safety level had increased to 6.2. The mayor proudly announced this at a press conference in the city hall in front of many national and regional media. The mayor and his alderman for safety expressed optimism (or in the mayor's words: realism).

The safety index was meant to show the Rotterdam citizens that the city's approach was working, but most citizens did not even know that it existed (Wemar Marketingstrategie en Onderzoek, 2004). The significance of the safety index therefore lies with its use by government actors: the approach provides common language to discuss safety issues and gives the Safety Committee a clear instrument to identify which actors are lacking where. When the index shows that extra effort is needed, the Safety Committee will direct extra resources to the city district or municipal service departments involved. When the index mark increases, the city districts and municipal service departments see the results of their efforts. After the successful index of 2004, the mayor and alderman did not forget to stress that success of the approach could not be reached without the help of all partners involved.

Facilitating the reform

Considering the barriers involved (policy inheritance, decision-making structures, and cultural constraints), the question rises how the safety reform could come about. Interestingly, the description in the previous section already shows that not one prime mover can be identified. There was a confluence of actors mutually supporting the safety policy reform in Rotterdam. They initiated the reform based on the urgency of the situation. These change agents were the policy entrepreneurs who effectively constructed and translated the growing concern surrounding safety into reform.

Sense of urgency

Mayor Opstelten often expressed that Rotterdam led the wrong lists: the highest number of unemployed, lowest level of education, cheapest stock of houses, and a high level of crime (cf. Rotterdams Dagblad, 12 November 1999; 4 January 2000). The 2000 Intraval Report confirms that the citizens in Rotterdam experienced more crime and felt more unsafe than citizens in other big Dutch cities (Stichting Intraval, 2000). Nevertheless, the time was right for more attention for safety problems in the whole country. The Christian Democratic mayor in Maastricht, for instance, made national news by ending illegal activities in a part of his city with a massive presence of police. Considering the national trend of focussing on safety, it is interesting to determine how typical Rotterdam barriers were overcome.

Rotterdam's safety concerns were mainly focused on neighbourhood problems. People increasingly worried about the social decline in numerous Rotterdam

---

neighbourhoods). With a complicated calculation, this results in a number from one to ten to indicate the change in safety within the city.

neighbourhoods and feared that the general state of safety in their city was deteriorating (Stichting Intraval, 2000; Stichting Intraval, 2001; Centrum voor Onderzoek en Statistiek Rotterdam, 2001). When the Intraval Report on the level of crime in Rotterdam was presented in October 2000, the mayor saw the need for a more integral approach to deal with safety problems confirmed yet again. According to the report, 49% of the Rotterdam citizens sometimes felt uncomfortable while walking the streets (Stichting Intraval, 2000). The mayor stressed these results in his call for more attention to safety issues: 'We should care about this and our ambitions should be higher' (Rotterdams Dagblad, 31 October 2000). During the safety conference, the mayor pointed to the citizens' petition and the citizens' desire for change. The mayor stated that the sense of urgency is deeply felt. The petition of neighbourhood organizations is fresh in everyone's memory' (City of Rotterdam, 2001: 6).

Another indication that the citizens wanted change was the rapid emergence of Leefbaar Rotterdam and Fortuyn. His electoral success and that of his party was unprecedented in Rotterdam (or Dutch) politics. Not to mention the trepidation that swept through the Netherlands – especially Rotterdam – after Fortuyn was murdered. A large number of people gathered in front of Fortuyn's house in Rotterdam, long lines of people queued in front of the Rotterdam city hall to sign the condolence register, and a massive crowd – including key national and local politicians – attended the funeral service. Mayor Opstelten led a silent procession a few days before the funeral. During and after these gatherings, the new coalition parties continued their work to formulate a new coalition program. After the new coalition came in place, the mayor was still stressing the sense of urgency, but with one difference: the argument that 'Rotterdam leads the wrong lists' had been replaced by a new recurring phrase: 'We are on the right track, but not there yet'.[9]

Change agents

There are different actors that operated as change agents when it came to reforming Rotterdam's safety policy. The citizens put the issue on the public agenda, whereas the mayor was quick to adopt it to his own agenda. Shortly after being appointed mayor of Rotterdam, Opstelten wanted to change the structure of the Rotterdam safety policy. Organizing the safety conference in Kaatsheuvel was his first step in achieving this. Considering his strategy, the citizens' protest occurred at a convenient time. During the conference, the mayor made good use of the petition received from citizens, as well as video footage, to show the participants the urgency of the problem. As chairman of the conference, the mayor was able to summarize the discussions and to conclude that safety is a top priority for all and that the much-

---

9   Expressed for instance at the presentation of the safety index, Rotterdam City Hall, 17 May 2004; the 'Day of Accountability', Rotterdam Central Library, 22 June 2004, and the mayor's New Year's Speech, 3 January 2005.

needed structure could only be achieved by developing a Five Year Action Program and neighbourhood safety action programs.

It is difficult to say what would have happened with these initiatives without the municipal elections of 2002. Fortuyn succeeded in turning citizens' unrest into a political victory for his party Leefbaar Rotterdam. The short amount of time between this success and his death make it impossible to judge what his role could have been, even though he was a change agent for a short amount of time. He succeeded in mobilizing and translating the broader societal worries and latent feelings of unrest in large parts of Rotterdam into a successful political movement. This sudden rise of Leefbaar Rotterdam and its electoral victory was the boost that made possible a quick adoptation of the safety reform. With the replacement of the social democrats by the new party Leefbaar Rotterdam, the mayor found a more willing partner to improve safety. Mayor Opstelten saw his ideas on safety realized in the new program of the municipal executive. The program made safety a top priority and directed most of the city's resources towards safety issues. These resources were used as incentives for the city districts and municipal service departments to comply with the municipal executive's safety approach. This was a huge change: it affected the way city districts made policy, since they were no longer able to make neighbourhood plans on their own. In the beginning this was not an easy process, but the happenings of 2002 made a big influence. The city districts were affected by Fortuyn as well. They were closer to the citizens' distress than the central city government. The extra resources were more than welcome to solve the problems of the districts on their own territory, but for this, they had to accept the coordination of the Safety Committee.

Combined forces

There appears to be a strong connection between the policy reform agenda of Mayor Opstelten and the external developments that made the reform possible. When Mayor Opstelten entered the Rotterdam government, he almost immediately started to focus on safety issues. He stressed the need for change on numerous occasions (Intraval research 2000, citizens' petition 2001, and municipal election 2002).

In the Netherlands, public safety is largely the responsibility of the mayor. The new coalition (with Leefbaar Rotterdam) felt strongly about safety, and their backing further boosted the mayor's ability to bring about change. The redirection of efforts and resources towards safety issues, the strict coordination of the Safety Committee (chaired by the mayor), combined with the traditional role of a mayor as head of the city, meant that the mayor became the central actor in the new approach on safety (Rekenkamer Rotterdam, 2005).

In the organization of the safety conference, the mayor operated as an effective policy entrepreneur (resulting in more structure through the Five Year Action Program and neighbourhood safety action programs). He made good use of the external development of the neighbourhood petition to show the participants the importance of an overall safety policy and stressed the urgency of the reform in the years to come. When the citizens of Rotterdam gave Fortuyn and his party a landslide-victory, the mayor again showed that he knew how to use this to his advantage. The new coalition program focused on safety and a substantial part of the budget was allocated to safety measures.

Entrepreneurship and external opportunities mutually influenced each other. The mayor was able to use external opportunities to realize his goal to increase control on safety policy. In doing so, he reinforced his own leadership and central role within the city government. It was this combination of facilitating factors that made a reform in Rotterdam's safety policy possible.

Conclusion

The Rotterdam safety reform, advertized by the Rotterdam city government as The Rotterdam Approach (*De Rotterdamse Aanpak*), began in the field of safety policy and spread out to adjacent policy sectors. The changes in Rotterdam correspond with the reform definition given in the first chapter. First of all the reform is fundamental; deviating from existing patterns. Before the reform, attention for safety was scattered, resulting in numerous different projects that lacked any coordination or overall structure. With the safety reform, Rotterdam entered a new era in which safety became a top priority and policy became structured and coordinated. A Five Year Action Program was developed and each city district had to create neighbourhood safety action programmes. The second characteristic of reform is that it is intended; the mayor took the initiative to restructure the safety policy field, while Fortuyn and Leefbaar Rotterdam voiced clear intentions in the same area. The last characteristic of a reform is that it is enforced. The safety changes have been adopted, largely as a consequence of the mayor's strong role in the reform process.

What made this reform so special? The Rotterdam reform involved a paradigm shift. For the first time, safety became a priority of local government in Rotterdam. The strongest barrier to reform had always been the existing organizational structure, which enforced the policy inheritance of safety not being an important issue. The ad hoc manner in which various projects were put together without any connection to existing programmes was the result of years of policy-making without big interferences from the municipal executive.

The key to the reform was a combination of external opportunities and entrepreneurship. Crucial pushes for reform came from outside local government. Citizens who protested and handed in a petition for a safer Rotterdam, combined with the electoral success of Fortuyn (an outsider) and the avid support of Opstelten (also an outsider when he started), accelerated the reform. For a newcomer it is easier to ignore the existing institutional structure, including its paradigm, and introduce reform because the newcomer has not yet become part of the norms and values dominant in an institution (Resodihardjo, 2006: 232–3).

However, having the desire to reform policy is not sufficient by itself. What is needed is opportunity. In this case, Opstelten was able to use the citizens' petition and the safety conference to amplify the sense of urgency. Moreover, he was able to use the phenomenal success of Fortuyn and Leefbaar Rotterdam to expand support for his safety policy. After the municipal election, the sense of urgency increased, and instead of a coalition blocking reform, a coalition advocating reform was created. It consisted of the mayor and the new municipal executive, which put safety as the number one priority. This shift in priority, which was also felt by the city districts, made it possible to direct more resources on the central level towards safety policy and make important players in Rotterdam safety policy accept a more central and coordinated structure. Since safety according to Dutch law is a core responsibility for Dutch mayors and Opstelten led the Safety Committee, the Rotterdam mayor played a key role in this reform.

References

Centrum voor onderzoek en statistiek te Rotterdam (2001) 'Rotterdam uit balans' *COS Courant*, vol. 4.

City of Rotterdam (2001) *Verslag Conferentie Integrale Veiligheid Rotterdam* 29–30 Maart 2001.

Elchardus, M. (2001) *De dramademocratie*, Tielt: Lannoo.

Hendriks, F., Tops, P.W. (2005) *Kroniek van de Rotterdamse aanpak in het Veiligheidsbeleid, 'De Eerste Helft'*, Tilburg: Tilburg School of Politics and Public Administration, Tilburg University.

Kreukels, T., Wever, E. (1996) 'Dealing with Competition: the Port of Rotterdam' *Tijdschrift voor Economische en Sociale Geografie*, vol. 87: 293–309.

Laar, P. van de, (2000) *Stad van Formaat. Geschiedenis van Rotterdam in de negentiende en twintigste eeuw*, Zwolle: Waanders Uitgevers.

Leun, J. van der, E. Snel, G. Engbersen (2001) 'Achterstandbuurten en onveiligheid' Engbersen, G., J. Burgers. (eds) *De verborgen stad. De zeven gezichten van Rotterdam*, Amsterdam: Amsterdam University Press: 229–8.

Municipal Executive of Rotterdam (2002) *Het nieuwe elan van Rotterdam ... en zo gaan we dat doen. College Programma 2002–2006*, Rotterdam.

The Netherlands School of Public Administration (2001) *Ellende wenden. Een bestuurlijke aanpak voor Rotterdam*.

Opstelten, I., (January 2004) Personal Interview.

Rekenkamer Rotterdam (2005) *Veilig zijn, veilig voelen. Uitvoering wijkveiligheidsbeleid op koers*, Rotterdam.

Resodihardjo, S.L. (2006) *Crisis and Change: Understanding Crisis-Reform Processes in Dutch and British Prison Services*, Dissertation: Amsterdam.

Rotterdams Dagblad (15 April 1999) *Opstelten klaar met eerste kennismakingsronde.*

Rotterdams Dagblad (12 November 1999) *Gemeenteraad Rotterdam van de straat.*

Rotterdams Dagblad (4 January 2000) *Opstelten zet 'n ideaalbeeld van Rotterdam neer.*

Rotterdams Dagblad (25 May 2000) *Wethouder Van der Tak wil veiligheid koppelen aan opzoomeren.*

Rotterdams Dagblad (31 October 2000) *Ambities voor veiligheid moeten hoger.*
Rotterdams Dagblad (27 March 2001) *Bewoners eisen veilige stad.*
Rotterdams Dagblad (28 March 2001) *Bewonersprotest komt Opstelten niet ongelegen.*
Rotterdams Dagblad (20 January 2002) *Fortuyn lijsttrekker Leefbaar Rotterdam.*
Samenwerkende Bewonersorganisaties Rotterdam (27 March 2001) *Petitie en Nota van Toelichting,* www.sbr-rotterdam.nl. Last accessed on 4 May 2005.
Stichting Intraval (2000) *Monitor Veiligheid Rotterdam 1999.*
Stichting Intraval (2001) *Monitor Veiligheid Rotterdam 2000.*
Wemar Marketingstrategie en Onderzoek (2004) *Onderzoekstraject Campagne Veilig Rapportage 0-meting,* Rotterdam.

Chapter 11

Explaining Reform in Europe: Comparisons, Patterns, and Reflections

Liesbet Heyse, Berber Lettinga and Martijn Groenleer

Introduction

Reform is often perceived to be difficult – if not impossible – to achieve. Three myths support this thought. One myth pertains to the idea that the institutional structure of a policy sector will make reform impossible; path dependencies, lock-in effects, and policy paradigms will block any possibility for reform. The second myth states that a substantial disruption of the policy process, such as a crisis, is required for reform to happen. The third myth holds that a strong leader is needed to initiate, design, and enforce reforms. These three myths imply that reform will hardly occur.

Yet, the cases in this volume show that reforms can be realized. Sometimes, governments succeed in carrying through fundamental changes in policy and organization. The case of the smoking ban in Ireland – a country inextricably bound up with the image of smoky pubs – made this compellingly clear. Whereas current research into public sector reforms has resulted in valuable insights into factors that hinder reform (March & Olsen, 1995; Bovens & 't Hart, 1998; Pollitt & Bouckaert, 2004), there is still little clarity as to what factors facilitate reform. This volume therefore examines how it is possible for reform to occur considering the formidable obstacles blocking its path.

This study started with a definition of reform: the fundamental, intended, and enforced change of the policy paradigm and/or organizational structure of (an organization within) a policy sector. Based on the existing literature on reform, a number of potential factors hampering and facilitating reform were listed in chapter 1 (see table 11.3 for an overview). Nine cases were then investigated to determine what barriers existed and how they were overcome, and which facilitators were present and what role they played in the reform process.

In this chapter, the case findings are compared to identify general patterns in the reform processes studied. First, we describe the reforms that have been addressed in the cases. Second, we offer an overview of the barriers and facilitators that appear from the cases and relate them to factors introduced in chapter 1. Third, we reflect on the paths to and phases of reform, based on an evaluation of how barriers either diminished or were overcome by facilitators. Fourth, we link our findings to the existing literature on change and reform. This chapter will conclude with putting the three pervading myths of reform in perspective.

Table 11.1   Barriers and facilitators to reform (Bannink & Resodihardjo)[1]

Barriers		Facilitators	
Opportunities	**Preferences**	**Structure**	**Agency**
Decision-making structures. Policy inheritance. Lock-in.	Paradigm, routinization, and internalized goals. Reform is disruptive. Vested interests and benefits from status quo.	Diminished barriers, such as a disruption in the policy-making process and the decline in support for the policy inheritance.	Change of preference. Leadership. Entrepreneurship. Go with the flow. Find support.

Reform in Europe

The cases analyzed in the chapters represent a wide variety of reform types, ranging from cases of constitutional reform (Germany) to New Public Management reform (home care). The cases occurred in diffent policy sectors (such as social security and agriculture), in different political systems (federal versus centralized) and on different levels (local level reforms in Germany, the Netherlands and the UK as well as national level reforms such as in Ireland and the Netherlands). Despite these differences, the policy changes studied in this project all fit the definition of reform used in this study: the studied changes were fundamental, intended, and enforced (see table 11.3 in the appendix for an overview of the cases).

The reforms were *fundamental* because they were accompanied by a deviation from existing paradigms and/or organizational structures (Keeler, 1993; Hall, 1993; Sabatier, 1998; Cortell & Peterson, 1999). Powerful national corporatist structures that existed in, for instance, the Dutch disability insurance and housing sectors, were replaced by new coordination structures characterized by market competition and privatization. In other cases, historically dominant values and norms lost their dominance and were replaced by values and norms that were contrary to the previous paradigm. In Germany, for example, immigrants were no longer welcomed but became subject to strict immigration regulations. In that very same country, views on how to conduct city planning shifted radically as the process was no longer seen as a bureaucratic exercise but as a participatory and integrative process.

The reforms were *intended* as they were the result of conscious decision-making and planning processes. Reform proposals were formulated and discussed, alternative plans were developed, and legislation was passed in Parliament. For

---

1   As introduced in chapter 1 of this book.

example, several proposals to solve the EU agricultural problems were discussed in EU ministerial committees and national parliaments were actively involved in discussing and deciding on reform proposals regarding asylum and smoking.

Finally, the reforms were *enforced* as they resulted in changed policies, organizational structures, or both. In the Dutch city of Rotterdam, organizational structures shifted as municipal departments were compelled to work together to tackle safety problems. English local authorities had to change their organizational structure to ensure a separation of powers in local government.

The extent to which these reforms achieved their aims was not the focus of this study. Numerous studies have shown that ascertaining whether reform measures have been consummately implemented or whether the implemented reforms have obtained the goals as intended by policy makers is simply impossible (Hogwood & Gunn, 1993; Fisher, 1995; Howlett & Ramesh, 2003). Various authors have pointed to the difficulties of objectively determining and evaluating the effects of reform due to time, space and culture (cf. 't Hart and Bovens, 1996; Bovens et al., 2001). Moreover, the evaluation of reform effects is a biased process. For example, a reform that was once perceived to be a failure might later be judged as a success, and vice versa. In the EU dairy and German asylum cases, reforms seem to have resulted in declined milk production and a smaller number of asylum seekers. However, whether this is perceived as a success or a failure is in the eye of the beholder and may change over time.

Instead of focusing on the effects of reform, we are interested in how reforms could have been initiated and executed in the first place. Before we address the factors that made the initiation and execution of reform possible, we first analyze which barriers played a role in the various cases.

Barriers to reform

In chapter 1, two types of barriers to reform were distinguished: those that affect the *opportunities* available to actors to push for reform, and those that affect the *preferences* of actors. The number of opportunities available to actors pushing for reform is limited by structural barriers such as decision-making structures, policy inheritance, and lock-in effects. The more complicated the decision-making procedure, for instance, the more difficult it is to push for reform because opponents to reform have more opportunities to veto the reform proposal. Whether or not actors prefer to opt for reform is determined by cultural barriers such as policy paradigms, the potentially disruptive nature of reform, vested interests, and benefits. Actors profiting from the status quo – because they receive subsidies or have access to the decision-making process – may not support changes that negatively affect their benefits.

In spite of the existence of these barriers in our cases, reform did occur. In this section, we analyze what barriers mattered in our cases and the role they played. Do both types of barriers always matter? Table 11.4 (see appendix) lists the barriers as described in the case studies. The table also shows whether these barriers dissolved or remained in place during the reform process.

Opportunities and preferences

Both opportunity and preference barriers can be discerned in the cases, especially veto-points in decision-making processes, vested interests, and attachment to the policy paradigm. This confirms the argument made in the literature that these are relevant factors hindering reform (Immergut, 1992; Hall, 1993; Rose & Davies, 1994; Cortell & Peterson, 1999). The Irish smoking ban case is the sole case where only one type of barrier was present; only preference-based barriers could be discerned as political and societal actors opposed the reform because it clashed with their belief system.

Interestingly, the disruptive nature of reform was only explicitly mentioned in one case, the English local authorities case. Actors indicated that the reform was upsetting and unsettling for them; they mourned for the loss of the old system. In other cases, the disruptive nature of reform implicitly played a role. Reform disrupts the life style, policy-making style, and administrative style of actors. In Ireland, for instance, people were hostile toward the smoking ban because the ban would interfere with their life style. Professionals and interest groups who were part of the disability insurance and home care policy sectors were afraid that the typical policy-making style of their sector would be undermined as the reforms led to the introduction of market competition which, in turn, would negatively affect their influence on the policy-making process. In the case of participative policy planning in Heidelberg, civil servants were reluctant to grant citizens participative rights in decision-making process, as they feared this would affect their administrative style.

Although our cases show that the disruptive nature of reform is not a factor to be ignored (cf. Leemans, 1976b), the cases also indicate that the upsetting and unsettling nature of reforms should not be regarded as a barrier in itself, but as an expression or manifestation of other barriers, such as internalized values, prevailing paradigms, and vested interests. The way in which EU member states responded to a possible change in the dairy policy is a case in point. National governments were reluctant to reform the dairy subsidy system as they knew how upsetting and unsettling the reform would be for their farmers. After all, a decrease in milk production would negatively affect farmers' monetary benefits intrinsic to the dairy subsidy system. The farmers' negative feelings originated from the interests they had in the milk increasing policy as they had invested immensely in their farms to improve milk production. Of course, political actors were mainly concerned about this because farmers are an important category of voters.

In addition to the barriers mentioned in the introductory chapter, one other barrier emerged from our cases: actors' low expectations of the reform's effects. A number of actors opposed the reform because they expected it to fail. The suggestion of an Irish smoking ban was met with scepticism. Minister Martin's own party opposed the ban because his party members did not expect it to work. In Heidelberg, the prospect of disappointment among citizens if participatory city planning failed served as an obstacle to reform.

Overcoming barriers

In order for reform to occur it is often assumed that either the barriers to reform have to diminish or other factors have to help to overcome the barriers. Whereas structural (or opportunity) barriers often remained in place (see table 11.4 in the appendix), our inventory of barriers present in the cases shows that preference barriers often diminished during the reform process as actors changed their preferences and came to favour reform. In fact, preference barriers in almost all cases diminished or disappeared during the reform process. Hence, preference barriers appear to be more important than opportunity barriers in determining whether reform is carried through.

The dairy policy case substantiates this claim: even when structural barriers diminished – qualitative majority voting replaced the rule of unanimity decision-making – reform remained difficult because the preferences of major actors had not changed. Despite a shared understanding on the need to control milk production as well as to curb the EU expenses for dairy policy, some member states strongly held on to the policy of production increase. Only financial compensation could eventually induce these states to change their position and go along with the quota system. A change in decision-making rules was insufficient for reform to occur; preferences had to change as well.

Additionally, the dairy case shows that dependency on decisions made in the past through policy inheritance and lock-in effects can be a strong barrier to reform when combined with vested interests. This combinatorial effect is also apparent from the case studies on home care and disability insurance. The interdependence of central government and local, professional and social actors in policy-making and implementation resulted in a consensus-seeking approach. This consensus-seeking approach put local, professional and social actors in a position to block reform imposed by central government.

Nevertheless, our cases show that if preferences change, decision-making structures, policy lock-ins, and policy inheritance cease functioning as barriers. In the German asylum case, for example, reform was possible without changing the decision-making structure regarding constitutional change, although in previous reform attempts political actors used this decision-making structure to block reform.

Diminishing barriers

In a number of cases studied, barriers that obstructed reform in the past did not do so in the reform process analyzed. In the case of the Irish smoking ban, the anti-reform coalition proved to be not as powerful, because the stakes of the various participants were too diverse. The resistance offered by this coalition therefore proved a weak barrier. In the case of the disability insurance, the societal actors' opposition to a decrease of income from benefits was weak as well. This was the result of an unexpected response by insurance companies: they introduced new insurance policies that compensated for the income loss. Although the insurance companies were not actively heading for reform, they influenced the reform process in such a way that a barrier which originally blocked reform diminished.

In a few other cases, barriers were neither activated nor removed. In some cases, for example, actors did not use their obstruction powers. In the home care case, central government did not use its power to coerce local actors to cooperate, in part because local actors anticipated a potential loss of autonomy by taking a cooperative stand in the reform process. In other cases actors did not try to break with policy inheritance or policy lock-ins because this would have taken too much energy or costs compared to the chance of success. As the dairy and housing cases illustrate, the support for reform, such as changing the production factors in the milk industry or selling the social housing stock, was not guaranteed at all. Thus reform can happen even though some barriers – deemed important in the literature – remain in place.

In sum, our analysis of barriers in reform demonstrates that not necessarily all barriers have to be overcome in order for reform to occur. Even though *opportunity* barriers remained in place in the majority of cases, reform did happen. Our findings thus do not fully support the claim that opportunity structures are important barriers to reform (Baumgartner & Jones, 1993; Immergut, 1992; Steinmo, Thelen & Longstreth, 1992). We conclude that reform is not likely to occur as long as *preference* barriers remain in place. After all, if actors prefer to stick with the status quo, nothing happens. Only when preferences change is reform possible. The next section addresses the factors that make preference changes possible.

Facilitating reform: Structural factors

As pointed out in chapter 1, if reform is to occur, structure has to break down: reform will be facilitated if barriers diminish. Yet, if no one acts upon this less structured environment nothing will happen. Moreover, barriers that remain in place can be overcome by agency. In the next two sections, we analyze what happened to the barriers, taking into account both types of facilitators (structural and agency) (see tables 11.5 and 11.6 in the appendix).

Disrupted policy processes

The facilitator most often referred to in the reform literature when explaining how barriers can diminish is a disruption of the policy-making process (Baumgartner & Jones, 1993). The policy-making process is normally characterized by incrementalism. At times, however, this process is disrupted when new problems catch the attention of the media, thereby demanding immediate attention of policy makers. One way for such a disruption to occur is through a crisis. When media, Members of Parliament (MPs), and civil servants interpret incidents as indicators of a failing policy sector, a crisis is born (Kuipers, 2006). Since this creates a pressure to end the crisis, it is possible to expedite decision-making procedures, thereby minimizing the number of veto-points accessible for opponents to reform.

In several cases, crisis proved an important factor. Four types of factors fuelled the various crises. First, *Parliamentary enquiries* acted as catalysts for crisis.

Parliamentary enquiry committees are usually installed during or after a crisis to establish what went wrong. However, enquiries can also contribute to crisis. In the disability insurance sector, for example, an enquiry fuelled the crisis in this sector by contributing to negative images of the policy sector and publicly disgracing key actors in the policy-making process. This gave Parliament leeway to abolish the corporatist policy-making model by excluding social partners from the policy-making process.

Second, *declining resources,* needed to support existing policies, resulted in a financial crisis and pressure to act. In the EU dairy case, the policy of providing subsidies to farmers to help them increase milk production led to financial obligations that could no longer be met. In the Dutch housing sector, the government provided substantial subsidies to provide for affordable housing. The budget constraints in the 1980s created a sense of urgency to diminish these subsidies. It was these declining resources that created a financial crisis and leverage to act.

Third, the Rotterdam and German asylum case exemplify that *societal upheaval* can facilitate the reform process. In Rotterdam, the Labour Party – a dominant partner in the council coalition – had ignored safety issues for years. Neglecting that citizens felt unsafe in their own city proved detrimental to their political survival. In contrast, Fortuyn's Leefbaar Rotterdam's acknowledgement of societal upheaval concerning safety issues was rewarded by electoral victory, allowing them to make safety the city's number one priority. The exceptionally large numbers of asylum seekers and the increasing number of violent attacks on foreigners in Germany made it necessary to change prevailing asylum policies: from generous admittance to a restriction on the number of asylum seekers allowed to enter the country.

Fourth, *the media* played a role in fuelling crises by highlighting the seriousness of problems. In the Danish home care sector, for example, the media portrayed the sector as malfunctioning and home care providers as indolent. Media coverage led to the loss of support for powerful actors such as the social partners in the disability insurance case, making it possible for reform-oriented actors to carry through with the reform.

The role of policy feedback

A structural facilitator not mentioned in chapter 1 was clearly present in some cases: policy feedback resulting in the erosion of support for existing policies and paradigms (see table 11.6 in the appendix). In the EU dairy case, for example, various attempts to control milk production included lowering the subsidies for milk production. Farmers tried to compensate for their loss of income by producing more milk. The negative policy effects clearly showed that existing policies were failing, thereby accelerating the reform process. The same dynamics were present in the Dutch disability insurance case, where attempts to adjust existing policies only resulted in increasing numbers of people receiving benefits.

Whereas the previous cases were characterized by negative policy feedback, the Dutch housing case illustrates that positive policy feedback can ultimately aid the adoption of reform. In this case, existing policies resulted in wealthy Dutch housing corporations that could afford to pay for their own housing stock. Consequently, these corporations no longer felt the need to cling to the existing policy in which national government paid for their housing stock. Instead, they started to support the idea of privatizing their housing stock.

Elections as windows of opportunity

Another observation from the cases – one not mentioned in the introductory chapter – is that elections can result in reform when new actors enter the political arena and act on their electoral mandate (cf. Keeler, 1993). Although elections do not necessarily disrupt policy processes, the cases show that they can be a structural facilitator in reform processes. In the three local reform cases, electoral mandates created windows of opportunity for reform, which were used by the newly elected officials. In Rotterdam (safety policy), Heidelberg (citizen participation), and the United Kingdom (local authority), political parties came to power pursuing radically different courses than their predecessors. The election of Mayor Weber in Heidelberg resulted in a clear mandate enabling her to carry through citizen participation in city planning practices. In the UK, New Labour came into office with Blair as its leader. His Third Way approach to governance combined with strong leadership and the electoral window of opportunity made the introduction of a Bill to separate powers at the local level possible. These findings are in line with existing research indicating that new incumbents are able to push for reform because they are not embedded in the institutional structure as much as their predecessors were, making it easier for them to change policies (Resodihardjo, 2006).

In sum, we found evidence confirming the pervading argument that disrupted policy processes facilitate reform processes in several cases. Consequently, in these cases, the *ability* for reform was present. In the other cases (Rotterdam, Heidelberg, local reform in the UK, and the home care case), disrupted policy processes did not play a role. We nevertheless conclude that in a majority of the cases structural facilitators – disrupted policies, policy feedback and elections – created opportunities for reform. We now turn to the other category of facilitators mentioned in this chapter's introductory section, i.e. agency facilitators, in order to understand the *willingness* of actors to reform.

Facilitating reform: Agency factors

Reform, it was argued in the introductory chapter, can only occur when actors act upon a structural opportunity for reform, resulting from diminished barriers or disrupted policy processes. Bannink and Resodihardjo list several interrelated agency facilitators that may be of importance, including leadership and entrepreneurship. Leaders and entrepreneurs can use a wide range of tactics to make public preferences change in favour in reform.

Leadership and entrepreneurship

Interestingly, and contrary to popular belief, reform entrepreneurship (i.e. by actors using the window of opportunity created by diminished constraints to push for reform) rarely occurred in the cases. Of the cases reviewed, entrepreneurs were only present in the Rotterdam safety reform, as well as in the home care case, where an entrepreneurial coalition of care providers and government arose. In the Rotterdam case Fortuyn acted as an entrepreneur by using latent feelings in society to present his new party as a political alternative to the Rotterdam electorate.

Except for the home care case, leaders did play an important role in all the reforms studied, especially by trying to find support for their ideas. Reformist actors used three tactics to find support for their reform proposals (see table 11.5 in the appendix): forming pro-reform coalitions, formulating an acceptable design, and forcing relevant actors to support reform.[2] The cases show that leaders used these tactics to contribute to reform in several ways.

First, leaders were actively engaged in convincing other actors that reform was needed by means of *building pro-reform coalitions*, thereby facilitating reform initiation (cf. Sabatier & Jenkins-Smith, 1999). In order to do so, leaders used symbolic politics or framed issues in such a way that a sense of urgency was created. The case of the Irish smoking ban exemplifies how framing contributed to building a pro-reform coalition (Caiden, 1991a; 1991b). The Irish pro-reform coalition started out with only a few members. This coalition – headed by Health Minister Martin – was capable of increasing the number of its members by changing the perception on smoking in public places. Instead of presenting the ban as an issue related to the private domain, the coalition presented it as a public matter by highlighting the negative effect of smoking on the health of employees. This broadened the debate to include clean and healthy working conditions for employees. Consequently, employee unions joined the pro-reform coalition.

Leaders also deliberately constructed and framed crises in order to create a sense of urgency and support for reform. The European Commission, for instance, presented the EU dairy crisis as a financial crisis linked to the survival of the EU as a whole, thereby creating pressure to act. In addition, some actors made use of symbolic politics (Edelman, 1964). Prime Minister Lubbers, for example, responded to the crisis in disability insurance by stating that 'the Netherlands were sick'. Fortuyn – the only entrepreneur found in the case studies – used symbolic politics in Rotterdam as well. He was able to present himself as an outsider fighting against the traditional political elite. In addition, once in power, the governing coalition

---

2   Our notion of pro-reform coalition partly coincides with Sabatier's advocacy coalitions. Both types of coalitions involve 'governmental and private organizations that engage in a non-trivial degree of coordinated activity over time' (Sabatier & Jenkins-Smith, 1999: 120). However, pro-reform coalitions may also consist of participants whose interests coincide, contrary to advocacy coalitions that only consist of participants sharing the same beliefs.

(including Fortuyn's political party) introduced the safety index as a symbolic instrument to show voters that problems were being solved.

A second tactic that leaders were actively engaged in was the process of *designing reform proposals*. Reformist actors were capable of formulating an acceptable reform design, i.e. designs that incorporated the wishes of opponents, which clearly showed that the proposal was feasible, or that it fit within a larger reform trend (cf. Leemans, 1976b; Olsen 1991). Mayor Weber of Heidelberg changed the rules of the participatory city planning process several times to meet the demands of some of her political opponents. For example, she accepted that the decisions made in the citizen participation workshops would still be discussed and decided on by the council – although this was not in the original plan. It was therefore decided that in the decision-making process concerning a new tramline, the council also had a say, instead of only the participants in the workshop, as it was originally intended. An additional way to formulate an acceptable design is by hiding the proposal's reform intentions. Junior minister Heerma's reform proposals for the Dutch housing sector were accepted because they seemed technical and incremental, unlike a reform.

Finally, some reformers were powerful enough to *force* other actors to back the reform plans (Leemans, 1976b). This characteristic is what distinguishes leaders from entrepreneurs: only the former are in the position to coerce other actors to comply with reform or have the formal legal powers to impose reform. The Labour government made mandatory the Act that reformed British local governments, thereby forcing local governments to separate executive and non-executive powers. In other cases, reformers used threats or sanctions to gather support. In the smoking ban and the Dutch disability insurance case, for example, politicians threatened to resign if their reform proposals were not accepted.

In conclusion, leadership was important in the reform cases studied, but it was not a necessary factor, as the home care case demonstrates. In order to achieve reform, reformist actors used the above-mentioned strategies: building pro-reform coalitions, creating an acceptable reform design, and procuring backing to guide the reform proposal through the decision-making process. Entrepreneurs and leaders identified in the cases used the same strategies, bar one. Leaders had an additional strategy at their disposal that entrepreneurs did not: the power (or threat) to coerce other actors to comply with the reform proposal. These findings confirm the ideas expressed in leadership literature as described in chapter 1.

The process of reform: Paths and phases

Simply stating which factors occurred in the various cases does not tell us which factors are necessary and sufficient conditions for reform. The existing literature points to a variety of factors that have to come together for reform to occur, but it remains unclear when, how and why these factors come together. In this section we reflect upon our findings and build upon existing reform literature to get a better insight in the various paths to reform that can be taken and the various phases that characterize reform.

Paths to reform

This study shows that reform is clearly not the result of a single facilitator. Rather, a combination of facilitators is needed for reform to occur (cf. Kingdon, 1995). The cases studied were characterized by unique combinations of factors interacting to enable reform – as is shown in table 11.2. Considering this wide variety of combinations, can we say anything about the variables that influence these various paths to reform? Do certain factors figure more prominently in the different reform paths than others?

Table 11.2   A summary of findings: Structural and agency facilitators

Cases	A	B	C	D	E	F	G	H
Dairy	1	1	1	0	1	1	0	1
Housing	1	0	1	0	0	1	0	0
Homecare	0	0	0	1	1	0	0	0
Asylum	1	0	1	1	1	1	0	0
Smoking	0	1	1	0	1	0	0	1
Disability	1	1	1	1	1	1	1	1
UK	0	0	1	0	1	0	0	0
Safety	1	0	1	1	1	0	1	0
Planning	1	0	1	1	1	0	0	0

Factors distilled from the literature
A=disruption/change in decision-making structures
B=diminished constraints
C=leadership/entrepreneurship
D=Reform tactic 1: go with the flow
E= Reform tactic 2: find support

Factors emerging from the case studies
F= Policy feedback
G= Reform tactic 3: symbolic politics
H= Reform tactic 4: issue linkage

Explanatory note: 1=presence of a certain factor, 0=absence of a certain factor; so, for example, in the smoking ban case we found that entrepreneurship was present, and in the safety policy case we found no evidence of decreasing returns or negative feedback.

This study shows that neither structural reform facilitators (such as crisis and policy feedback) nor agency reform facilitators (such as leadership) sufficiently explain the occurrence of reform. What we did find is that a combination of leadership and reform strategies to procure backing is the most prominent facilitator of reform. Leaders played a crucial role in the process by initiating the reform, changing other actors' preferences, designing reform proposals, and courting or enforcing the support for a reform. However, most leaders could also do this because of crises, negative policy feedback, or electoral outcomes to press for reform. Only in the Irish smoking ban and home care case did leaders enforce reform without the windows of opportunity resulting from crises, policy feedback or elections.

Moreover, our cases also reveal that some factors can be both barriers and facilitators (see table 11.7 in the appendix). Consider, for instance, policy inheritance, which is mentioned as a reform barrier in the literature (Rose & Davies, 1994). Nevertheless, in a number of cases, policy feedback also functioned as a facilitator. For example, negative policy feedback showed that existing policies were malfunctioning, thereby increasing the pressure to change that very same policy. Whether such factors serve as a barrier or a facilitator is likely to depend on the particular combination with other factors. Thinking of factors as potentially being both barriers and facilitators may prove a useful avenue for further research, because it points to the dynamics characterising the reform process. These dynamics will be addressed in the remainder of this section.

Phases of reform

The cases demonstrate that not only can we identify different paths to reform, but we can also distinguish among different phases of reform. Reform is not a single event occurring at a certain moment in time. Rather, it is a process taking place over a period of time (cf. Mahoney & Rueschemeyer, 2003; Pierson, 2004). This process can be characterized by two analytically different phases: a first phase of increasing awareness that something needs to be changed followed by a second phase in which reforms are actually initiated and executed (see figure 11.1). In reality, these phases are, of course, closely related and cannot be easily disentangled.

In the first phase of reform, actors become aware that something needs to be fundamentally changed. This phase mainly involves leaders and entrepreneurs. The case findings suggest that various factors affect reformist actors' preferences: a fear of electoral loss and thereby loss of political power, a crisis provoking the sense that urgent action is needed, or a failed previous attempt to adjust existing policies. Once these reformist actors have changed their own preferences, they can try to change the preferences of other actors. Potential tactics in order to achieve this include: invoking a crisis, gathering support, using symbols, and framing issues. When actors succeeded in increasing awareness and changing preferences, the second phase of reform can begin: initiating and executing reform.

Leaders and entrepreneurs also play a crucial role in the second phase of reform. If they do not initiate, design, manipulate, and enforce the reform proposal in an acceptable manner, the reform process may come to a halt and eventually fail, as the opportunity for initiation and execution of a reform is usually restricted in time and scope. Various tactics proved to be effective in ensuring the adaptation of reform. These strategies included drafting a reform proposal with an acceptable design, finding support, and following trends instead of creating them.

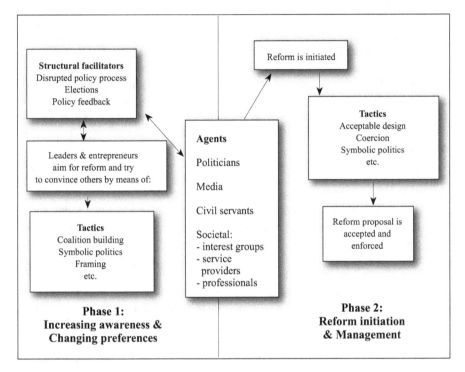

Figure 11.1   The process of reform

Theoretical reflections

How does all this compare to existing reform literature? In the cases provided, previous reform attempts were characterized by a process Lindblom refers to as 'muddling through' (1959; 1979). In the asylum, housing, disability insurance, and dairy cases, actors initially tried to solve problems incrementally within the existing policy paradigm and organizational structures. When these incremental policy changes did not lead to the desired results, reform was initiated (cf. Hall, 1993). A number of reforms, however, were not preceded by failing incremental policy-making. Instead, they were the result of changing ideas on how to act on a certain policy issue. In the city planning, home care and smoking ban case, the reform was initiated without incremental processes.

Interestingly, the cases also show characteristics of Kingdon's multiple-streams theory regarding reform (1995). Kingdon distinguishes three process streams: problem recognition, the formulation and refining of policy proposals, and politics. If these processes are joined, or coupled, policy change can occur. These streams were present in our cases as well. Problem recognition through negative policy feedback and crises played a crucial role in various cases. Without the skill to design and refine an acceptable reform proposal, backing could not be procured in the politics stream.

According to Kingdon, however, 'no one factor *dominates* or *precedes* the others. Each has its own life and its own dynamics' (1995: 179; italics added, LH/BL/MG). In some of our case studies, we find confirmation for Kingdon's thesis that no one factor always precedes another. For example, in some cases structure preceded agency: a crisis developed, and leaders acted upon this crisis. Yet in other cases, we find that agency preceded structure: for example, a crisis was purposefully constructed. Thus, it would appear as if Kingdon is correct in stating that *no factor precedes another*.

Yet, we find evidence that there is one type of factor dominating the others, contrary to Kingdon's statement: *agency dominates structure*. Some cases reveal that in absence of structural changes, reform was still initiated as a result of agency. In Kingdon's terminology, if windows of opportunity are not construed and/or seized by leaders or entrepreneurs, reform simply does not occur. Thus, whereas structure may create opportunities for reform, agency is a sine qua non for reform to happen.

This puts all the more emphasis on the actions of agents in general, and leaders and entrepreneurs in particular. In the introductory chapter, Bannink and Resodihardjo noted that while a policy entrepreneur is always dependent on the occurrence of a window of opportunity to push for reform, leaders can push for reform with or without this window. Reformist leaders do not have to wait for a window of opportunity to open: they can open it themselves by creating a crisis. Moreover, leaders can act without the aid of a window of opportunity by changing other actors' preferences, procuring backing, or forcing the reform through.

Conclusion: Demystifying reform

We began this volume by outlining three myths of reform that illustrate how reform is nearly impossible to accomplish. These myths state that reform can only occur when the institutional make-up of a policy sector is disrupted by, for instance, a crisis and only when a strong leader is willing and able to garner support for reform. This study sought to demystify the pervading idea that reform is almost unattainable. The case studies in this volume provide substantial evidence for the argument that reform can and does occur. While the institutional structure of a policy sector makes reform difficult, it is not impossible to achieve. We have also shown that severe crises and strong leadership, although important explanatory factors, are neither necessary nor sufficient for reform to be brought about.

In this volume, we have attempted to demystify reform and to unravel the factors behind reform. Our findings indicate that a myriad of factors contribute to the reform process. However, this volume shows that we do not have to be pessimistic. Precisely because there is no single path to reform, we should be optimistic about the possibilities of governments to carry through reform.

References

Baumgartner, F.R., Jones, B.D. (1993) *Agendas and Instability in American Politics*, Chicago: University of Chicago Press.

Bovens, M.A.P., 't Hart, P. (1998) *Understanding policy fiascoes*, New Brunswick: Transaction Publishers.

Bovens, M., P. 't Hart, G.B. Peters (2001) *Success and Failure in Public Governance: A Comparative Analysis*, Cheltenham: Edward Elgar.

Caiden, G.E. (1991a) 'Doing Something Different'. Caiden, G.E. (ed.) *Administrative Reform Comes of Age*, Berlin: Walter de Gruyter pp. 131–149.

Caiden, G.E. (1991b) 'Guarding against Failure'. Caiden, G.E. (ed.) *Administrative Reform Comes of Age*, Berlin: Walter de Gruyter pp. 151–169.

Cortell, A.P., Peterson, S. (1999) 'Altered States: Explaining Domestic Institutional Change'. *British Journal of Political Science* vol. 29 pp. 177–203.

Edelman, M.J. (1964) *The Symbolic Uses of Politics*, Urbana: University of Illinois Press.

Fisher, F. (1995) *Evaluating Public Policy*, Chicago: Nelson-Hall Publishers.

Hall, P.A. (1993) 'Policy Paradigms, Social Learning, and the State: The Case of Economic Policymaking in Britain'. *Comparative Politics* vol. 25 (3) pp. 275–296.

Hogwood, B., Gunn, L. (1993) 'Why 'Perfect Implementation' is Unattainable'. Hill, M. (ed.) *The Policy Process: A Reader*, New York: Harvester Wheatsheaf pp. 238–247.

Howlett, M., Ramesh, M. (2003) *Studying Public Policy: Policy Cycles and Policy Subsystems*, Ontario: Oxford University Press (2nd edition).

Immergut, E. (1992) 'The Rules of the Game: The Logic of Health Policy-making in France, Switzerland, and Sweden'. Steinmo, S., Thelen, K., and Longstreth, F. (eds.) *Structuring politics: Historical Institutionalism in Comparative Analysis*, Cambridge: Cambridge University Press pp. 57–89.

Keeler, J.T.S. (1993) 'Opening the Window for Reform: Mandates, Crises and Extraordinary Policy-Making'. *Comparative Political Studies* vol. 25 (1) pp. 433–486.

Kingdon, J.W. (1995) *Agendas, Alternatives, and Public Policies*, New York: Longman (2nd edition).

Kuipers, S. L. (2006) *The Crisis Imperative: Crisis Rhetoric and Welfare State Reform in Belgium and the Netherlands in the Early 1990s*, Amsterdam: Amsterdam University Press.

Leemans, A.F. (1976a) 'Overview'. Leemans, A.F. (ed.) *The Management of Change in Government*, The Hague: Martinus Nijhoff pp. 1–62.

Leemans, A.F. (1976b) 'A Conceptual Framework for the Study of Reform of Central Government'. Leemans, A.F. (ed.) *The Management of Change in Government*, The Hague: Martinus Nijhoff pp. 65–98.

Lindblom, C.E. (1959) 'The Science of 'Muddling Through''. *Public Administration Review* vol. 19 pp. 79–88.

Lindblom, C.E. (1979) 'Still Muddling, Not Yet Through'. *Public Administration Review* vol. 39 pp. 517–526.

Mahoney, J., Rueschemeyer, D. (eds.) (2003) *Comparative Historical Analysis in the Social Sciences,* Cambridge: Cambridge University Press.

March, J. J. Olsen (1995) *Democratic Governance*, New York: Free Press.

Olsen, J.P. (1991) 'Modernization Programs in Perspective: Institutional Analysis of Organizational Change'. *Governance: An International Journal of Policy and Administration* vol. 2 (2) pp. 125–149.

Pierson, P. (2004) *Politics in Time: History, Institutions and Social Analysis*, Princeton: Princeton University Press.

Pollitt, C., G. Bouckaert (2004) *Public Management Reform. A Comparative Analysis*, Oxford: Oxford University Press.

Resodihardjo, S.L. (2006) *Crisis and Change: Understanding Crisis-Reform Processes in Dutch and British Prison Services*, Dissertation: Amsterdam.

Rose, R., Davies, P.L. (1994) *Inheritance in Public Policy: Change without Choice in Britain*, New Haven: Yale University Press.

Sabatier, P.A., Jenkins-Smith, H.C. (1999) 'The Advocacy Coalition Framework: An Assessment'. Sabatier, P.A. (ed.), *Theories of the Policy Process,* Boulder: Westview Press, pp.117–166.

Steinmo, S., Thelen, K., Longstreth, F. (eds.) (1992) *Structuring Politics: Historical Institutionalism in Comparative Analysis,* Cambridge: Cambridge University Press.

Appendix to Chapter 11

Table 11.3 Reform in Europe

Case	Level	Shift in paradigm?	Shift in structures?
EU dairy reform	Trans-national	From promoting milk production to discouraging milk production	From incentives to produce milk to quotas and fines to restrict milk production From unanimous to majority decision-making
Housing reform in the Netherlands	National	From housing policy as a public emergency exit to housing policy as a public burden	Creation of financial independence of the housing organizations, government steps back
Home care reform in Denmark & the Netherlands	National Local	From acknowledging professional autonomy to determine quality standards to imposing a national quality policy regulating organizational aspects of care	In the Dutch case: from strict and detailed quality provisions to conditioned and structured self-regulation
German's constitutional change in asylum law	National	From welcoming immigration to discouraging immigration	A restrictive asylum law
Irish ban on smoking	National	From smoking as a way of life to smoking as a health hazard on the work floor	From voluntary agreements to statutory measures
Dutch disability insurance reform	National	From a generous, universal benefit system to a restricted benefit system	From bureaucracy to privatization A loss of influence of social partners – disappearance of the corporist structure
Local government reform in the UK	National Local	Introduction of the Third Way approach: more focus on transparency and accountability	A separation of powers between executive and non-executive actors
Safety policy reform in Rotterdam	Local	Towards a broader understanding of the concept of safety	From fragmented policy making and implementation to integrative policy making and implementation
Participative city planning in Heidelberg	Local	From city planning as a technical matter to city planning as a participatory matter	The introduction of integrative and participative planning procedures

Table 11.4 Barriers to reform (mentioned in introductory chapter)

| | Opportunity | | Policy lock-in | Preferences | Benefits, vested interests | Disruption | Other barriers |
	Decision-making rules	Policy inheritance		Paradigm, routines, internalized goals			Low expectations
EU Dairy	*Rule of unanimity*		Immobile production		*Beneficial financial allocation system*		
Dutch Housing		Social housing stock	Housing as capital good (investment)	*Housing as emergency exit*	*Object subsidy*		
Dutch and Danish home care	Corporative policy-making			*Autonomy municipalities / professionals*	Autonomy municipalities / professionals		
German asylum	Rule of majority Länder Government; Federal system			Moral obligation			*Internal political disagreement laws and campaigns*
Irish smoking Ban				*Accepted life style*	*Anti-reform coalition*		
Dutch disability insurance	Formal vote social partners in SER; *Corporatist policy-implementation*			*High sensitivity of cutbacks in level of provision*	Social partners' focus on the volume and bipartite organization		
UK local government national level				Party control	Fear of losing support on the local level		
local level			Sunk costs Committee structure	Committee structure as routine		*Experience of form of bereavement*	
Heidelberg city planning	Majority rule			No (working) participation culture			*Cynical disillusionment*
Rotterdam safety policy		*Lack of attention Lack of formal coordination*		*Management and civic culture (incomprehensive paradigm)*			

Italicized barriers have been addressed during the reform process.

Table 11.5 Facilitators of reform (mentioned in introductory chapter)

| Cases | Structure | | Agency | | Reform tactic 2: Procure backing | | |
	Disrupted policy-making process	Diminished constraints	Leadership Entrepreneurship	Reform tactic 1: Go with the flow	a) coalition building	b) acceptable design	c) force
EU dairy	Financial crisis as an opportunity for reform	Temporarily changed rules of decision making	Leadership exerted by French Presidency of the EU				- Acceptance of quota system by farmers due to fear of renationalization - financial payments were stopped
Dutch housing	Parliamentary enquiry and crisis of legitimacy		Leadership by Heerma			Trial and error strategy	
Dutch and Danish home care			Entrepreneurship of home care actors: suggested blueprint	Dutch national association took charge by creating a blueprint model	National governments implementing actors in decision-making and implementation process		Anticipation on a potential loss of autonomy fostered cooperation of local actors
German asylum policy	An ongoing, deepening crisis		Pro-reformative attitude of political leaders, especially Minister of Internal Affairs	Deeply felt crisis in society; majority supported change of Constitution		Civil servants visited commissions all over Germany to explain plans	
Irish smoking ban		Anti-reform coalition proved to be weak	Leadership by Minister Martin		Expanding pro-reform coalition		Political actors threatened to resign if reform failed

Table 11.5   Continued.

Cases	Structure		Agency	Reform tactic 1: Go with the flow	Reform tactic 2: Procure backing		
	Disrupted policy-making process	Diminished constraints	Leadership Entrepreneurship		a) coalition building	b) acceptable design	c) force
Dutch disability insurance	Parliamentary inquiry made drastic reform recommendations	Opportunity to insure for loss of income due to new, lower benefits.	Lubbers, prime minister at the time, intervened to push for reform	Increasing political and societal criticism on corporatist decision making	An ad hoc political coalition by-passed support for corporatism		Political actors threatened to resign if reform failed
UK local government **National level**			National level: Blair's personal position benefited the decision-making process on the Bill	Local government reform fitted national Third Way politics		National level: Various amendments of the Bill included wishes of other political actors	National level: Bill was mandatory, however with options to choose from for various models
Local level						Local level: New way of working benefited executive councillors & local bureaucrats	
Heidelberg city planning			Communitarian leadership of Mayor Weber	.		- Creating a supportive organizational environment - Managing resistance of political actors by means of compromise	
Rotterdam Safety policy			Fortuyn (entrepreneur) and Mayor Opstelten (leadership)	Latent feeling in society	Safety conference		

Table 11.6   Additional facilitators of reform (not mentioned in introductory chapter)

Case	Structure Impact of policy inheritance	Elections	Agency Reform tactic 3: Framing	Reform tactic 4: Symbolic politics
EU dairy	Impact was negative: previously failed attempts induced fundamental reform		Preventing bankruptcy of the EU instead of decreasing milk production	
Dutch housing policy	Impact was positive so that a win-win situation emerged			
Dutch and Danish home care				
German asylum	Impact was negative: previously failed policies induced fundamental reform			
Irish smoking ban			Smoking was presented as a health hazard on the work floor (scientific information was used to support this argument)	
Dutch disability insurance	Impact was negative: previously failed policies induced fundamental reform			One million people in the disability insurance system became a symbolic threshold
UK local government		New Labour government pushing for the Third Way politics		
Heidelberg city planning		Newly elected Mayor Weber campaigns for participatory city planning		
Rotterdam safety policy		Fortuyn and Leefbaar Rotterdam are elected newcomers in the city council coalition		Fortuyn presented himself as an outsider to the traditional political culture. The newly elected council highlighted problems and positive developments; safety index; use of media and of new jargon

Reform in Europe

Table 11.7   Factors functioning as barriers *and* facilitators of reform

		Barrier	Facilitator
Structure	Policy inheritance	Increasing returns: vested interests are damaged by removal of the policy creating these returns	Increasing returns: win-win situation is created that makes reform acceptable Decreasing returns: pressure is created to go beyond first and second order changes
Agency	Paradigm Preferences	If one profits from status quo	If one benefits from reform or if one gets punished for doing nothing
	Leadership/ Entrepreneurs	To obstruct change	To initiate change
	Tactics - go with the flow - procure support - symbolic politics	Obstruction tactics	Reform tactics

Chapter 12

Epilogue: Friction, Resistance, and Breakthroughs

Frank R. Baumgartner

The studies included in this volume have amply demonstrated the contingent nature of reform. They also clearly show that large-scale and purposeful reforms are, indeed, successfully implemented in a wide range of countries and in many policy areas. There are many lessons from these studies. Most lessons are explained in chapter 11, which draws out the common themes across the various successful reforms included in this volume. The purpose of this epilogue is to link these findings to the broader literature, that is, to general policy change.

Reform, status quo bias, and policy change

Most policies, most of the time, do not change much. The status quo is developed through adaptation to changing circumstances, and reflects all the previous historical adjustments in a policy. This being the case, the status quo is typically not so far off from where it should be (at least in the eyes of those in charge) and so, when adaptation is called for, it is usually only marginally adjusted. If this were not the case, then we would be living in a world of constant policy failure and crisis. We can see this status-quo bias in every political system. The bias stems from many causes, but perhaps the most fundamental reason to keep the status quo is because it functions above some acceptable level, even if few would argue that it does so perfectly. Still, even with this status quo orientation for most issues most of the time, dramatic policy changes do occur on a regular basis in all political systems. In fact, because we are overly attuned to the status quo, when changes do finally occur they are often dramatic. In other words, we lurch from periods of under-reaction to new conditions to over-reactions. Because of the power of the status quo, governmental reactions are often not proportionate to the crisis at hand. The status quo is privileged for many reasons, but perhaps the most important is the relative stability of decision-makers. To change the status quo policy is typically to ask that governmental leaders, civil servants, and others involved in the administration of a program admit that their own policies are failing. Naturally, they prefer incremental adjustments and fixes rather than over-arching reforms. Such reforms require an admission of the failure of the previous policy regime. Yet over-arching reforms are regularly adopted; they are a constant and important part of the policy process.

The objects of the studies in this book are large-scale reforms that were purposefully and successfully implemented. These is a subset of more general large-scale policy changes which includes both changes resulting from purposive reform as well as those stemming from other sources. Some dramatic policy changes occur by policy drift or by accident, with no purposeful institutional reform consciously imposed from the top. That is to say, simply, that policy changes can come from sources other than purposeful reform. Such sources may include reactions to changing circumstances, or the slow accumulation of new norms and practices. Similarly, the cases included in this book exclude failed reform attempts, those that were not implemented, or which were small in scale or scope. What can we say, more generally, about dramatic policy changes? Moreover, are the lessons from this study of successful, purposeful, large-scale reforms applicable to this broader class of events?

First, there is strong and growing evidence that the nature of policy change in many countries follows a pattern of punctuated equilibrium. This occurs when strong forces act to reinforce the power of the status quo, but are occasionally overcome so that substantial policy changes occur.

Substantial evidence for this can be found in the US case, which was based on comprehensive analyses of budgeting data for over 60 categories of spending from 1947 to present (Jones & Baumgartner, 2005). The distribution of policy changes, reflected in the budget, has a characteristic pattern. When we count the number of cases with large decreases, marginal adjustments, and large increases, we see that the vast majority falls in the central peak of the distribution (reflecting only slight adjustments to the budgets of the previous year), but also that quite substantial numbers fall far out in the tails of the distribution (reflecting substantial reallocations of funds to a subset of the budget categories). The missing element here is moderate adjustment. Something about the process produces an over-abundance in both the smallest and the largest degrees of change, while under-producing moderate adjustment.

Interestingly, such *fat tailed* distributions have been noted in a wide range of natural processes, from earthquakes to avalanches. Typically, there is some process that imposes friction on the system so that changing inputs to the process of government (e.g., social pressures, stochastic events, economic changes, technological advance, or anything that affects the series of problems and issues that governments face) are dampened out for the vast majority of cases (where the input pressures are below some threshold), but where the inputs are amplified in those cases which pass the threshold. So geologists and seismologists note that the earth's tectonic plates generate massive numbers of extremely small earthquakes almost on a routine bases, responding to small pressures with even smaller adjustments. Eventually those pressures build up and, when they pass a threshold, a massive shift occurs. Such themes in natural disaster may offer an accurate metaphor for the processes associated with the implementation of reforms.

Bryan Jones and I (Jones & Baumgartner, 2005) have argued that the mechanisms in governance that lead to punctuated equilibrium have to do with the overwhelming complexity of the policy environment. Governments deal with thousands of real and potential problems, each with a different magnitude, clarity, urgency, and familiarity. Each of these many problems can be understood in multiple ways; most issues of public policy are internally complex. In turn, each dimension of the issue may be related to many policy choices. So we lay out a multiple-stage model of cognitive complexity (Jones & Baumgartner, 2005). The key insight is that the scarcity of attention – at both the individual and the organizational level – creates a process similar to natural friction. It is not possible to pay attention to everything concomitantly. Rather, attention is given to those issues that seem most urgent. The result of our model, laid out in *The Politics of Attention* (2005), is an understanding of why most issues are routinely renewed with only the slightest adjustments to the status quo, while a smaller number of them are subject to dramatic change.

Evidence is growing that punctuated equilibrium processes are common across the policy processes in Western democracies. In a recent special issue of the *Journal of European Public Policy,* various authors have explored these processes in Canada, the US, Britain, Denmark, France, the Netherlands, Belgium, and the European Union (Baumgartner, Green-Pedersen, & Jones, 2006). Figure 12.1 gives a sense of a common finding. It shows the distribution in the sizes of annual changes in the budget of the French state, from 1820 to 2002 (see Baumgartner, Foucault & François, 2006).

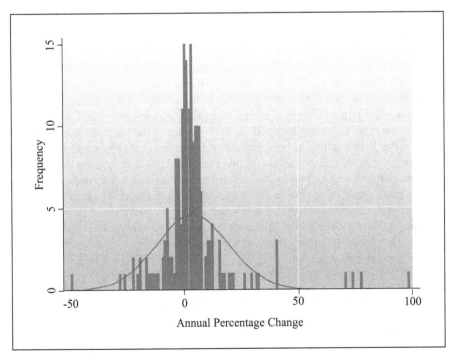

Figure 12.1 The distribution of annual percent changes in the French state budget, 1820–2002

This figure illustrates the combination of modest adjustments and also radical departures from the status quo that characterize the budgetary process. This is virtually the same as was found in both the entire US government budget and for more detailed classifications of spending by category (Jones & Baumgartner, 2005). The pattern has been found in municipal, state, and national governments in many systems, and appears to be a common characteristic of policy changes in a wide range of settings and at many levels of scale.

What is the relevance of all this to the policy reforms that are the object of this book? The broader analysis of policy change in general illustrates that policies can be considered as one of two possible regimes – a status-quo regime, or a dramatic change. There is virtually no middle ground. Successful reforms are rare but not so rare that they can be ignored, as the chapters in this book have pointed out. They are subject to powerful threshold effects and depend heavily on contextual factors where each individual decision-maker bases his/her actions partially on his/her estimate of the expected behaviour of others. Naturally, these processes are inherently unstable. The cases described in the previous chapters have no single cause, but result from the complex interaction of multiple sources, some related to leadership efforts and some related to contextual factors beyond the control of leaders. They occur at all levels of scale. Thus the work reported here corresponds well with important themes in the broader literature on policy change in general.

The power of the status quo

Most efforts at reform fail. The cases included in this book were chosen because they were extraordinary. The logic is that we can learn a lot from exploring the commonalities of such extraordinary cases. But, it is important to keep in mind that the successful implementation of a large-scale and purposive reform is the exception, and not the rule. There are many ideas for reform, but only a small percentage of these make it through to being adopted and implemented. Ideas can be snuffed out along the way, in any number of places. Indeed, each chapter in this book of extraordinary reform catalogues previous reform failures; the actors in extraordinary reform could easily offer cases where they had attempted to, or would have liked to, enact reforms in previous time periods when it was not possible. So the cases here, paradoxically, show the power of the status quo in two ways: first, by the unusual nature of successfully implemented reforms, and second, by comparison to previous efforts in many cases.

The weakness of the powerful and the power of the weak

During periods when status quo policies are routinely reviewed and only marginally adjusted, those benefiting from the policy may be seen as politically powerful. Often it seems foolhardy for political leaders to contemplate challenging these *entrenched interests*. Thus, for example, the many stories of lobbying and the economic, financial, and political power of the tobacco industry over the decades. Similarly, the German understanding of nationhood and citizenship, a fundamental matter of identity and national self-definition, represented an entrenched interest. French farmers and the Common Agricultural Policy in the EU also represented entrenched interests. The list is long, and the point is clear: cases in this book show how entrenched and powerful interests were routed. The policy reversals detailed in this book, typically, did not come about through continual chipping away at the policies. Rather, a process of large social diffusion is a more accurate depiction of how reform occurred. More and more actors concluded that the war could be won, and therefore were willing to mobilize resources to fight it. So, for example, as long as it appeared hopeless to challenge smoking in public establishments, few actors would do so. As it becomes clear that the reform might actually work, greater numbers of actors are willing to engage. Such processes focus on cue-taking, mimicking, and note the contingent nature of human behaviour. These threshold models of behaviour can show disruptive patterns such as those observed here. The entrenched interests of today suddenly find themselves upended. Such a set of observations flows naturally from the cases included here and also figures prominently in the literature on policy change (see Jones & Baumgartner, 2005).

The contingent nature of reform

In chapter 11, Heyse, Lettinga, and Groenleer illustrate clearly the multiple paths to reform. No single combination of variables was consistent across all the cases, and very few individual variables were in common across all the cases. It is tempting (and follows a long research tradition) to look for the effects of *leadership* in such cases. The subject of leadership shows the greatest similarity across the cases, since almost all the reforms included here involved substantial leadership by a policy entrepreneur. Still, it is important to remember that such leadership is contingent on many other values. If leadership alone was sufficient, then we would see many more successful reforms across many countries and policy domains. Instead, we see failed efforts by individual entrepreneurs sometimes leading to an eventual breakthrough, when other factors are favourable. The most effective *leader* may be that entrepreneur who knows best when to promote the right idea – an idea whose time has come, as Kingdon (1984) wrote.

The multiple contingencies of reform imply that specifying the necessary and sufficient conditions for reform may not be very easy. Reform may result from the combination of many different factors. The matrix laid out in table 11.6 makes clear that there is no single necessary condition for reform, there being no single variable present in all cases. Similarly, there is certainly no single factor which by itself is a sufficient condition. Every case exhibited a combination of several different facilitating variables; none had just one facilitating feature. The multiple possible combinations of factors to promote reform are typically not often present, and so large-scale reforms are rare. But the multiplicity of avenues that can lead to a successful reform implies two things: one, reforms are likely to take place, and two, we cannot look to simple models to explain them. No single facilitating factor need be present; most, if not all, inhibiting factors can be overcome with the right combination of facilitators.

How can the analyst proceed in such a complex environment? First, we need to avoid drawing too many general lessons from individual case studies. That is, as the chapters included in this book make clear, there is great value in structured and comparable studies of a number of cases of reform. This systematic comparison of a dozen or so reforms shows that there are multiple paths to reform, that reform is highly contingent on the particular context. Still we can see some general patterns from these comparisons even as we avoid over-generalizing from the process in any particular case. Clearly there is no single typical pattern. Second, we must be attuned to complex causation and rare events. Most reforms fail or are never even attempted. But looking at successful cases and viewing things over significant periods of time, as the studies in this book do, we can see that a wide range of unrelated factors may indeed come together to provide the opportunity for dramatic changes to be implemented.

Perhaps the most straightforward way of thinking about the contingent nature of policy change is to consider political leadership on the one side and the environment on the other. Reform may be rare because it (usually) requires both effective leadership and favourable circumstances. Favourable circumstances imply both urgency about the problem and agreement about a set of policy solutions. For most issues most of the time, no amount of leadership would be sufficient to create a given policy reform. This is because there is either insufficient consensus about the available policy solutions, or else inadequate concern about the severity of the underlying problem. The availability of feasible policy solutions with substantial leadership, but with no sense of urgency about the severity of the problem may lead to some policy change, but not the kind of large-scale reform discussed here (and even this conclusion must be tempered since there are cases, as the Irish smoking ban, where there was no particular increase in the urgency of the health-care problem, though other barriers to reform fell away). A sense of urgency about the severity of a problem, but with no consensus on feasible solutions may not lead to substantial reform either, even with a strong leader.

So we can get a sense of the multiple contingencies of reform by considering three variables: *urgency* (or the perception of the severity of the problem the reform would potentially address), *consensus* on solutions, and *leadership*. While the discussion above made clear that there is no single combination that leads inevitably to successful reform, we can better understand the frustrations and opportunities available to political leaders if we understand the multiple contingencies of their work. This includes the combination of things within their control, and contextual factors outside their control, that must come together for a successful reform to be possible. Sometimes the most effective leader is the one who can read the environment most effectively. But if the environment is not propitious to reform, then leadership alone will not change that. Moreover, there is no clear mathematical formula where positive values on urgency, solution, and leadership point inevitably to reform. It is much more complex. The discussions in this book have made clear these multiple contingencies.

Invariance to scale

The cases included in this book illustrate successful implementation of large-scale reforms ranging from those affecting a single policy arena in a local community to those changing constitutional structures for an entire nation. They involve relatively technical areas and highly charged moral areas. They involve behaviours by millions of citizens, in some cases, and are limited to professional actions by service providers, in other cases. Yet they all have important characteristics in common. These facts illustrate an important commonality with the literature on large-scale policy change in general: invariance with respect to scale. This means that the processes and interactions that we observe between actors in one case are expected to be similar to those in other cases, even if the cases are at substantially different levels of aggregation. A *dramatic* shift of policy within the context of a single bureau in a municipality can be an important reform, but it is at a different level of scale than a reform affecting millions of citizens in their daily lives, as for example in a smoking ban or a revision of a nation's basic laws concerning citizenship. The complex interactions of many unrelated factors that can combine in various ways are common features of the policy process at all these different levels of scale, however. The chapters included in this book clearly illustrate this fundamental point of complexity.

Two approaches to understanding policy change

Political entrepreneurs successfully implement policy changes on a routine basis, and they take rightful credit for their accomplishments. Still, reform cannot be said to be due only to political leadership; it is highly contingent. In fact, statistical approaches to studying policy change indicate that the distribution of changes in public policy (in a very wide array of settings across many levels of government, and in various democratic regimes) seems to correspond to a punctuated-equilibrium model similar to those found in biological and physical settings, where there is no single cause for policy change, and no relation between the size of an input and the size of the output (e.g., the degree of policy change). The chapters and case studies in this book illustrate clearly both the contingent and probabilistic nature of policy change, as well as the strategic and goal-oriented behaviours of those political leaders who operate within these complex and constantly evolving environments.

This book brings together detailed case studies of how dramatic and successful reforms were adopted in various settings. The authors have described the individuals involved attempting to push or inhibit the reforms, the motivations of the various actors, the political and policy considerations that were relevant in each case, and the idiosyncrasies of each case study. Such detailed analyses are absolutely fundamental to our understanding of how policy changes come about. In this short commentary, I have noted that these micro-level analyses have not only contributed to a useful comparison (as the authors of the book have clearly drawn out in their theoretical structure and conclusion), but also that the case studies included here correspond in many ways with very similar ideas that are simultaneously being developed using a completely different research approach. Large-scale empirical projects assessing the nature of policy change, over many decades and in many countries, by definition cannot go into detail about the precise mechanisms of each policy change they observe; they look for general patterns. Such studies do not always correspond in their theoretical approach or most important findings to more detailed micro-level studies of bureaucratic behaviour within agencies. In the case of this volume, however, we see a synergy between the two. The studies included here individually and collectively constitute a major contribution to the study of policy change more generally and not only, as the authors set out, to the study of policy reform.

References

Baumgartner, F.R., M. Foucault, A. François (2006) 'Punctuated Equilibrium and French Budgeting Processes' *Journal of European Public Policy* Forthcoming.

Baumgartner, F.R., C. Green-Pedersen, B.D. Jones (eds) (2006) Agenda-Setting in Comparative Public Policy. Special Issue of the *Journal of European Public Policy*. Forthcoming.

Jones, B.D., F.R. Baumgartner (2005) *The Politics of Attention: How Government Prioritizes Problems*. Chicago: University of Chicago Press.

Kingdon, J.W. (1984) *Agendas, Alternatives, and Public Policies*. Boston: Little, Brown.

Index